Macmillan McGraw-Hill

Math Connects

5

Reteach and Skills Practice Workbook

Macmillan/McGraw-Hill

TO THE STUDENT This *Reteach and Skills Practice Workbook* gives you additional examples and problems for the concept exercises in each lesson. The exercises are designed to help you study mathematics by reinforcing important skills needed to succeed in the everyday world. The materials are organized by chapter and lesson, with one Reteach and Skills Practice worksheet for every lesson in *Math Connects, Grade 5*.

Always keep your workbook handy. Along with you textbook, daily homework, and class notes, the completed *Reteach and Skills Practice Workbook* can help you in reviewing for quizzes and tests.

TO THE TEACHER These worksheets are the same ones found in the Chapter Resource Masters for *Math Connects, Grade 5*. The answers to these worksheets are available at the end of each Chapter Resource Masters booklet.

The McGraw·Hill Companies

Macmillan/McGraw-Hill

Send all inquiries to:
Macmillan/McGraw-Hill
8787 Orion Place
Columbus, OH 43240

ISBN: 978-0-02-107306-1
MHID: 0-02-107306-6 *Reteach and Skills Practice Workbook, Grade 5*

Printed in the United States of America.

10 MAL 14 13

CONTENTS

Name ______________________________

1-1

Reteach

Place Value Through Billions

A place-value chart can help you read greater numbers. Say the number in each period followed by the name of the period, except for the ones.

Billions Period			**Millions Period**			**Thousands Period**			**Ones Period**		
H	**T**	**O**	**H**	**T**	**O**	**H**	**T**	**O**	**H**	**T**	**O**
	4	7	3	0	2	0	1	6	2	9	4

Standard form: 47,302,016,294

Word form: 47 **billion**, 302 **million**, 16 **thousand**, 294
Read: forty-seven billion, three hundred two million, sixteen thousand, two hundred ninety-four

Expanded form: 40,000,000,000 + 7,000,000,000 + 300,000,000 + 2,000,000 + 10,000 + 6,000 + 200 + 90 + 4

Write the word form and the expanded form of each number. For help, complete the place-value chart.

1.

Billions Period			**Millions Period**			**Thousands Period**			**Ones Period**		
H	**T**	**O**	**H**	**T**	**O**	**H**	**T**	**O**	**H**	**T**	**O**

Standard form: 27,006,593

Word form: ______________________________

Expanded form: ______________________________

2. Standard form: 6,020,700,510

Word form: ______________________________

Expanded form: ______________________________

Name ____________________

1-1

Skills Practice

Place Value Through Billions

Name the place value and write the value of the underlined digit.

1. 2,346 ________ **2.** 65,893 ________

3. 763,406,594 ________

4. 407,356,138,920 ________

5. 64,321,008 ________

6. 117,927,724,417 ________

7. 903,004,200,006 ________

Write each number in standard form.

8. 3 thousand, 125 ________

9. 52 thousand, 40 ________

Write each number in expanded form.

10. 7,450,693 ________

11. 531,017 ________

Write each number in word form.

12. 9,000,000,006 ________

13. 273,273 ________

Solve.

14. Mercury is the planet closest to the Sun. It orbits the Sun from a distance of about 28 million, 600 thousand miles. Write the number in standard form.

____

15. Neptune is the planet farthest from the Sun. It orbits the Sun from a distance of about 4 billion, 497 million miles. Write the number in standard form.

____

1–2

Name ______________________________

Reteach

Compare Whole Numbers

You can write numbers in expanded form to compare them.

Compare 43,058 and 48,503.
Write the numbers in expanded form.

43,058 = 40,000 + 3,000 + 50 + 8
48,503 = 40,000 + 8,000 + 500 + 3

Compare the numbers, starting with the greatest place.

40,000 = 40,000   3,000 < 8,000
So, 43,058 < 48,503.

Write the numbers in expanded form. Replace each ◯ with <, >, or = to make a true sentence.

1. 3,505 = ______________

3,055 = ______________

3,505 ◯ 3,055

2. 432 = ______________

4,322 = ______________

432 ◯ 4,322

3. 8,296 = ______________

596 = ______________

8,296 ◯ 596

4. 5,324 = ______________

9,736 = ______________

5,324 ◯ 9,736

5. 4,000,976 = ______________

4,009,076 = ______________

4,000,976 ◯ 4,009,076

6. 1,104 = ______________

1,140 = ______________

1,104 ◯ 1,140

7. 9,076 = ______________

1,942 = ______________

9,076 ◯ 1,942

8. 4,103 = ______________

4,130 = ______________

4,103 ◯ 4,130

Name ____________________

1–2

Skills Practice

Compare Whole Numbers

Replace each ◯ with <, >, or = to make a true sentence.

1. 1,040 ◯ 10

2. 14,092 ◯ 19,812

3. 840 ◯ 480

4. 1,001 ◯ 101

5. 123,778 ◯ 123,778

6. 9,879 ◯ 9,798

7. 6,823 ◯ 682

8. 5 ◯ 13

9. 190 ◯ 19

10. 71 ◯ 98

11. 192 ◯ 291

12. 611 ◯ 611

13. 314 ◯ 3,140

14. 657 ◯ 567

15. 324 ◯ 452

16. Michael ran 7 miles during one week. Krista ran 9 miles during one week. Who ran more miles?

____

17. Jerry is 55 inches tall. Tom is 56 inches tall. Who is taller?

____

1-3

Name ______________________________

Reteach

Problem-Solving Investigation: Use the Four-Step Plan

The three tallest buildings in Boston are the Prudential Tower (750 ft), the John Hancock Tower (790 ft), and the Federal Reserve Building (604 ft). List these buildings from tallest to shortest.

Step 1 **Understand**	**Be sure you understand the problem.** Read carefully. Identify what you need to do. • What do you know? ______________ • What have you been asked to do? ______________
Step 2 **Plan**	You can compare the heights of the buildings. **Plan a strategy.** • Decide what actions you will take and in what order.
Step 3 **Solve**	**Solve the problem.** Follow your plan. Compare Prudential Tower and John Hancock Tower. $750 < 790$ Compare Prudential Tower and the Federal Reserve Building. $750 > 604$ The order from tallest to shortest is John Hancock Tower, Prudential Tower, Federal Reserve Building.
Step 4 **Check**	**Did you answer the question? Is the solution reasonable?** Yes, you have listed the buildings from tallest to shortest.

Solve. Use the four-step plan.

1. Scotia Plaza in Toronto is 902 feet tall. First Canadian Place in Toronto is 978 feet tall. Which building is taller?

____

____

2. Dallas' Renaissance Tower is 886 feet, Bank of America Plaza is 921 feet, and Bank One Center is 787 feet. List the buildings from shortest to tallest.

____

____

1–3

Name ______________________________

Reteach

Problem-Solving Investigation: Use the Four-Step Plan

(continued)

3. The Andersons are buying a paddle boat for $540. They plan to pay in four equal payments. How much will their payments be?

____

4. Lynn can walk two miles in 24 minutes. At this rate, how long will it take her to walk 6 miles?

____

5. Bridgit plays on the basketball team. The table shows the number of baskets she made in the first three days of practice. If the pattern continues, how many baskets will she make on Thursday and Friday?

Day	Baskets
Monday	21
Tuesday	22
Wednesday	24
Thursday	
Friday	

6. The Glendale Plaza Building in Glendale, California is 353 feet tall. The U.S. Bank Tower in Los Angeles, California is 1,017 feet tall. Which building is taller?

7. After going on vacation, you come home with $5. You spent $6 on a pair of sunglasses, $10 on snacks, $4 on a book, and $5 on arcade games. How much money did you start with?

____

1–3

Name ______________________________

Skills Practice

Problem-Solving Strategy: Use the Four-Step Plan

Solve. Use the four-step plan.

1. The three highest mountains in Colorado are Mount Massive (14,421 ft), Mount Harvard (14,420 ft), and Mount Elbert (14,433 ft). Which mountain has the greatest height?

____

2. Hoover Dam, in the United States, is 223 meters high. Ertan Dam, in China, is 240 meters high. In Canada, Mica Dam is 243 meters high. List the dams by height from greatest to least.

____

____

3. The Akshi Kaikyo suspension bridge in Japan has a span of 6,570 feet. The Humber suspension bridge in England has a span of 4,626 feet. The Izmit Bay suspension bridge in Turkey has a span of 5,538 feet. Which bridge has the shortest span?

____

4. There are three long tunnels that go under Boston Harbor. The Sumner Tunnel is 5,653 feet long. The Callahan Tunnel is 5,070 feet long. The Ted Williams Tunnel is 8,448 feet long. List the tunnels from shortest to longest.

____

____

5. List the tunnels in the table at the right by name in order from shortest to longest.

____

____

____

Land Tunnels in the United States

Tunnel	State	Length (ft)
Liberty Tubes	Pennsylvania	5,920
Devil's Side	California	3,400
E. Johnson Memorial	Colorado	8,959
Squirrel Hill	Pennsylvania	4,225

Name ______________________________

1–4

Reteach

Represent Decimals

You can write a fraction as a decimal. Think of place value.

Fractions that name tenths, hundredths, and thousandths have one digit, two digits, and three digits to the right of the decimal point.

$\frac{1}{10}$	one tenth	0.1
$\frac{1}{100}$	one hundredth	0.01
$\frac{1}{1,000}$	one thousandth	0.001

Write each fraction as a decimal.

1. $\frac{65}{100}$ ____________

2. $\frac{6}{10}$ ____________

3. $\frac{86}{100}$ ____________

4. $\frac{57}{100}$ ____________

5. $\frac{5}{10}$ ____________

6. $\frac{68}{100}$ ____________

7. $\frac{25}{100}$ ____________

8. $\frac{15}{100}$ ____________

9. $\frac{4}{10}$ ____________

10. $\frac{9}{10}$ ____________

11. $\frac{2}{1,000}$ ____________

12. $\frac{7}{10}$ ____________

13. $\frac{11}{1,000}$ ____________

14. $\frac{31}{100}$ ____________

15. $\frac{19}{1,000}$ ____________

16. $\frac{3}{1,000}$ ____________

17. $\frac{3}{10}$ ____________

18. $\frac{29}{1,000}$ ____________

19. $\frac{4}{1,000}$ ____________

20. $\frac{5}{1,000}$ ____________

1–4

Name ____________________

Skills Practice

Represent Decimals

Write each fraction as a decimal.

1. $\frac{3}{10}$ ________ **2.** $\frac{498}{1,000}$ ________ **3.** $\frac{7}{10}$ ________

4. $\frac{1}{10}$ ________ **5.** $\frac{947}{1,000}$ ________ **6.** $\frac{3}{10}$ ________

7. $\frac{18}{20}$ ________ **8.** $\frac{1}{50}$ ________ **9.** $\frac{11}{20}$ ________

10. $\frac{1}{10}$ ________ **11.** $\frac{256}{1,000}$ ________ **12.** $\frac{3}{100}$ ________

13. $\frac{77}{100}$ ________ **14.** $\frac{3}{100}$ ________ **15.** $\frac{13}{50}$ ________

16. $\frac{999}{1,000}$ ________ **17.** $\frac{9}{50}$ ________ **18.** $\frac{751}{1,000}$ ________

19. $\frac{7}{10}$ ________ **20.** $\frac{2}{10}$ ________ **21.** $\frac{1}{20}$ ________

22. $\frac{357}{1,000}$ ________ **23.** $\frac{4}{20}$ ________ **24.** $\frac{632}{1,000}$ ________

Solve.

25. The largest butterfly in the world is found in Papua, New Guinea. The female of the species weighs about 0.9 ounce. Use a fraction to write the female's weight.

____

26. The shortest fish ever recorded is the dwarf goby found in the Indo-Pacific. The female of this species is about 0.35 inch long. Use a fraction to write the female's length.

____

Name ______________________________

1–5

Reteach

Place Value Through Thousandths

The decimal 1.56 can be shown in several ways. The models below will show you different ways to represent 1.56.

You can use a place-value chart like the one below to represent 1.56.

1,000	100	10	1	0.1	0.01	0.001
Thousands	Hundreds	Tens	Ones	Tenths	Hundredths	Thousandths
0	0	0	**1**	**.5**	**6**	

You can also represent 1.56 using a decimal model:

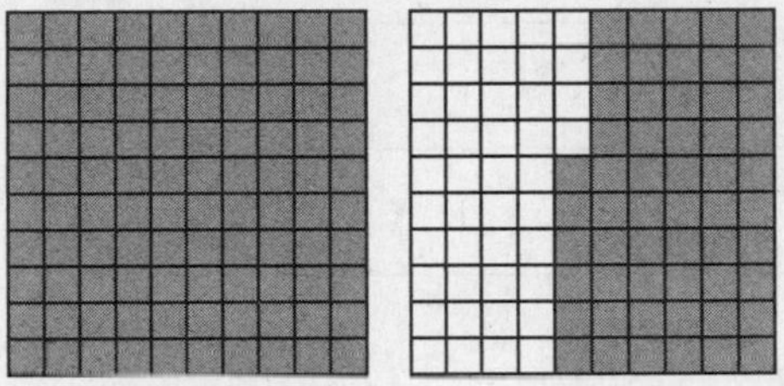

Represent the following decimals.

1. Use the place-value chart to show 0.87.

1,000	100	10	1	0.1	0.01	0.001
Thousands	Hundreds	Tens	Ones	Tenths	Hundredths	Thousandths
				.		

2. Use the decimal model to show 1.03.

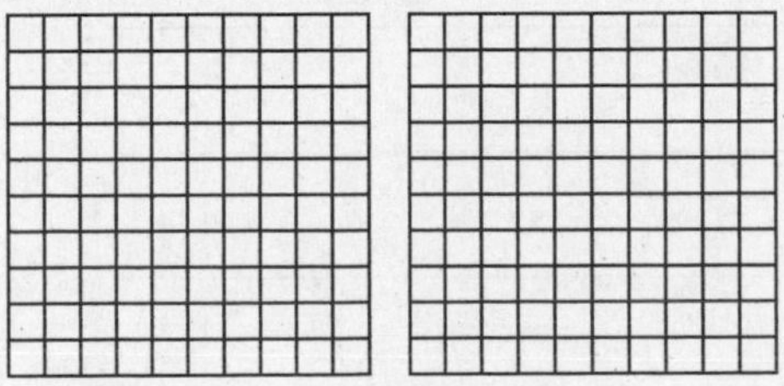

Name ________________________

1–5

Skills Practice

Place Value Through Thousandths

Write the place value and the value of each underlined digit.

1. 2.<u>8</u> ________________

2. 1.42<u>7</u> ________________

3. 2.5<u>3</u>1 ________________

4. 35.<u>0</u>52 ________________

5. 5.3<u>5</u> ________________

6. 24.00<u>2</u> ________________

Write each number in standard form.

7. 5 and 34 thousandths ________________

8. 34 and 12 hundredths ________________

9. 20 + 4 + 0.7 + 0.04 + 0.005 ________________

10. 100 + 7 + 0.05 + 0.007 ________________

Write each number in expanded form and word form.

11. 23.5 ________________________________

____

12. 164.38 ________________________________

____

13. 4.292 ________________________________

____

14. 53.007 ________________________________

____

Name ______________________________

1–6

Reteach

Compare Decimals

Compare 12.1 and 9.8.

Method 1

Use a number line.

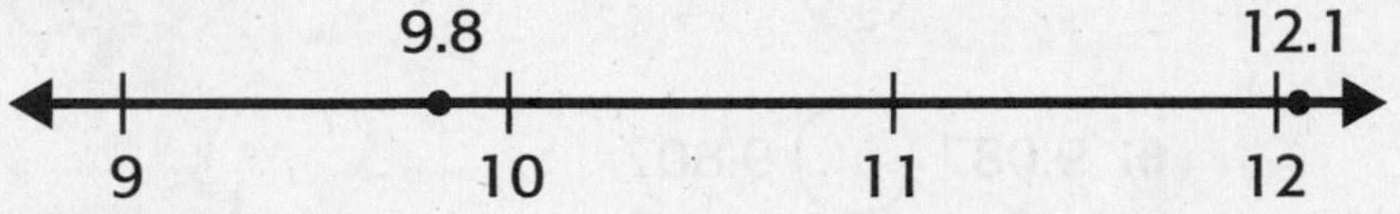

Numbers to the right are greater than numbers to the left.
Since 12.1 is to the right of 9.8, 12.1 > 9.8.

Method 2

Use place value.

Line up the decimal points.

If the numbers have a different number of digits, be sure to line them up correctly.

```
12.1
 9.8
```

Only the number 12.1 has a digit in the tens place. So, 12.1 > 9.8.

Replace each ◯ with <, >, or = to make a true sentence.

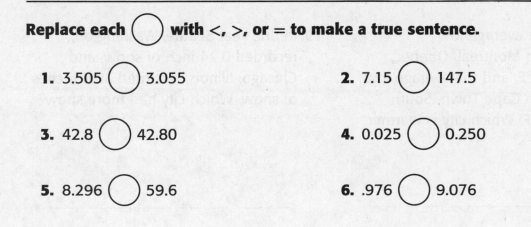

1. 3.505 ◯ 3.055

2. 7.15 ◯ 147.5

3. 42.8 ◯ 42.80

4. 0.025 ◯ 0.250

5. 8.296 ◯ 59.6

6. .976 ◯ 9.076

1–6

Name ____________________

Skills Practice

Compare Decimals

Replace each ◯ with <, >, or = to make a true sentence.

1. 3.976 ◯ 4.007

2. 89.001 ◯ 89.100

3. 126.698 ◯ 126.689

4. 5.052 ◯ 5.052

5. 3.674 ◯ 6.764

6. 9.087 ◯ 9.807

7. 0.256 ◯ 0.256

8. 2.7 ◯ 2.82

9. 6.030 ◯ 6.03

10. 7.89 ◯ 7.189

11. 12.54 ◯ 1.254

12. 0.981 ◯ 2.3

13. 0.004 ◯ 0.040

14. 8.26 ◯ 8.6

15. 5.085 ◯ 5.805

16. 0.86 ◯ 0.168

17. 5.309 ◯ 5.003

Solve.

18. In January, the average low temperature in Montreal, Quebec, Canada, is 5.2°F, and the average low temperature in Cape Town, South Africa, is 60.3°F. Which city is warmer in January?

____

19. In one year Seattle, Washington, recorded 0.24 inch of snow, and Chicago, Illinois, recorded 30.9 inches of snow. Which city had more snow?

____

1–7

Name ________________________________

Reteach

Order Whole Numbers and Decimals

You can write numbers in expanded form to compare them.

- Compare 43,058 and 48,503.
  Write the numbers in expanded form.

  43,058 = 40,000 + 3,000 + 50 + 8

  48,503 = 40,000 + 8,000 + 500 + 3

  Compare the numbers, starting with the greatest place.

  40,000 = 40,000 | 3,000, < 8,000

  So, 43,058, < 48,503.

- Compare 12.106 and 9.837.
  If the numbers have a different number of digits, be sure to line them up correctly.

  12.106 = 10 + 2 + 0.1 + 0.006

  9.837 = 9 + 0.8 + 0.03 + 0.007

  Only the number 12.106 has a digit in the tens place. So, 12.106 > 9.837.

Write the numbers in expanded form. Replace each ◯ with >, < or = to compare each pair of numbers.

1. 3,505 = ____________________

3,055 = ____________________

3,505 ◯ 3,055

2. 7.15 = ____________________

17.5 = ____________________

7.15 ◯ 17.5

3. 42.8 = ____________________

42.80 = ____________________

42.8 ◯ 42.80

4. 0.025 = ____________________

0.250 = ____________________

0.025 ◯ 0.250

5. 8,296 = ____________________

596 = ____________________

8,296 ◯ 596

6. 4,000,976 = ____________________

4,009,076 = ____________________

4,000,976 ◯ 4,009,076

Name ______________________________

1–7

Skills Practice

Order Whole Numbers and Decimals

Replace each ○ with >, <, or = to compare each pair of numbers.

1. 3,976 ○ 4,007

2. 89,001 ○ 89,100

3. 126,698 ○ 126,689

4. 1,435,052 ○ 145,052

5. 19,463,674 ○ 29,436,764

6. 4,303,259,087 ○ 4,033,259,807

7. 2.7 ○ 2.82

8. 6.030 ○ 6.03

9. 7.89 ○ 7.189

10. 12.54 ○ 1.254

11. 0.981 ○ 2.3

12. 0.004 ○ 0.040

Order each set of numbers from *least* to *greatest*.

13. 17,639; 3,828; 45,947 ______________________

14. 890,409; 890,904; 809,904 ______________________

15. 0.186; 0.1; 0.86; 0.168 ______________________

16. 5.309; 5.003; 0.53; 0.9 ______________________

Solve.

17. In City A, the average low temperature is 7.4°F, and the average low temperature in City B is 54.1°F. Which city is warmer?

____

18. In one year Seattle recorded 0.24 inch of snow, Chicago recorded 30.9 inches of snow, and Birmingham recorded 1 inch of snow. Write these amounts in order from least to greatest.

____

1–8

Name ______________________________

Reteach

Problem-Solving Strategy: Guess and Check

Guess and Check

During summer vacation, Sanjay writes letters and postcards to his friends at home. A letter costs $0.41 to mail, and a postcard costs $0.21 to mail. Sanjay writes to 8 friends and spends $2.08. How many letters and postcards does he send?

Step 1 Understand	**Be sure you understand the problem.** Read carefully. Identify what you need to do. What facts do you know? • A letter costs ________ and a postcard costs ________ to mail. • Sanjay writes to ________. • He spends ________. What do you need to find? • The number of ________________.
Step 2 Plan • Use Logical Reasoning • Draw a Diagram • Make a Graph • Make a Table or List • Find a Pattern • Guess and Check	**Make a plan.** Choose a strategy. You can solve the problem by making a guess. Then check the guess. If it is not the correct answer, adjust the guess and check again until you find the correct answer.

Name ____________________

1–8 Reteach

Problem-Solving Strategy: Guess and Check (continued)

Step 3 Solve	**Follow your plan.** Make a guess about the number of letters and the number of postcards. Suppose you guess 4 letters and 4 postcards. Check the amounts for the guess. Letters: ______ × ______ = ______ Postcards: ______ × ______ = ______ Total Cost: ______ + ______ = ______ Does the guess check with the total that Sanjay spent? ______ Should you adjust the number of letters up or down? Explain. ____________________ ____________________ Adjust your guess. Check your guess. Did the guess check? ______ If your guess did not check, adjust it again. How many letters does Sanjay send? ______ How many postcards does Sanjay send? ______
Step 4 Check	**Look back. Did you answer the question?** Is the solution reasonable? Reread the problem. Have you answered the question? ______ How can you check your answer? ____________________ ____________________

Practice

1. Nelson has 7 coins. All the coins are dimes and quarters. He has a total of $1.15. How many dimes and how many quarters does he have?

____

2. The library charges $0.75 a day for overdue videos and $0.12 a day for overdue books. Emily returns a video and a book and pays a total of $3.48 in late fees. How many days late were her items?

____

1-8

Name ____________________

Skills Practice

Problem-Solving Strategy: Guess and Check

Use the guess and check strategy to solve.

1. The Bactrian camel has two humps and the Dromedary camel has one hump. In a group of 15 camels, the total number of humps is 21. How many camels of each type are there?

____

2. The circus orders bicycles and unicycles for a new act. It orders a total of 12 cycles. The cycles have 16 tires altogether. How many bicycles and unicycles did the circus order?

____

3. Anja buys a magazine and a pizza. She spends $8.10. The magazine costs $2.40 less than the pizza. How much does the pizza cost?

____

4. A letter to Europe from the United States costs $0.80 to mail. A letter mailed within the United States costs $0.41. Nancy mails 5 letters for $2.83, some to Europe and some to the United States. How many letters did she send to Europe?

____

5. Warren spent $8.50 at the store. He spent $2.40 on paper, $0.88 on pencils, and $2.65 on markers. He spent the rest on a notebook. How much did the notebook cost?

____

6. Ms. Baxter takes a group of 8 children to a concert. Tickets for children 12 years and older cost $3.50. Tickets for children under 12 cost $2.25. She spends a total of $21.75 on tickets for the children. How many children are 12 and older?

____

Name ________________________________

2–1

Reteach

Round Whole Numbers and Decimals

Rounding Whole Numbers and Decimals

You can round whole numbers and decimals the same way:

Step 1

Underline the digit of the place value being rounded.

Step 2

Look at the digit to its right. If it is 4 or less, the underlined digit stays the same. If it is 5 or greater, add 1 to the underlined digit.

Step 3

After rounding, replace the remaining digits to the right with zeros.

Round 2,876,301 to the nearest million.

Step 1: Underline the digit to be rounded: ____________________

Step 2: Look at the digit to its right. Is it 4 or less or 5 or greater? ______

Step 3: The rounded number is: ____________________

Round 67.01 to the nearest tenth.

Step 1: Underline the digit to be rounded: ____________________

Step 2: Look at the digit to its right. Is it 4 or less or 5 or greater? ______

Step 3: The rounded number is: ____________________

Round each whole number to the place indicated.

1. 4,583,304; thousand ____________________

2. 62,893,665; million ____________________

3. 12,887,329; ten million ____________________

4. 7,623,873; ten thousand ____________________

Round each decimal to the place indicated.

5. 90.763; ones ____________________

6. 0.337; hundredths ____________________

7. 42.7456; thousandths ____________________

8. 55.23; tenths ____________________

2–1

Name ______________________

Skills Practice

Round Whole Numbers and Decimals

Round each decimal to the place indicated.

1. 0.463; tenths ________

2. 32.877; hundredths ________

3. 5.65689; thousandths ________

4. 3.48; ones ________

5. 56.45; tens ________

6. 4.67; tenths ________

7. 13.8908; tenths ________

8. 21.9; tens ________

9. The price of a gallon of milk is $3.75. How much is this to the nearest dollar?

____

Round each whole number to the place indicated.

10. 3,579; thousand ________

11. 29,342; hundred ________

12. 433,231,292; million ________

13. 711,900; hundred thousand ________

14. 33,110; ten thousand ________

15. 132,509; ten ________

16. 559,308; ten thousand ________

17. 14,663; hundred ________

18. 8,413; thousand ________

19. There are about 77,621,001 pet cats in the United States. How many pet cats are there rounded to the nearest hundred thousand?

____

Name ______________________________

2–2 Reteach

Estimate Sums and Differences

To estimate a sum or difference, you can round the numbers first. This can make it easier to add or subtract mentally.

$$\begin{array}{rcr} 18.7 & \rightarrow & 19 \\ \underline{-4.2} & \rightarrow & \underline{-4} \\ & & 15 \end{array}$$

Find the lesser number. Circle the digit in the greatest place. Round each number to that place. Add or subtract.

Estimate each sum or difference by rounding.

1. $\begin{array}{r} 4.204 \rightarrow \\ \underline{+\ 2.779} \rightarrow \end{array}$

2. $\begin{array}{r} \$189 \rightarrow \\ \underline{-\ \ 53} \rightarrow \end{array}$

3. $\begin{array}{r} 4.567 \rightarrow \\ \underline{-\ 1.788} \rightarrow \end{array}$

4. $\begin{array}{r} 31.53 \rightarrow \\ \underline{+\ 42.07} \rightarrow \end{array}$

5. $\begin{array}{r} 15.497 \rightarrow \\ \underline{+\ 8.38} \rightarrow \end{array}$

6. $\begin{array}{r} 47.1 \rightarrow \\ \underline{-11.66} \rightarrow \end{array}$

7. $\begin{array}{r} 5.087 \rightarrow \\ \underline{+\ 9.615} \rightarrow \end{array}$

8. $\begin{array}{r} 794 \rightarrow \\ \underline{+\ 3{,}157} \rightarrow \end{array}$

9. $\begin{array}{r} 4{,}780 \rightarrow \\ \underline{-\ \ 103} \rightarrow \end{array}$

10. $\begin{array}{r} \$42.46 \rightarrow \\ \underline{+\ \ 8.23} \rightarrow \end{array}$

11. $\begin{array}{r} 58.9 \rightarrow \\ \underline{-\ 7.1} \rightarrow \end{array}$

12. $\begin{array}{r} 32.78 \rightarrow \\ \underline{-\ 6.6} \rightarrow \end{array}$

Name ______________________________

2–2

Skills Practice

Estimate Sums and Differences

Estimate each sum or difference by rounding.

1. 68.99 + 22.31 ______________

2. 39.57 + 18.34 ______________

3. 81.25 − 23.16 ______________

4. 21.56 − 19.62 ______________

5. 34.87 − 29.12 ______

6. 69.45 − 44.8 ______

7. $78.69 + $31.49 ______

8. $258.32 + $378.60 ______

9. 5.69 + 3.47 + 8.02 ______________

10. 6.6 + 1.22 + 5.54 ______________

11. $4.56 + $4.79 + $5.21 + $5.38

____

12. 9.7325 + 9.55 + 10.333

____

13. 39.8 + 39.6 + 40.21 + 40.47

____

14. $69.72 + $70.44 + $70.59 + $69.56

____

Solve.

15. Miriam bought a basketball for $24.99 and basketball shoes for $47.79. About how much did Miriam spend on the ball and shoes?

____

16. Albuquerque gets an average of 6.35 inches of precipitation a year. Phoenix gets an average of 6.82 inches a year. About how many more inches of precipitation does Phoenix get than Albuquerque?

____

2–3

Name ______________________________

Reteach

Problem-Solving Strategy: Work Backward

A scientist plans to study exotic birds in the rain forest. The helicopter flight to and from the rain forest costs $499. Supplies cost $112 for each day. How many days can the scientist spend in the rain forest on a $1,283 budget?

Step 1 **Understand**	**Be sure you understand the problem.** Read carefully. What do you know? • A helicopter flight costs __________. • Supplies cost __________. • The budget is __________. What do you need to find? • The ____________________ in the rain forest.
Step 2 **Plan**	You can work backward to find the number of days the scientist can stay in the rain forest. Use math operations to undo each step.

Name ____________________

2–3

Reteach

Problem-Solving Strategy: Work Backward (continued)

Step 3
Solve

Carry out your plan.

Decide which operation undoes each step.

Undo the addition of the cost of the helicopter.

Which operation undoes addition? ____________________

____________________ the cost of the helicopter from the total budget: ____________________

The scientist has ____________________ left after paying for the helicopter.

Undo the multiplication of the number of days the scientist can stay in the rain forest.

Which operation undoes multiplication? ____________________

____________________ the amount remaining by the cost of supplies for each day.

How many days can the scientist stay in the rain forest? __________ days

Step 4
Check

Is the solution reasonable?

Reread the problem.

Have you answered the question? __________

How can you check your answer?

____

Solve. Use the *work backward* strategy.

1. Ms. Robin's class is planting trees for Arbor Day. They raise a total of $80 to buy trees and supplies. A local nursery has offered to provide trees for $7 each. They spend $17 on supplies. How many trees do they buy?

____

2. Mr. Stone's class visits the aquarium. Mr. Stone has $46 for the trip. The entrance fee for the class is $34. The rest of the money is used to buy posters for the classroom. Each poster costs $3. How many posters does Mr. Stone buy?

____

2–3

Name ____________________

Skills Practice

Problem-Solving Strategy: Work Backward

Solve. Use the *work backward* strategy.

1. Joel spent $6 for a movie ticket and $4 for a drink. He also played some video games that each cost $2.

   He spent $16 in all. How many video games did he play.

   ____

2. Patrick arrived at school at 8:30 A.M. If it took him 45 minutes to get ready, 10 minutes to wait for the school bus, and 20 minutes to get to school, what time did he wake up?

   ____

3. Lauro collects baseball cards. He had a total of 542 cards, but sold some of them so that he could buy a DVD. He now has 489 cards.

   If he made $106, and he charged the same amount for each card, how much did he charge for each card?

   ____

4. Carol is thinking of a number. If the number is increased by 6, then doubled, and 9 is subtracted from the product, the result is 23. What is the original number?

   ____

5. Teresa owns a pet shop. She has 24 dogs, 32 cats, 84 lovebirds, 24 parakeets, and 62 canaries. Each dog has its own cage, and there are two cats per cage. The birds are divided equally among the birdcages.

   If Teresa has a total of 34 birdcages, how many birds are together in each cage?

   ____

6. Julia, Paul, and Mel helped their mother make jelly. Julia filled one third of the jars, and Paul filled twice as many as Mel did. They filled a total of 27 jars.

   How many jars did Julia fill? _____ jars

   How many jars did Mel fill? _____ jars

   How many jars did Paul fill? _____ jars

Name ______________________________

2–4

Reteach

Add and Subtract Whole Numbers

To add or subtract whole numbers, add or subtract the digits in each place-value position, starting with the ones place. Regroup if necessary.

Add 287 + 162.

Step 1

Add the ones.

$$\begin{array}{r} 287 \\ +\ 162 \\ \hline 9 \end{array}$$

Step 2

Add the tens.

$$\begin{array}{r} 1 \\ 287 \\ +\ 162 \\ \hline 49 \end{array}$$

Step 3

Add the hundreds.

$$\begin{array}{r} 1 \\ 287 \\ +\ 162 \\ \hline 449 \end{array}$$

So, 287 + 162 = 449.

Add or subtract.

1. $\begin{array}{r} 4{,}691 \\ +\ 8{,}056 \\ \hline \end{array}$

2. $\begin{array}{r} 491{,}394 \\ +\ 17{,}698 \\ \hline \end{array}$

3. $\begin{array}{r} 32{,}681 \\ -\ 4{,}095 \\ \hline \end{array}$

4. $\begin{array}{r} 498 \\ -\ 311 \\ \hline \end{array}$

5. 67,430 + 25,875 = ______________

6. 7,043 + 39,605 = ______________

7. 80,000 − 18,550 = ______________

8. 40,000 − 398 = ______________

9. 163 + 139 = ______________

10. 82 + 679 = ______________

11. 725 − 16 = ______________

12. 93 − 45 = ______________

Name ______________________

2–4

Skills Practice

Add and Subtract Whole Numbers

Add or subtract.

1. 9,868 + 6,329

2. 3,136 − 473

3. 87 + 612

4. 445 − 102

5. 3,007 − 1,980

6. 4,672 + 1,531

7. 31,043 + 56,691

8. 285 − 58

9. 4,609 − 281

10. 124,543 + 96,883

11. 12,974 + 4,734

12. 20,431 − 17,642

13. 5,802 + 4,289

14. 30,048 − 9,338

15. 109 − 65

16. 34,504 + 5,712 = ______

17. 1,265 + 877 = ______

18. 5,954 − 4,883 = ______

19. 2,980 + 135,618 = ______

20. 4,465 − 219 = ______

21. 78,327 − 59,912 = ______

22. 33 + 579 = ______

23. 210,336 − 89,481 = ______

Name ______________________________

2–5

Reteach

Problem-Solving Investigation: Estimate or Exact Answer

The Selden School buys 28 boxes of pencils. Each box holds 32 pencils. About how many pencils does the school buy?

Step 1 Understand	**Be sure you understand the problem.** Read carefully. • What do you know? You know the number of boxes that the school buys, and the number of pencils in each box. • What do you need to find? You need to find about how many pencils the school buys. Choose an Estimate or an Exact Answer. • Some problems need an exact answer. Find an exact answer when the problem asks for one. Find an exact answer when you need to be sure if a result is greater or less than a number. • Some problems need only an estimate. Estimate when you do not need to know the exact number. Estimate when an exact number is too hard to find. Some problems use words like *about* or *approximately*. Such words are clues that you can use an estimate.
Step 2 Plan	**Plan a Strategy.** You need to find *about* how many pencils the school buys. So, you can use an estimate to solve the problem.
Step 3 Solve	**Solve the problem.** Use your plan. Estimate. Round each factor to the nearest ten. $28 \times 32 \longrightarrow 30 \times 30 = 900$ The school buys about 900 pencils.
Step 4 Check	**Did you answer the question?** Yes, you have found about how many pencils the school buys.

For each problem, determine whether you need an estimate or exact answer. Then solve.

1. Robert earns $9 each hour. If he works 24 hours in a week, how much money does he earn that week?

____

2. A theater has 36 rows. Each row has 24 seats. About how many seats does the theater have?

____

2–5

Name ___________________

Reteach

Problem-Solving Investigation: Estimate or Exact Answer (continued)

3. Kallie has 9 books of stamps. If each book has about 42 stamps, about how many stamps does she have?

____

4. You have to be 48 inches tall to get on the roller coaster. Emma is 45 inches tall. If she grows 2 inches each year, will she be able to ride the roller coaster in 2 years?

____

5. Six friends split the cost of dinner. If the total cost of dinner was $35.25, about how much will each friend have to pay?

____

6. A family is staying in a hotel for 6 nights. The hotel costs 79.99 a night. About how much will they pay for the hotel?

____

7. Erin needs $59 to buy new boots that she wants. If she saves 5 dollars a week, will she be able to buy the boots in 11 weeks?

____

8. A puppy weighs 4 pounds. If the puppy gains 1.7 pounds every 2 weeks, about how much will the puppy weigh in 8 weeks?

____

2–5

Name ______________________

Skills Practice

Problem-Solving Investigation: Estimate or Exact Answer

For each problem, determine whether you need an estimate or an exact answer. Then solve.

1. The ski team has a race at 9:00 A.M. The race is 120 miles away. The team leaves at 6:00 A.M. and drives about 50 miles each hour. Will they arrive at the race on time?

____

2. The ski team travels in 4 vans. Each van holds 9 team members. How many members are on the team?

____

3. School raffle tickets cost $8 apiece. The school's goal is to raise at least $3,000 from the raffle. If 424 tickets are sold, will the school meet its goal?

____

4. Students at Tuscan School filled out a survey. The survey showed that of 374 students, 195 speak a second language. How many students speak only one language?

____

5. Book World receives 12 boxes of books. Each box contains 16 copies of the new best-seller, *Norton's Last Laugh*. How many copies of *Norton's Last Laugh* does the store receive?

____

____

6. At the beginning of the last year, there were 368 students at the elementary school. By the beginning of this year, 72 of those students had moved. About how many students started the school year this year?

____

____

Name ____________________

2–6 Reteach

Add and Subtract Decimals

Add 3.25 + 12.6 + 18.93

Step 1
Line up the decimal points. Write an equivalent decimal if necessary.

```
  03.25
  12.60
+ 18.93
```

Step 2
Add as you would add whole numbers. Regroup if necessary.

```
  11
  03.25
  12.60
+ 18.93
  34 78
```

Step 3
Place the decimal point.

```
  11
  03.25
  12.60
+ 18.93
  34.78
```

To subtract decimals, follow similar steps. Work from right to left and regroup if necessary. Place the decimal point to complete the subtraction.

Add.

1. 0.9 + 6.7 = ________

2. 3.1 + 9.4 = ________

3. 4.88 + 8.19 = ________

4. 14.05 + 9.2 = ________

5. 6.008 + 0.22 = ________

6. 9.104 + 5.2 + 7.99 = ________

Subtract.

7. 8.5 − 4.2 = ________

8. 7.2 − 3.05 = ________

9. 5.07 − 2.8 = ________

10. 6.347 − 2.986 = ________

11. 14.2 − 9.86 = ________

12. 13.45 − 5.001 = ________

13. 22.7 − 12.06 = ________

14. 16.1 − 10.88 = ________

Add or subtract.

15.
```
  40.6
−  3.7
```

16.
```
  45.67
+ 33.9
```

17.
```
   6.41
  12.1
+ 13.43
```

18.
```
  10.9
−  0.726
```

2–6

Name ______________________

Skills Practice

Add and Subtract Decimals

Add or subtract.

1. 9.868 + 6.329

2. 3.136 − 2.473

3. 0.87 + 6.12

4. 4.45 − 1.02

5. 3.007 − 1.980

6. 4.672 + 15.31

7. 31.043 + 56.691

8. 2.85 − 0.58

9. 4.609 − 2.81

10. 124.543 + 96.883

11. 12.974 + 4.734

12. 20.431 − 17.642

13. 5.8 + 4.289

14. 30.048 − 9.338

15. $1.09 − 0.65

16. 76.509 + 120.306

17. 321.658 − 197.369

18. 3.472 + 7.810

19. 3.65 − 0.824

20. $28.99 + 1.75

21. 34.504 + 5.712 = __________

22. 1.265 + 8.77 = __________

23. 9.54 − 4.883 = __________

24. 2.980 + 135.618 = __________

25. $44.65 − $2.19 = __________

26. 78.327 − 59.912 = __________

27. $0.33 + $5.79 = __________

28. 210.336 − 89.481 = __________

Solve.

29. Gasoline prices are given to the nearest thousandth of a dollar. If gasoline rises in price from $1.499 to $1.589, what is the amount of the increase?

____

30. The area of Max's room, including his closet, is 695.676 square feet. The area of his closet is 10.463 square feet. What is the area of his room, not including the closet?

____

Name ____________________

2–7

Reteach

Addition Properties

On Monday, Simone did math homework for 30 minutes and science homework for 20 minutes. On Tuesday, she did science homework for 20 minutes and math homework for 30 minutes. On which day did she do more homework?

In this situation, the order in which Simone did math and science homework did not change the total amount of time she did homework.

This is an example of the Commutative Property. The definition of this property and other properties of addition appear below:

Commutative Property: The order in which numbers are added does not change the sum.

Associative Property: The way in which numbers are grouped does not change the sum.

Identity Property: The sum of any number and 0 equals the number.

Identify the addition property used to rewrite each problem.

1. 21 + 36 + 17 = 36 + 17 + 21

____

2. (5 + 9) + 2 = 5 + (9 + 2)

____

3. 46.8 + 0 = 46.8

____

4. 77 + (31 + 15) = (77 + 31) + 15

____

5. 46 + 13 + 8 = 13 + 8 + 46

____

6. 15 + 0 = 15

____

Name ______________________

2–7

Skills Practice

Addition Properties

Identify the addition property used to rewrite each problem.

1. $7 + (26 + 13) = (7 + 26) + 13$

____

2. $18 + 12 + 7 = 12 + 7 + 18$

____

3. $57 + 0 = 57$

____

4. $22 + 5 + 3 = 3 + 22 + 5$

____

Use properties of addition to find each sum mentally. Show your steps and identify the properties that you used.

5. $15 + 5 + 6$ ______________________

____

____

6. $12 + 18 + 7$ ______________________

____

____

7. $4.3 + 1 + 5.7$ ______________________

____

____

____

For exercises 8–9, find the value that makes the sentence true.

8. $45 + (10 + 34) = (10 + \square) + 34$

9. $1.1 + (3.9 + 12) = (3.9 + 1.1) + \square$

Solve.

10. Sasha spent $1.05 on a soda, $5.25 on a sandwich, $0.75 on a piece of fruit, and $4.95 on a magazine. Use mental math to find the total amount she spent.

____

Name ______________________________

2–8

Reteach

Add and Subtract Mentally

Compensation is a method of adjusting numbers you're adding or subtracting to make them easier to add or subtract mentally.

When adding mentally, adjust either number to make it a whole number or multiple of 10:

<u>Whole numbers</u>

37	+	34	
+ 3		− 3	Add 3 to 37. Adjust by subtracting 3 from 34.
40	+	31	= 71

<u>Decimals</u>

3.8	+	1.5	
− 0.5		+ 0.5	Add 0.5 to 1.5. Adjust by subtracting 0.5 from 3.8.
3.3	+	2.0	= 5.3

When subtracting mentally, adjust the second number to make it a whole number or multiple of 10:

<u>Whole numbers</u>

242	−	198	
+ 2		+ 2	Add 2 to 198. Adjust by adding 2 to 242.
244	−	200	= 44

<u>Decimals</u>

6.7	−	3.3	
− 0.3		− 0.3	Subtract 0.3 from 3.3. Adjust by subtracting 0.3 from 6.7.
6.4	−	3.0	= 3.4

Add or subtract mentally. Use compensation.

1. 26 + 94 ____________ **2.** 6.8 + 5.2 ____________

3. 325 − 218 ____________ **4.** 56.7 − 32.7 ____________

5. 423 + 118 ____________ **6.** 13.5 − 2.4 ____________

Name ____________________

2–8

Skills Practice

Add and Subtract Mentally

Add or subtract mentally. Use compensation.

1. 46 + 27 ________

2. 9.4 + 1.8 ________

3. 647 − 498 ________

4. 26.4 − 20.1 ________

5. 171 + 204 ________

6. 7.4 − 1.3 ________

7. 105 + 278 ________

8. 347 + 8.9 ________

9. 415 − 196 ________

10. 51.3 − 23.7 ________

11. 309 + 265 ________

12. 9.5 − 1.4 ________

13. 56 + 24

14. 7.2 + 3.9

15. 216 − 173 ________

16. 42.8 − 25.3 ________

17. 369 + 76 ________

18. 25.4 − 11.7 ________

Solve.

19. Sarah skipped rope 335 times in a row. Katie skipped rope 296 times in a row. Use mental math to find how many times more Sarah skipped rope than Katie.

____

20. When Jonah was born, he weighed 7.4 pounds. His twin brother, James, weighed 7.8 pounds when he was born. Use mental math to find how much they weighed altogether.

____

3–1

Name ______________________________

Reteach

Multiplication Patterns

To multiply by multiples of 10, 100, and 1,000, you can use basic facts and patterns.

Multiply 40 × 800.

Start with the basic fact.	4	×	8	=	32
Count the number of zeros in each factor and add them together.	40 ↑	×	800 ↑		
	1 zero	+	2 zeros	=	3 zeros
Write that number of zeros in the product.	40	×	800	=	32,000

Multiply 50 × 80.

Start with the basic fact.	5	×	8	=	40
Count the number of zeros in each factor and add them together.	50 ↑	×	80 ↑		
	1 zero	+	1 zero	=	2 zeros
Write that number of zeros in the product.	50	×	80	=	4,000

Complete.

1. 20 × 60

Basic fact: 2 × 6 = __________

Number of zeros in each factor:

__________ + 1 = __________

Product: 20 × 60 = __________

2. 9 × 80

Basic fact: ____________________

Number of zeros in each factor:

0 + __________ = __________

Product: ____________________

Find each product mentally.

3. 5 × 9 = __________

5 × 90 = __________

5 × 900 = __________

5 × 9,000 = __________

4. 3 × 6 = __________

3 × 60 = __________

3 × 600 = __________

3 × 6,000 = __________

5. 4 × 12 = __________

40 × 12 = __________

400 × 12 = __________

4,000 × 12 = __________

6. 6 × 60 = __________

60 × 60 = __________

600 × 60 = __________

6,000 × 60 = __________

7. 7 × \$3 = __________

70 × \$3 = __________

700 × \$3 = __________

7,000 × \$3 = __________

8. 5 × 40 = __________

50 × 40 = __________

500 × 40 = __________

5,000 × 40 = __________

3-1

Name ____________

Skills Practice

Multiplication Patterns

Find each product mentally.

1. 8 × 2= ________

8 × 20 = ________

8 × 200 = ________

8 × 2,000 = ________

2. 6 × 4 = ________

6 × 40 = ________

6 × 400 = ________

6 × 4,000 = ________

3. 4 × 5 = ________

4 × 50 = ________

4 × 500 = ________

4 × 5,000 = ________

4. 3 × 80 = ________

30 × 80 = ________

300 × 80 = ________

3,000 × 80 = ________

5. 5 × 60 = ________

50 × 60 = ________

500 × 60 = ________

5,000 × 60 = ________

6. 9 × $70 = ________

90 × $70 = ________

900 × $70 = ________

9,000 × $70 = ________

7. 90 × 3 = ________

8. 7 × $4,000 = ________

9. 200 × 6 = ________

10. 30 × 40 = ________

11. 600 × 70 = ________

12. 40 × 800 = ________

13. 4 × $1,000 = ________

14. 500 × 80 = ________

15. 70 × 100 = ________

16. 3 × 30 = ________

17. 5 × 1,000 = ________

18. 7 × $900 = ________

19. 50 × 80 = ________

20. 100 × 80 = ________

21. 50 × 20 = ________

Solve.

22. The 9 members of a music club in Indianapolis want to fly to New York to see several musicals. The cost of a round trip ticket is $300. How much would the airfare be altogether?

____

23. During one week, an airport shop sold 70 New York City travel guides for $9 each. How much was the total received for the guides?

____

3–2

Name ____________________

Reteach

The Distributive Property

The Distributive Property combines addition and multiplication. To mulitiply a sum by a number, multiply each addend of the sum by the number. Then add.

Multiply 3 × 26. Multiply and add (3 × 20) + (3 × 6).

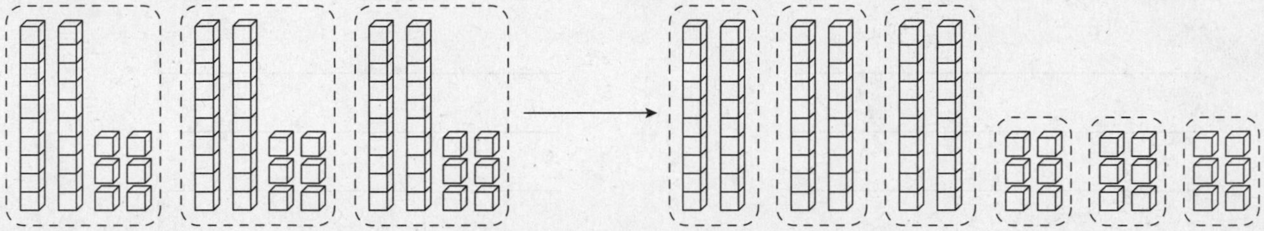

3 × 26 = 3 × (20 + 6) (3 × 20) (3 × 6)

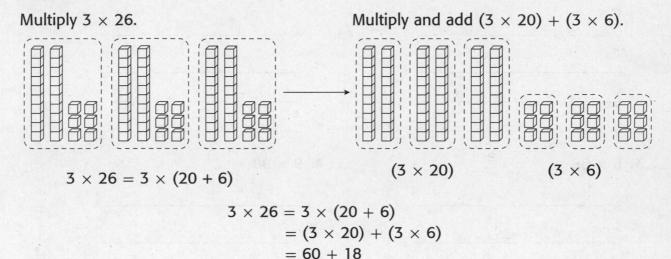

$$3 \times 26 = 3 \times (20 + 6)$$
$$= (3 \times 20) + (3 \times 6)$$
$$= 60 + 18$$
$$= 78$$

Rewrite each expression using the Distributive Property. Then evaluate.

1. 3 × (15 + 6)

2. 6 × (14 + 3)

Find each product mentally using the Distributive Property. Show the steps that you used.

3. 2 × 48

4. 3 × 88

Name ______________________________

3–2

Skills Practice

The Distributive Property

Find each product mentally using the Distributive Property. Show the steps that you used.

1. 7 × 19

____

____

____

____

2. 2 × 27

____

____

____

____

3. 6 × 88

____

____

____

____

4. 9 × 98

____

____

____

____

Rewrite each expression using the Distributive Property. Then evaluate.

5. 3 × 13

____

6. 8 × 68

____

7. 7 × 32

____

8. 9 × 35

____

9. 8 × 17

____

10. 4 × 71

____

Solve.

11. Each of 6 hikers were allowed to bring 24 pounds of gear on a cross-country hike. How many pounds of gear was that altogether?

____

12. The hikers plan to travel an average of 12 miles each day for 9 days. How many miles do they plan to travel in all?

____

3-3

Name ______________________________

Reteach

Estimate Products

To estimate a product, round each number. Then use a basic fact and a multiplication pattern to multiply mentally.

	Estimate 27 × 643.	Estimate 54 × 761
Round each number to its greatest place.	27 × 643 ↓ ↓	54 × 761 ↓ ↓
Write the basic fact. Then, write the same number of zeros in the product as are in both factors.	**3**0 × **6**00 = **18**,000 ↑ ↑ ↑ 1 zero + 2 zeros = 3 zeros	**5**0 × **8**00 = **40**,000 ↑ ↑ ↑ 1 zero + 2 zeros = 3 zeros

Estimate by rounding. Show your work.

1. 54 × 68
↓ ↓
_____ × _____ = _____

2. 61 × 239
↓ ↓
_____ × _____ = _____

3. 697 × 43
↓ ↓
_____ × _____ = _____

4. 364 × 28
↓ ↓
_____ × _____ = _____

5. 8 × 674 ______________

6. 9 × 458 ______________

7. 43 × 104 ______________

8. 19 × 74 ______________

9. 84 × 13 ______________

10. 21 × 663 ______________

11. 38 × 573 ______________

12. 18 × 264 ______________

13. 184 × 48 ______________

14. 26 × 904 ______________

3–3

Name ______________________

Skills Practice

Estimate Products

Estimate by rounding. Show your work.

1. 34 × 10 ______________

2. 59 × 32 ______________

3. 446 × 682 ______________

4. 21 × 663 ______________

5. 98 × 32 ______________

6. 91 × 32 ______________

7. 334 × 847 ______________

8. 929 × 8 ______________

9. 43 × 58 ______________

10. 186 × 92 ______________

11. 342 × 86 ______________

12. 396 × 23 ______________

13. 8,547 × 836

14. 603 × 29

15. 408 × 46

16. 3,045 × 38

Estimate by using compatible numbers. Show your work.

17. 6 × 24 __________

18. 8 × 48 __________

19. 12 × 26 __________

20. 12 × 52 __________

21. 110 × 97 __________

22. 120 × 11 __________

Solve.

23. Tickets to a basketball game cost $22 each. Mr. Reynolds bought 17 tickets to give away as prizes at an assembly. About how much did the tickets cost altogether?

____

24. There are 514 students at Scioto Elementary. Each of the students donated 7 food items for a charity food drive. About how many items were collected altogether?

____

Name ______________________

3–4

Reteach

Multiply by One-Digit Numbers

Find 32 × 6.
Estimate: 32 × 6 = 180

Step 1

Multiply the ones.

$$\begin{array}{r} \scriptstyle 1 \\ 32 \\ \times\ 6 \\ \hline 2 \end{array}$$

6 × 2 = 12 ones

Step 2

Multiply the tens.

$$\begin{array}{r} \scriptstyle 1 \\ 32 \\ \times\ 6 \\ \hline 192 \end{array}$$

6 × 3 = 18 tens
18 + 1 = 19 tens

The product is 192. This is close to the estimate of 180, so the answer is reasonable.

Multiply.

1. 53 × 4   **2.** 26 × 3   **3.** 38 × 5   **4.** 47 × 4

5. 12 × 3   **6.** 28 × 6   **7.** 144 × 3   **8.** 615 × 4

9. 262 × 5   **10.** 811 × 2   **11.** 501 × 6   **12.** 149 × 7

13. 5 × 78   **14.** 24 × 6   **15.** 704 × 3   **16.** 8 × 92

Name ______________________

3–4

Skills Practice

Multiply by One-Digit Numbers

Multiply.

1. 83 × 5

2. 66 × 6

3. 32 × 4

4. 44 × 3

5. 56 × 5

6. 14 × 7

7. 28 × 4

8. 89 × 2

9. 557 × 9

10. 732 × 6

11. 645 × 3

12. 312 × 2

13. 564 × 4

14. 623 × 7

15. 769 × 3

16. 293 × 6

17. 4 × 39 ______

18. 19 × 8 ______

19. 344 × 7 ______

20. 3 × 51 ______

21. 2 × 99 ______

22. 63 × 3 ______

23. 519 × 4 ______

24. 4 × 89 ______

25. 2 × 67 ______

26. 42 × 5 ______

27. 716 × 8 ______

28. 6 × 191 ______

29. The math club at Southview Elementary School sold 443 rolls of wrapping paper during the holiday fundraiser. If the price of each roll was $4, how much money did they earn?

____

30. Andrea made 28 flowerpots to sell at the craft fair. Jenna made twice as many flowerpots. How many flower pots does Jenna have?

____

3–5

Name ____________________

Reteach

Problem-Solving Strategy: Draw a picture

You are making a seating chart for a math center. If one person can sit on each side of a square table, how many people can sit at four tables pushed together in a square?

Step 1 Understand	**Be sure you understand the problem.** Read carefully. What do you know? • There are ________ square tables. • __________ can sit on each side of a square table. What do you need to find? • You need to find the number of people ________
Step 2 Plan • Draw a Picture • Guess and Check • Work Backward	**Make a plan.** Choose a strategy. You can draw a picture to solve the problem. You can use four small squares to represent the tables. You can use a circle to represent each chair.

Name ____________________

3–5

Reteach

Problem-Solving Strategy: Draw a Picture (continued)

Draw a picture.

Step 3 Solve	Draw four small squares so that they form one large square. Draw one circle at each exposed edge of each small square. 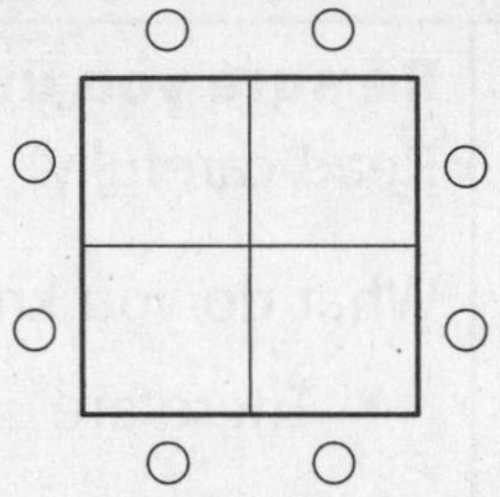 How many people can sit at four tables pushed together in a square? ____________________
Step 4 Check	**Is the solution reasonable?** Reread the problem. Have you answered the question? __________ How can you decide if your results are reasonable? ____________________ ____________________ ____________________ ____________________ ____________________

Solve.

1. A restaurant has some circular tables and three large square tables. Two people can sit on each side of a large square table. If the three large square tables are pushed together to form a rectangle, how many people can sit at the rectangle?

____

2. A house has a rectangular porch that is 15 feet by 20 feet. One of the long sides of the porch is connected to the house. The other sides of the porch have a 2-foot high railing. What is the total length of the railing?

____

3–5

Name ____________________

Skills Practice

Problem-Solving Strategy: Draw a Picture (continued)

Solve. Use the *draw a picture* strategy.

1. Maria wants to tack three rectangular pictures in a row on the bulletin board. The edges of the pictures can overlap. Maria wants to put a tack in each corner of each picture. How many tacks does she need?

____

2. Jack builds a patio from square tiles that are 2 feet on each side. The patio is 10 feet by 16 feet. How many tiles does Jack need in order to build the patio?

____

3. Howard leaves the dock and sails 2.5 miles west. He turns south and sails 3.5 miles. Then he turns east and sails 2.5 miles. In what direction should Howard turn if he wants to use the most direct route to return to the dock? If Howard uses this route, how many miles will he have sailed in all?

____

4. The main lawn of a college is a rectangle with one building on each side. There is a path from each building to each of the other buildings. How many paths are there?

____

5. Akira cut triangles of the same size out of different colors of cloth. She is going to use the pieces to make a quilt. She places the triangles together around one point until they form a hexagon. How many of the triangles did she have to use?

____

6. For every two steps her dad takes, Heidi takes 4 steps. How many steps will she takes if her dad takes 30 steps?

____

Name ______________________________

3–6

Reteach

Multiply by Two-Digit Numbers

Find 265 × 21.
Estimate: 300 × 20 = 6,000

Step 1 Multiply the ones.	Step 2 Multiply the tens.	Step 3 Add.
265 × 21 265 265 × 1 = 265	265 × 21 265 265 × 20 = 5,300	265 × 21 265 5300 265 + 5,300 = 5,565 5,565

So, 265 × 21 = 5,565.

Multiply.

1. 45 × 12 **2.** 68 × 33 **3.** 57 × 19 **4.** 24 × 39 **5.** 72 × 46

6. 68 × 34 **7.** 25 × 25 **8.** 82 × 58 **9.** 93 × 37 **10.** 81 × 93

11. 364 × 87 **12.** 617 × 62 **13.** 703 × 29 **14.** 548 × 95 **15.** 277 × 38

16. 229 × 43 **17.** 326 × 55 **18.** 449 × 39 **19.** 622 × 12 **20.** 882 × 59

Name ______________________

3–6

Skills Practice

Multiply by Two-Digit Numbers

Multiply.

1. 32 × 517 = ________

2. 466 × 21 = ________

3. 83 × 13 = ________

4. 43 × 65 = ________

5. 458 × 26 = ________

6. 329 × 72 = ________

7. 601 × 24 = ________

8. 728 × 68 = ________

9. 188 × 46 = ________

10. 250 × 27 = ________

11. 45 × 371 = ________

12. 70 × 686 = ________

13. 67 × 211

14. 30 × 456

15. 170 × 55

16. 824 × 19

17. 345 × 42

18. \$740 × 16

19. 92 × 301

20. 262 × 39

21. 114 × 48

22. 653 × 20

23. 49 × 700

24. 318 × 52

25. 202 × 96

26. 79 × 349

27. 26 × 781

28. 176 × 45

29. 500 × 19

30. 241 × 67

31. 82 × 820

32. 199 × 36

Solve.

33. A basketball player scored an average of 23 points per game. He played 82 games during the season. How many points did he score that season?

____

34. A basketball arena has 36 sections of seats. Each section contains 784 seats. How many people can the arena seat?

____

Name ______________________________

3–7

Reteach

Multiplication Properties

You can use these multiplication properties to find products mentally.

Commutative Property	Associative Property	Identity Property
The order of the factors does not change the product.	The way the factors are grouped does not change the product.	The product of any number and 1 is that number.
$25 \times 4 = 4 \times 25$ $100 = 100$	$(9 \times 4) \times 5 = 9 \times (4 \times 5)$ $36 \times 5 = 9 \times 20$ $180 = 180$	$87 \times 1 = 87$ $1 \times 6.5 = 6.5$

Identify the multiplication property used to rewrite each problem.

1. $(3 \times 5) \times 2 = 3 \times (5 \times 2)$

____

2. $6 \times 2 \times 18 = 6 \times 18 \times 2$

____

3. $13 \times 24 \times 9 = 9 \times 24 \times 13$

____

4. $(15 \times 6) \times 3 = 15 \times (6 \times 3)$

____

Use properties of multiplication to find each product mentally. Show your steps and identify the properties that you used.

5. $25 \times 9 \times 4$

____

____

____

____

6. $(19 \times 5) \times 2$

____

____

____

____

7. $9 \times 29 \times 0$

____

____

____

____

8. $(4 \times 15) \times 2$

____

____

____

____

3–7

Name ______________________________

Skills Practice

Multiplication Properties

Identify the multiplication property used to rewrite each problem.

1. (185 × 6) × ____ = 185 × (6 × 2)

____

2. 9 × (60 + 7) = (__ × 60) + (9 × 7)

____

3. 124 × ____ = 14 × 124

____

4. 3.41 × ____ = 3.41

____

Use properties of multiplication to find each product mentally. Show your steps and identify the properties that you used.

5. 5 × 24 × 2

____

____

____

____

6. 200 × (4 × 7)

____

____

____

____

7. 483 × 10 × 1

____

____

____

____

8. 5 × 3 × 20

____

____

____

____

3–8

Name ________________________

Reteach

Extending Multiplication

Margaret would like to buy 4 notebooks that cost \$3.08 a piece. The total cost will be 4 × \$3.08. You can estimate the total cost using rounding.

4 × \$3.08	
4 × \$3	Round \$3.08 to \$3 because \$3.08 is closer to \$3 than \$4.
4 × \$3 = \$12	Multiply mentally.

So, the total cost of the notebooks is about \$12.

Estimate each product.

1. \$0.94 × 9

2. \$3.92 × 5

3. \$3.79 × 8

4. \$2.82 × 4

5. \$7.25 × 6

6. \$2.67 × 2

7. \$1.75 × 7

8. \$68.70 × 4

9. \$9.85 × 8

10. 20.1 × 9

11. 10.8 × 7

12. 79.3 × 40

13. 61.2 × 5

14. 23.4 × 60

15. 87.5 × 42

3–8

Name ______________________________

Skills Practice

Extending Multiplication

Estimate each product.

1. $1.80 × 8

2. $2.83 × 7

3. $14.75 × 4

4. $31.15 × 4

5. $4.80 × 5

6. $1.67 × 4

7. $1.79 × 6

8. $2.26 × 14

9. $9.72 × 15

10. 8.4 × 41

11. 48.2 × 31

12. 14.7 × 305

13. 42.3 × 31

14. 104.6 × 411

15. 21.3 × 72

Solve.

16. Each Sunday during his nine week summer vacation, Ray buys a newspaper. The Sunday paper costs $1.85. About how much did Ray spend on the Sunday newspaper during his vacation?

____

17. Jorge buys 8 pounds of ground beef for $3.29 a pound. About how much did he pay altogether?

____

Name ______________________________

3–9

Reteach

Problem-Solving Investigation: Extra or Missing Information

Benjamin was in charge of selling tickets to the school play. On Monday he sold 10 tickets. He sold 8 tickets on Tuesday and again on Wednesday. On Thursday he sold 10 tickets, and on Friday he sold 5. The play was on Saturday at noon.

Find the amount of money Benjamin collected selling tickets to the school play.

Understand	**What facts do you know?** You know how many tickets Benjamin sold Monday–Friday. You also know when the play was. **What do you need to find?** How much money Benjamin collected selling tickets to the school play.
Plan	**Is there any information that is not needed?** The day and time of the play **Is there any information that is missing?** You do not know the cost of a ticket.
Solve	Since you do not have enough information, the problem cannot be solved.
Check	Read the question again to see if you missed any information. If so, go back and rework the problem. If not, the problem cannot be solved.

Solve each problem. If there is extra information, identify it. If there is not enough information, tell what information is needed.

1. Julia drinks 5 glasses of water on day 1 and 4 glasses of water on day 2. She also drank 4 glasses of water on day 3. She drank 7 glasses on day 4. She also had some juice on day 4. What is the total number of glasses of water she drank at the end of the four days.

____

3–9

Name ______________________________

Reteach

Problem-Solving Investigation: Extra or Missing Information (continued)

Solve each problem. If there is extra information, identify it. If there is not enough information, tell what information is needed.

2. Susan bikes 3 miles round-trip from home to school, Monday through Friday. On Saturday and Sunday she does not ride her bike, but skateboards around her neighborhood. How many miles total does she bike to and from school each week?

____

3. Jason's goal is to wash 30 cars on the day of his scout troop's car wash fundraiser. If he washes 5 cars between 9:00 and 11:00 A.M. and 10 more cars between noon and 2:30, will he meet his goal? And Explain.

____

4. Carl is planting an herb garden. If his garden has 3 rows and he can plant three herbs in each row, how many herbs can he grow?

____

5. Mr. Davis has too much stuff so he is having a yard sale. He wants to make at least $200 from the sale. If he has sold $20 worth of his belongings to five different people, has he reached his goal? Explain

____

6. Marissa can run 1 mile in 10 minutes. How many miles will she run in a half hour?

____

7. Zach really enjoys listening to music. If Zach listens to 3 hours of music a day, how many total hours of music will he listen to in 7 days?

____

3–9

Name ____________________

Skills Practice

Problem-Solving Investigation: Extra or Missing Information

Solve each problem. If there is extra information, identify it. If there is not enough information, tell what information is needed.

1. Mrs. Blackwell gives each of her students two pencils. How many pencils did she hand out?

____

2. Mary has saved $50. If she wants to buy an mp3 player that costs $250, will she have enough money in six months?

____

3. Marco does 10 extra math problems each school night. How many extra problems does he do each school week?

____

4. Juan's family is from Houston. They want to go to Florida for vacation. If they need $100 for each person in the family in order to be able to make the trip, will they have enough?

____

5. Shannon has five red shirts, three blue shirts, and four purple shirts. She has three more white shirts than she does brown shirts. How many brown shirts does she have?

____

6. If David plays 3 tennis matches every week for 9 weeks, how many matches will he play altogether?

____

4–1

Name ______________________

Reteach

Division Patterns

A **quotient** is the result of dividing one number by another. A **dividend** is the number that is divided. The **divisor** is the number by which the dividend is divided.

Basic facts and patterns can help you divide by multiples of 10. Look at the patterns below:

$28 \div 7 = 4$	← basic fact →	$28 \div 7 = 4$
$280 \div 7 = 40$		$280 \div 70 = 4$
$2{,}800 \div 7 = 400$		$2{,}800 \div 700 = 4$
$28{,}000 \div 7 = 4{,}000$		$28{,}000 \div 7{,}000 = 4$

Find 420 ÷ 60.

Since 420 is a multiple of 10, you can use the basic fact and continue the pattern:

$42 \div 6 = 7$

$420 \div 60 = 7$

You can also cross out zeros to make division easier:

$42\not{0} \div 6\not{0} =$

$42 \div 6 = 7$

Be sure to cross out the same number of zeros in the dividend and divisor.

Divide mentally.

1. 630 ÷ 7 = ________ **2.** 810 ÷ 90 = ________ **3.** 480 ÷ 4 = ________

4. 240 ÷ 20 = ________ **5.** 550 ÷ 50 = ________ **6.** 400 ÷ 8 = ________

7. 360 ÷ 6 = ________ **8.** 800 ÷ 10 = ________ **9.** 270 ÷ 30 = ________

10. 4,900 ÷ 7 = ________ **11.** 5,600 ÷ 80 = ________ **12.** 6,300 ÷ 9 = ________

13. 2,500 ÷ 5 = ________ **14.** 1,600 ÷ 20 = ________ **15.** 900 ÷ 3 = ________

Name ______________________________

4–1

Skills Practice

Division Patterns

Divide mentally.

1. 210 ÷ 3 = ____ **2.** 560 ÷ 7 = ____ **3.** 500 ÷ 5 = ____ **4.** 360 ÷ 6 = ____

5. 100 ÷ 2 = ____ **6.** 250 ÷ 5 = ____ **7.** 140 ÷ 2 = ____ **8.** 280 ÷ 4 = ____

9. 720 ÷ 9 = ____ **10.** 180 ÷ 3 = ____ **11.** 480 ÷ 8 = ____ **12.** 360 ÷ 4 = ____

13. 350 ÷ 5 = ____ **14.** 450 ÷ 9 = ____ **15.** 700 ÷ 10 = ____ **16.** 480 ÷ 12 = ____

17. $8\overline{)640}$ **18.** $4\overline{)320}$ **19.** $9\overline{)900}$ **20.** $9\overline{)360}$ **21.** $11\overline{)990}$

22. $3\overline{)240}$ **23.** $5\overline{)300}$ **24.** $2\overline{)180}$ **25.** $9\overline{)990}$ **26.** $7\overline{)630}$

27. $6\overline{)420}$ **28.** $8\overline{)400}$ **29.** $4\overline{)2{,}400}$ **30.** $8\overline{)3{,}200}$ **31.** $6\overline{)6{,}000}$

32. $9\overline{)810}$ **33.** $5\overline{)4{,}000}$ **34.** $10\overline{)5{,}000}$ **35.** $7\overline{)490}$ **36.** $9\overline{)450}$

Solve.

37. Corey has saved 60 files on the hard drive of his computer. He wants to divide them equally among 10 folders. How many files will go in each folder?

____

38. Jasmine has 50 computer disks. She has just enough cases to place 5 disks in each case. How many cases does she have?

____

39. Ten friends paid a total of $80 for movie tickets. How much did one movie ticket cost?

____

40. The Millers drove 300 miles in two days. On average, how many miles did they drive each day?

____

Name ____________________

4–2

Reteach

Estimate Quotients

You can use compatible numbers to estimate quotients. Compatible numbers are easy to divide mentally. They are often members of fact families.

Estimate 4,396 ÷ 6.

Circle the first two digits of the dividend and the divisor. — (43)96 ÷ (6)

Think of a division fact that is close to 43 ÷ 6. — 43 ÷ 6 ↓ 42 ÷ 6

Write zeros in the dividend of the basic fact so it has as many digits as the original dividend. — 4,200 ÷ 6

Divide mentally to find the estimated quotient. — 4,200 ÷ 6 = 700

So, 4,396 ÷ 6 is about 700.

Estimate. Show your work.

1. 133 ÷ 4
↓ ↓
_____ ÷ _____ = _____

2. 694 ÷ 8
↓ ↓
_____ ÷ _____ = _____

3. 2,461 ÷ 5
↓ ↓
_____ ÷ _____ = _____

4. 1,732 ÷ 6
↓ ↓
_____ ÷ _____ = _____

5. 61,191 ÷ 91
↓ ↓
_____ ÷ _____ = _____

6. 34,212 ÷ 8
↓ ↓
_____ ÷ _____ = _____

7. 1,149 ÷ 2 _____

8. 286 ÷ 5 _____

9. 592 ÷ 7 _____

10. 1,359 ÷ 5 _____

11. 43,089 ÷ 8 _____

12. 2,425 ÷ 3 _____

13. 10,126 ÷ 6 _____

14. 29,453 ÷ 4 _____

15. 78,264 ÷ 9 _____

Name ______________________

4–2

Skills Practice

Estimate Quotients

Estimate. Show your work.

1. 2,117 ÷ 7 ______________
2. 2,001 ÷ 19 ______________
3. 2,100 ÷ 708 ______________
4. 540 ÷ 90 ______________
5. 270 ÷ 9 ______________
6. 3,515 ÷ 49 ______________
7. 1,621 ÷ 19 ______________
8. 3,493 ÷ 698 ______________
9. 6,028 ÷ 293 ______________
10. 8,405 ÷ 121 ______________
11. 15,997 ÷ 395 ______________
12. 45,112 ÷ 5,010 ______________
13. 6,000 ÷ 48 ______________
14. 1,800 ÷ 27 ______________
15. 4,200 ÷ 60 ______________
16. 150,175 ÷ 3 ______________
17. 480,000 ÷ 59,997 ______________
18. 18,106 ÷ 289 ______________
19. 717 ÷ 9 ______________
20. 638 ÷ 8 ______________
21. 463 ÷ 90 ______________
22. 249 ÷ 81 ______________
23. 162 ÷ 4 ______________
24. 534 ÷ 9 ______________
25. 481 ÷ 64 ______________
26. 34 ÷ 4 ______________
27. 57 ÷ 9 ______________
28. 468 ÷ 8 ______________
29. 409 ÷ 48 ______________
30. 363 ÷ 3 ______________
31. 311 ÷ 5 ______________
32. 364 ÷ 69 ______________

Solve.

33. Jane makes 20 equal payments to buy a CD player that sells for $170. About how much is each payment? Show your work.

____

34. Justine makes 30 equal payments to buy a car that sells for $14,000. About how much is each payment? Show your work.

____

Name ____________________

4–3

Reteach

Divide by One-Digit Numbers

You can think of the dividend in expanded form to help you divide.

Divide $6\overline{)394}$.

$$\begin{array}{r} \mathbf{6} \\ 6\overline{)394} \end{array}$$

Since there are not enough hundreds to be divided by 6, rename 3 hundreds 9 tens as 39 tens. Divide 39 tens by 6. Write the first digit of the quotient above the tens digit of the dividend.

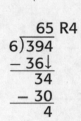

$$\begin{array}{r} 6 \\ 6\overline{)394} \\ -36\downarrow \\ \hline 34 \end{array}$$

Multiply: $6 \times 6 = 36$
Subtract: $39 - 36 = 3$
Compare the difference to the divisor: $3 < 6$
Bring down the next digit of the dividend.

$$\begin{array}{r} 65 \text{ R4} \\ 6\overline{)394} \\ -36\downarrow \\ \hline 34 \\ -30 \\ \hline 4 \end{array}$$

Divide 34 by 6.
Multiply: $5 \times 6 = 30$
Subtract: $34 - 30 = 4$
Compare the difference to the divisor: $4 < 6$
Write the remainder.

Check:

$$\begin{array}{r} 65 \\ \times\ 6 \\ \hline 390 \\ +\ \ 4 \\ \hline 394 \end{array}$$

← Multiply the quotient by the divisor.
← Add the remainder.
← Should equal the dividend.

Divide.

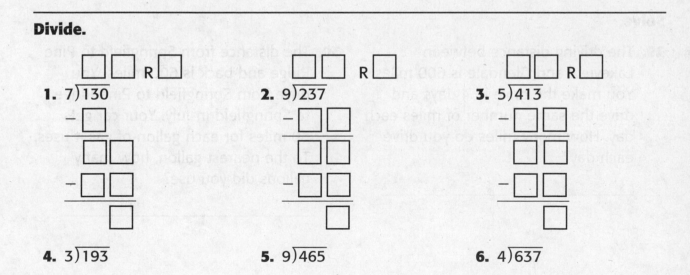

1. $7\overline{)130}$ __ __ R __

2. $9\overline{)237}$ __ __ R __

3. $5\overline{)413}$ __ __ R __

4. $3\overline{)193}$

5. $9\overline{)465}$

6. $4\overline{)637}$

4–3

Name ______________________________

Skills Practice

Divide by One-Digit Numbers

Divide.

1. $3\overline{)385}$ **2.** $7\overline{)511}$ **3.** $9\overline{)179}$ **4.** $5\overline{)254}$

5. $6\overline{)407}$ **6.** $8\overline{)167}$ **7.** $4\overline{)131}$ **8.** $9\overline{)852}$

9. $5\overline{)123}$ **10.** $3\overline{)304}$ **11.** $7\overline{)224}$ **12.** $9\overline{)782}$

13. $4\overline{)299}$ **14.** $8\overline{)207}$ **15.** $5\overline{)632}$ **16.** $3\overline{)819}$

17. 463 ÷ 5 = ________ **18.** 606 ÷ 8 = ________ **19.** 615 ÷ 2 = ________

20. 103 ÷ 9 = ________ **21.** 618 ÷ 3 = ________ **22.** 968 ÷ 6 = ________

23. 53 ÷ 2 = ________ **24.** 55 ÷ 4 = ________ **25.** 27 ÷ 8 = ________

26. 98 ÷ 3 = ________ **27.** 22 ÷ 9 = ________ **28.** 54 ÷ 5 = ________

Solve.

29. The driving distance between Lakeview and Glendale is 600 miles. You make the drive in 4 days and drive the same number of miles each day. How many miles do you drive each day?

____

30. The distance from Springfield to Pine Ridge and back is 600 miles. You drive from Springfield to Pine Ridge to Springfield in July. Your car gets 30 miles for each gallon of gas it uses. To the nearest gallon, how many gallons did you use?

____

Name ______________________

4–4

Reteach

Divide by Two-Digit Numbers

Find $30\overline{)592}$.

$$\begin{array}{r} 1 \\ 30\overline{)592} \end{array}$$

You cannot divide 5 by 30. But you can divide 59 by 30. The first digit in the quotient will be in the tens place.

$$\begin{array}{r} 1 \\ 30\overline{)592} \\ -30\downarrow \\ \hline 292 \end{array}$$

59 ÷ 30 is less than 2. Write the 1 above the tens digit of the dividend. Multiply: 1 × 30 = 30

Subtract 59 − 30 = 29.
Compare the difference to the divisor: 29 < 30
Bring down the next digit of the dividend.

$$\begin{array}{r} 19 \\ 30\overline{)592} \\ -30\downarrow \\ \hline 292 \end{array}$$

292 ÷ 30 is about 10.
Multiply 10 × 30 = 300.
You cannot subtract because 300 > 292.

$$\begin{array}{r} 19 \text{ R22} \\ 30\overline{)592} \\ -30\downarrow \\ \hline 292 \\ -270 \\ \hline 22 \end{array}$$

Try a lesser number in the divisor.
Multiply 9 × 30 = 270.
Subtract 292 − 270 = 22.
Compare the difference to the divisor: 22 < 30
There are no more digits in the dividend, so write the remainder.

Estimate. Then divide.

1. $23\overline{)595}$ = ☐☐ R ☐☐
− ☐☐
☐☐☐
− ☐☐☐
☐☐

2. $38\overline{)190}$ = ☐
− ☐☐☐
☐

3. $23\overline{)156}$

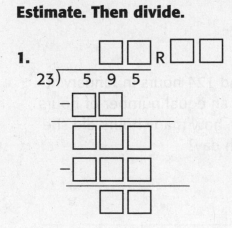

4. $58\overline{)575}$

Name ______________________________

4–4

Skills Practice

Divide by Two-Digit Numbers

Divide.

1. $58\overline{)94}$ **2.** $78\overline{)161}$ **3.** $23\overline{)491}$

4. $47\overline{)539}$ **5.** $21\overline{)390}$ **6.** $96\overline{)694}$

7. $73\overline{)521}$ **8.** $88\overline{)755}$ **9.** $39\overline{)388}$

10. $37\overline{)120}$ **11.** $54\overline{)254}$ **12.** $82\overline{)215}$

13. $84\overline{)275}$ **14.** $22\overline{)416}$ **15.** $32\overline{)224}$

16. $204 \div 33 =$ ______ **17.** $649 \div 84 =$ ______

18. $129 \div 95 =$ ______ **19.** $720 \div 45 =$ ______

20. $201 \div 70 =$ ______ **21.** $639 \div 87 =$ ______

22. $488 \div 96 =$ ______ **23.** $289 \div 54 =$ ______

24. $205 \div 75 =$ ______ **25.** $878 \div 42 =$ ______

Solve.

26. Members of the Bladerunners skating club collected $950 from fundraising activities. They want to buy Ultrablade skates, which are $50 a pair. How many pairs of skates can they buy?

____

27. Emily read 124 hours in January. If she read an equal number of hours each day, how many hours did she read each day?

____

4–5

Name ____________________

Reteach

Problem-Solving Strategy: Act It Out

***Act It Out* Strategy**

Akio and Mei began the project of repainting and covering the seats of old dining room chairs. To cover one seat, they need 0.75 of a yard of fabric. How much fabric do they need to buy to cover the seats of 4 chairs?

Understand	**What facts do you know?** There are 4 chairs to cover. 0.75 of a yard of fabric is needed to cover the seat of each chair. **What do you need to find?** How much fabric is needed to cover the seats of 4 chairs?
Plan	Act out the problem by marking the floor to show a length of 0.75 of a yard. Then, continue to mark 0.75 of a yard of fabric until you have done this 4 times.
Solve	0.75 + 0.75 + 0.75 + 0.75 = 3 yards of fabric
Check	You can estimate by rounding 0.75 to 1. Each chair needs about 1 yard of fabric. 1 + 1 + 1 + 1 = 4, which is close to your answer of 3.

Name ______________________

4–5

Reteach

Problem-Solving Strategy: Act It Out (continued)

Solve. Use the *act it out* strategy.

1. The girls need 0.25 can of paint to paint one chair. How many cans of paint will they need to paint 4 chairs?

____

2. The girls found 6 more chairs. Each chair needs 0.75 yard of fabric to cover its seat. How much more fabric do they need to buy?

____

3. Since each of the 6 chairs needs 0.25 can of paint, how much more paint will they need?

____

4. Jean reads one chapter of her book each day. If she starts reading on Monday, on what day will she complete chapter seven?

____

5. Robert lives 0.3 mile from school. Al lives 0.7 mile from school. Who lives farther from school? How much farther?

____

6. A puppy eats a can of food at each meal. If he eats two times a day, how long will it take him to eat 4 cans of food?

____

Name ___________________________

4–5

Skills Practice

Problem-Solving Strategy: Act It Out

Solve. Use the *act it out* strategy.

1. The ceramics class is designing mugs with three colored stripes. The colors are red, yellow, and green. How many different ways can students in the class arrange the three colored stripes?

____

2. Meg and Matt are painting all 4 walls of a room. Each person is painting 2 walls. After one hour, Meg has painted $\frac{1}{2}$ of one wall, and Matt has painted 1 wall. How much longer will it take Meg to paint her 2 walls than it will take Matt to paint his?

____

3. Twenty-four students are in study hall. Eight more arrive. At the same time, 12 leave. Then, 16 leave and 8 more arrive. How many students are left in study hall?

____

4. Ellen is decorating a wall with family pictures. She has 2 different pictures that are 10 inches and 2 different pictures that are 8 inches. If she keeps all the pictures in one row, how many ways can she arrange the pictures?

____

5. Dolores has 6 quarters, 5 dimes, 4 nickels, and 10 pennies. How many different combinations of coins can she make to have $1?

____

Name ____________________

4–6

Reteach

Interpret the Remainder

Ms. Douglas takes 179 students to the science museum. The students eat lunch in the museum cafeteria. Each table in the cafeteria seats 8 people. How many tables do the students use?

Divide 179 students into groups of 8. $179 \div 8 = 22$ R3

There are different ways to interpret a remainder in the context of the problem.

- **Sometimes you use only the quotient.** Think: How many tables will be full? There will be 22 full tables.
- **Sometimes you use only the remainder.** Think: How many students are left after those tables are filled? There will be 3 students left.
- **Sometimes you add 1 to the quotient.** Think: Where will the remaining students sit? Another table is needed. $22 + 1 = 23$. They will need 23 tables.

So, Ms. Douglas needs 23 tables.

Solve. Explain how you interpreted the remainder.

1. A total of 140 students visit the science museum. They tour the museum in groups of 9. How many groups of students are there?

____

____

____

2. A scientist has 70 sheets of paper. He wants to put the paper in packs of 6. How many packs can he make?

____

____

____

4–6

Name ________________________________

Skills Practice

Interpret the Remainder

Solve. Explain how you interpreted the remainder.

1. At the Science Fair, a hall featuring an electronics exhibit holds 30 people. How many groups will need to be formed if 460 people want to see the electronics exhibit?

____

____

2. Students from four local schools are bussed to the Science Fair. The number of students and teachers attending is 290. Each bus holds 50 passengers. How many buses will be needed?

____

____

3. The Natural History Museum is open 10 hours each day. A 9-minute movie about dinosaurs plays continuously. How many times does the complete movie play each day? (*Hint*: 10 hours = 600 minutes)

____

____

4. The Natural History Museum sells postcards for $3 each. Morris has $29 to spend. If he buys as many postcards as he can, how much money will he have left?

____

____

5. A museum curator has 203 wildlife photographs. She wants to display them in groups of 8. How many groups of 8 can she make?

____

____

6. Each museum tour can have a maximum of 20 people. There are 110 students and teachers who want to take a tour. How many groups will they need?

____

____

7. An artist makes models of dinosaurs. He has 59 dinosaurs. He packages them in boxes of 4. After the artist fills as many boxes as he can, how many dinosaurs will be left?

____

____

8. At the Discovery Center, students work in groups of 5 or fewer. There are 89 students who want to use the center. What is the least number of groups that will need to be formed?

____

____

Name ______________________________

4–7 Reteach

Extending Division

You can use compatible numbers to estimate quotients of decimals.

Estimate 47.6 ÷ 4.

↓ ↓

48 ÷ 4 — Change 47.6 to 48 because 48 and 4 are compatible numbers.

48 ÷ 4 = 12 — Divide mentally.

Technology can be useful for dividing greater numbers.

The Atlantic Ocean has an average depth of 11,730 feet. The Black Sea has an average depth of 3,906 feet. About how many times greater is the average depth of the Atlantic Ocean than the Black Sea?

Then use a calculator to find the exact answer rounded to the nearest whole number.

Estimate 11,730 ÷ 3,906.

↓ ↓

12,000 ÷ 4,000 — 12 and 4 are compatible numbers.

12,000 ÷ 4,000 = 3 — Divide mentally.

Use a calculator.

Enter: [1] [1] [7] [3] [0]

Press: [÷]

Enter: [3] [9] [0] [6]

Press: [=]

Solution: [3.003072197]

So, the Atlantic Ocean is 3 times greater than the Black Sea.

1. $42.60 ÷ 8 ____________ **2.** $23.30 ÷ 6 ____________

3. 17.9 ÷ 3 ____________ **4.** 34.6 ÷ 5 ____________

For Exercises 5 and 6, estimate the quotient. Then use a calculator.

5. 46,212 ÷ 15 ____________ **6.** 9,750 ÷ 40 ____________

____________ ____________

Name ____________________

4–7

Skills Practice

Extending Division

Estimate each quotient.

1. 21.9 ÷ 3 ________

2. 36.3 ÷ 6 ________

3. 12.5 ÷ 5 ________

4. 17.2 ÷ 8 ________

5. 23.7 ÷ 6 ________

6. 20.6 ÷ 4 ________

7. 24.3 ÷ 8 ________

8. 118.1 ÷ 10 ________

9. 13.2 ÷ 6 ________

10. 32.3 ÷ 3 ________

11. 65.1 ÷ 2 ________

12. 13.5 ÷ 5 ________

13. $18.01 ÷ 9 = ________

14. $16.48 ÷ 4 = ________

15. $13.64 ÷ 7 = ________

16. $240.50 ÷ 6 = ________

17. $62.70 ÷ 8 = ________

18. $22.90 ÷ 7 = ________

19. $30.87 ÷ 4 = ________

20. $44.40 ÷ 5 = ________

Solve.

21. Nine students each ordered a different meal from a fast food restaurant as part of a science project. When they finished eating, they weighed all the packaging. They found that the packaging weighed a total of 46.1 ounces. Estimate the average weight of the packaging from each meal.

____

22. Population density is found by dividing the number of people by the area. Pecos County, Texas, has a population of 16,039 and a land area of 4,764 square miles. Estimate the population density of Pecos County. Then use a calculator to find the exact answer rounded to the nearest whole number.

____

Name ______________________________

4-8

Reteach

Problem-Solving Investigation: Choose the Best Strategy

Marissa is helping her mother set up tables for the family reunion. Each table seats 4 people. They have 16 tables to set up. If 70 people are attending the reunion, will they have enough tables to seat everyone?

Understand	**What facts do you know?** You know Marissa and her mother have 16 tables and each table seats 4 people. **What do you need to find?** If they have enough tables to seat everyone.
Plan	You can multiply 16 by 4 to see how many seats they have. Then we can subtract the product from 70 to see if any additional tables are needed.
Solve	**Use your plan to solve the problem.** $16 \times 4 = 64$ $70 - 64 = 6$
Check	Look back at the problem. Check your work. There are 6 more people than there are seats. If each table seats 4 people, it means Marissa and her mother need 2 more tables to seat everyone.

Solve. Use any strategy shown below to solve each problem.

- Draw a picture
- Guess and check
- Work backward
- Act it out

1. The department store sells scarves at 2 for $35. How much will 12 scarves cost?

____

2. On Sunday, Justine and her sister Rowena checked out 14 books at the library. This is 4 less than twice the amount of books they checked out the previous Sunday. How many books did they check out last Sunday?

____

Name ______________________________

4-8

Reteach

Problem-Solving Investigation: Choose the Best Strategy (continued)

3. Ms. Robin's class is planting trees for Arbor Day. They raise a total of $80 to buy trees and supplies. A local nursery has offered to provide trees for $7 each. They spend $17 on supplies. How many trees do they buy?

____

4. Akiko is 5 years older than her brother Tai. Tai is 3 years older than their sister Kin. Kin is 6 years older than their brother Taro. If Taro is 15 years old, how old is Akiko?

____

5. A farmer is putting up fence around his front yard. The yard is 60 feet long and 70 feet wide. How much fencing will the farmer need?

____

6. Jennifer bought tennis shoes and a pack of socks. The tennis shoes cost $51.25 more than the socks. The total for the two items, before tax, was $57.24. How much did the pack of socks cost?

____

7. Anthony arrives home from school at 4:00 P.M. He spends 20 minutes eating a snack and doing the dishes. Next he works on his homework for 2 hours. Then he spends 15 minutes practicing his music and getting ready for choir practice. If it takes Anthony 10 minutes to walk to choir practice and he needs to arrive at choir practice at 6:45 P.M., what time does he need to leave his house?

____

8. Mr. Stone's class visits the aquarium. Mr. Stone has $46 for the trip. The entrance fee for the class is $34. The rest of the money is used to buy posters for the classroom. Each poster costs $3. How many posters does Mr. Stone buy?

____

4–8

Name ______________________________

Skills Practice

Problem-Solving Investigation: Choose the Best Strategy

Solve. Use any strategy shown below to solve each problem.

- **Draw a picture**
- **Work backward**
- **Guess and check**
- **Act it out**

1. Kelly buys 12 packs of postcards and 3 packs of souvenir photos while on vacation. One pack of postcards costs \$3. Kelly spends \$54 total. How much does each pack of souvenir photos cost?

____

2. 58 passengers each checked 2 pieces of luggage at the airport. 122 passengers each checked 1 piece of luggage. How many pieces of luggage did the passengers check in all? If the plane holds 250 pieces of luggage, will there be enough room for the luggage the passengers checked?

____

3. Mr. Stinson took his classes to the community theater for a play. Mr. Stinson spent \$290 on tickets. Adult tickets cost \$8 and student tickets cost \$5. If Mr. Stinson brought 4 adult chaperones along, how many students went to the play?

____

4. It is 11:30 A.M. and Patrick needs to finish reading a 145-page book before returning it to the library at 6:30 P.M. Patrick has already read 54 pages of the book. How many pages an hour does he need to read to return the book on time?

____

5. Madeline is saving up to buy a new pair of rollerblades. The rollerblades she would like to buy cost \$90. She has \$34 saved from her birthday. She needs to earn the rest of the money by saving her weekly allowance. If she earns \$7 a week, how many weeks will she need to save her allowance to buy the rollerblades?

____

6. Mario is packing his backpack for a camping trip. He has to fit a flashlight, a bag of snacks, a water bottle, and a sweatshirt in to his backpack. The sweatshirt must go in the bag first. In how many different ways can the remaining items go into the backpack?

____

Name ____________________

5-1

Reteach

Addition Expressions

A box contains some baseballs. There are 2 baseballs on the ground. How many baseballs are there altogether?

You can draw models to show the total number of baseballs if the box contains certain numbers of baseballs.

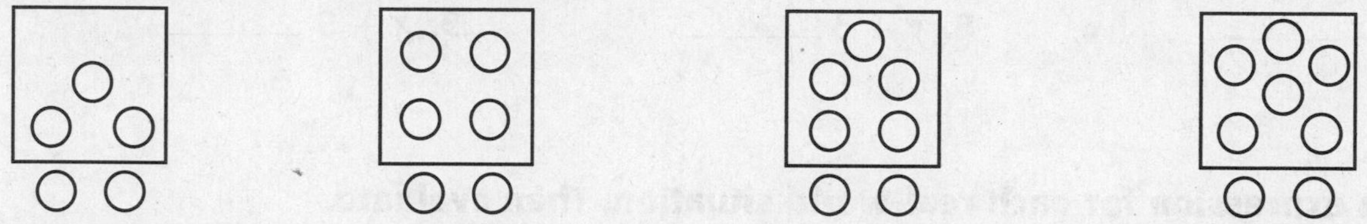

5 baseballs   6 baseballs   7 baseballs   8 baseballs

You can also write an algebraic expression to represent the total number of baseballs.

- The number of baseballs in the box changes, so represent it with the **variable**, b.
- The number of baseballs on the ground stays the same: 2
- Add the number of baseballs in the box and the number on the ground to find the number of baseballs altogether.

So, $b + 2$ represents the total number of baseballs.

Suppose there are 9 baseballs in the box.	$b = 9$
You can find the total number of baseballs	$b + 2$
by **evaluating** the expression.	$9 + 2 = 11$ baseballs

Write an expression for each real-world situation. Then evaluate.

1. Laura had 5 more hits than Susan. How many hits did Laura have?

What number changes? ____________________

Write a variable to represent the number that changes. ____________________

What number stays the same? ____________________

Write the number that stays the same. ____________________

What operation do you need to use to find the number of hits Laura had? ____________________

Write an expression to represent the number of hits Laura had. ____________________

Suppose Susan had 2 hits. Evaluate the expression for $s = 2$. ____________________

2. The Mustangs scored 8 runs in the softball game. The Rangers scored m more runs than the Mustangs. If $m = 3$, how many runs did the Rangers get?

____

3. During the softball season, the Patriots won y games. They lost 4 more games than they won. How many games did the Patriots lose during the season?

____

Name ______________________________

5–1

Skills Practice

Addition Expressions

Evaluate each expression if $x = 6$ and $y = 4$.

1. $x + 1$ ________ **2.** $9 + y$ ________ **3.** $17 + y$ ________

4. $y + 19$ ________ **5.** $12 + x$ ________ **6.** $15 + x$ ________

7. $7 + x$ ________ **8.** $y + 3$ ________ **9.** $x + 9$ ________

Write an expression for each real-world situation. Then evaluate.

10. John worked x hours planting bushes. Kim worked 2 more hours than John. If $x = 5$, how many hours did Kim work?

____

11. A rose bush costs x dollars. A lilac bush costs $2.50 more than a rose bush. If $x = 40$, how much does a lilac bush cost, in dollars?

____

12. The lilac bush is x feet tall now. By next year, it should be 3 feet taller. If $x = 3$, how tall will the lilac bush be then, in feet?

____

13. John has planted x bushes. He needs to plant 8 more. If $x = 10$, how many bushes will John plant altogether?

____

Solve.

14. This year the troop planted 15 more bushes than last year. Write an expression for the number planted this year. Let y represent the number planted last year.

____

15. Last year the troop planted 12 bushes. Evaluate the expression you wrote in problem 14 to find how many bushes they planted this year.

____

Name ____________________

5–2

Reteach

Problem-Solving Strategy: Solve a Simpler Problem

A rectangular backyard measures 50 feet by 60 feet and is covered with grass. A rectangular pool will be installed that covers 30 feet by 20 feet. How many square feet of grass will be left after the pool is built? The area of a rectangle can be found by multiplying length by width.

Step 1 Understand	**Be sure you understand the problem.** Read carefully. What do you know? • The dimensions of the backyard are ____________. • The dimensions of the pool are ____________. What do you need to find? • You need to find how many ____________ ____________ after the pool is built.
Step 2 Plan **• Draw a Picture** **• Guess and Check** **• Work Backward** **• Solve a Simpler Problem** **• Act it Out**	**Make a plan.** Choose a strategy. Think of the problem in simpler parts to help solve it. It is easier to solve the problem in pieces instead of all at once. Find the area of the backyard. Find the area of the pool. Then you can subtract to find the area that will be left.

5–2

Name ______________________________

Reteach

Problem-Solving Strategy: Solve a Simpler Problem (continued)

Solve a Simpler Problem

Step 3

Solve

Carry out your plan.

Find the area of the backyard.

A = *length* × *width*

= ________ × ________

= ________ square feet

Find the area of the pool.

A = *length* × *width*

= ________ × ________

= ________ square feet

What must you do to find how many square feet of grass are left after the pool is built?

____

____

________ − ________ = ________

How many square feet of grass will be left?

Step 4

Check

Is the solution reasonable?

Reread the problem.

Does your answer make sense?

____

____

Practice

1. A rectangular park is 80 meters by 70 meters. A square piece of land next to the park is purchased to enlarge the park. The land is 30 meters on each side. What will the total area of the enlarged park be?

____

2. A rectangular rock garden is 18 feet by 15 feet. Ms. Smithson wants to put a rectangular pond that measures 6 feet by 4 feet in one corner of the garden. How many square feet of the rock garden will not be covered by the pond?

____

Name ______________________________

5–2

Skills Practice

Problem-Solving Strategy: Solve a Simpler Problem

Solve a Simpler Problem

Solve. Use the *solve a simpler problem* strategy.

1. What is the area of the fenced-in garden shown in the plan below?

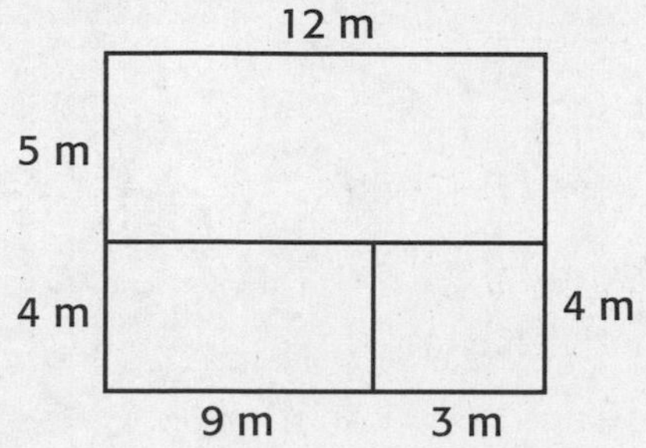

____

____

2. How much wood is needed to make the deck shown in the plan below?

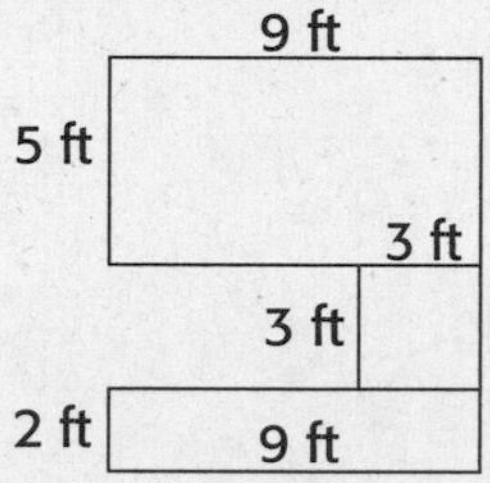

____

____

3. Five farmers can plow five fields in five hours. How many fields can ten farmers plow in ten hours?

____

4. Enriqué has a board that is 20 feet long. He needs to cut it into 2 foot long pieces to make shelves. How many shelves can he make from the board he has?

____

5. Constance is cutting ribbon to make bows to put on gift boxes. The roll of ribbon she has is 3 feet long. Each ribbon needs to be 6 inches long. How many 6 inch bows can she make? (*Hint:* 1 foot = 12 inches.)

____

6. Four people can make 8 bracelets in one hour. How many bracelets can 12 people working at the same rate make in a $\frac{1}{2}$ hour?

____

7. The total land area of four states is listed in the table. How much greater is the area of New Hampshire than the other states combined?

____

State	Total Land Area (square miles)
Delaware	1,955
New Hampshire	8,969
Rhode Island	1,045
Connecticut	4,845

Name ______________________

5-3

Reteach

Multiplication Expressions

Joe takes a bag containing 3 cookies to eat with his lunch at school. How many cookies are needed for lunch for one week?

You can draw models to show the total number of cookies needed.

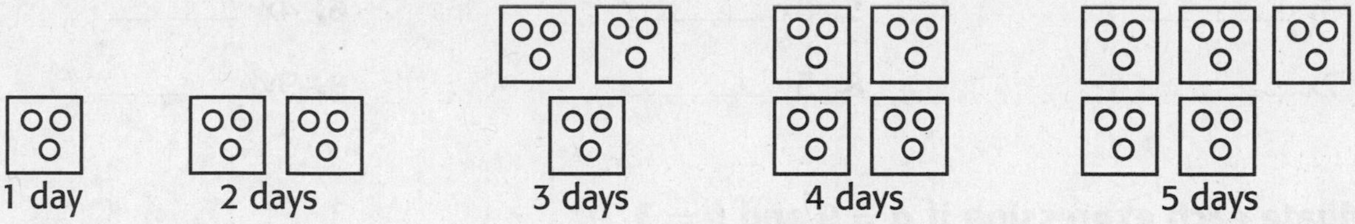

You can also write an algebraic expression to represent the total number of cookies.

- The number of cookies in each bag stays the same: 3.
- The number of bags of cookies changes, so represent it with the variable *c*.
- Multiply the number of cookies in the bag by the number of bags to find the total number of cookies.

So, $3 \times c$, or $3c$ represents the total number of cookies.

Suppose Joe needs cookies for lunch for 9 days. You can find the number of cookies he needs by evaluating the expression.

$c = 9$

$3c$

$3 \times 9 = 27$ cookies

Write an expression for each real-world situation. Then evaluate.

1. Mrs. Cook is making sliced turkey sandwiches for the football team . She puts 3 slices of turkey on each sandwich. How many total slices of turkey does she need?

What number changes in this situation? ______________

Write a variable to represent the number that changes. ______________

What number stays the same? ______________

Write the number that stays the same. ______________

Write an expression to represent the slices Mrs. Cook needs. ______________

2. Sandy uses 2 slices of bread for each of *s* sandwiches for lunch. If $s = 5$, how many slices does she need?

____

3. Sam drinks 3 servings of juice everyday. Each serving is *x* ounces. If $x = 8$, how many ounces of juice does Sam drink a day?

____

5–3

Name ______________________

Skills Practice

Multiplication Expressions

Evaluate each expression if $x = 5$ and $y = 8$.

1. $6x$ ________ **2.** $10x$ ________ **3.** $7y$ ________

4. $3y$ ________ **5.** $8x$ ________ **6.** $4x$ ________

7. $2x$ ________ **8.** $5y$ ________ **9.** $9y$ ________

Evaluate each expression if $a = 9$ and $b = 3$.

10. $11a$ ________ **11.** $2a$ ________ **12.** $4b$ ________

13. $6b$ ________ **14.** $12b$ ________ **15.** $6a$ ________

16. $4a$ ________ **17.** $9b$ ________ **18.** $7b$ ________

Write an expression for each real-world situation. Then evaluate.

19. Every year the school's Science Club builds b bird feeders. If $b = 7$, how many bird feeders will the club build in 3 years?

____

20. A hiker walks 3 miles per hour. He walks for y hours. If $y = 9$, how many miles does the hiker walk?

____

21. Scott kicked g field goals this football season. Each field goal is 3 points. If $g = 5$, how many points did Scott score?

____

22. Used DVDs are on sale for $8 each. Sandra bought d DVDs. If $d = 5$, how much did Sandra spend for DVDs?

____

Name ______________________________

5-4 Reteach

More Algebraic Expressions

A bag contains some marbles. There are 5 marbles on the table. How many marbles are there altogether?

You can draw models to show the total number of marbles if the bag contains certain numbers of marbles.

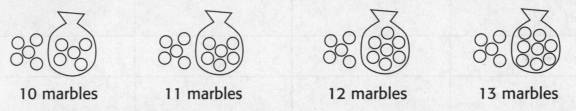

10 marbles   11 marbles   12 marbles   13 marbles

You can also write an algebraic expression to represent the total number of marbles.

- The number of marbles in the bag changes, so represent it with the variable, m.
- The number of marbles on the table stays the same: 5.
- Add the number of marbles in the bag and the number on the table to find the number of marbles altogether.

So, $m + 5$ represents the total number of marbles.

Suppose there are 13 marbles in the bag.	$m = 13$
You can find the total number of marbles	$m + 5$
by evaluating the expression.	$13 + 5 = 18$ marbles

Write an expression to represent each real-world situation. Then evaluate.

1. Jamal earned $5 dollars an hour mowing lawns. He mowed lawns for 13 hours. He spent $25 on a DVD. How much money does he have left?

What number changes? ______________________________

Write a variable to represent the number that changes. ______________

What number stays the same? ______________________________

Write the number that stays the same. ______________

What operation do you need to use to find the amount left? ______________

Write an expression to represent how much money is left. ______________

Solve the expression using the information given. ______________

2. Marisol wants to buy some board games for a party. Each game costs $15. If she has $75, how many games can she buy?

____

Name ______

5–4

Skills Practice

More Algebraic Expressions

Complete the table.

Algebraic Expressions	Variables	Numbers	Operations
1. $5d + 2c$			
2. $5w - 4y$			
3. $xy \div 4$			

Evaluate each expression if $a = 3$ and $b = 4$.

4. $10 + b$ ______ **5.** $2a + 8$ ______ **6.** $4b - 5a$ ______

7. $a \times b$ ______ **8.** $7a \times 9b$ ______ **9.** $8a - 9$ ______

10. $18 \div 2a$ ______ **11.** $ab \div 3$ ______ **12.** $15a - 4b$ ______

13. $ab + 7$ ______ **14.** $36 \div 6a$ ______ **15.** $7a + 8b$ ______

Evaluate each expression if $x = 7$, $y = 15$, and $z = 8$.

16. $x + y + z$ ______ **17.** $x + 2z$ ______ **18.** $xz + 3y$ ______

19. $4x - 3z$ ______ **20.** $xz \div 4$ ______ **21.** $6z - 5z$ ______

22. $9y \div 3$ ______ **23.** $15y + x$ ______ **24.** $xy + 2z$ ______

25. $13y - zx$ ______ **26.** $xz - 2y$ ______ **27.** $3y \times 40x$ ______

Name ______________________________

5–5

Reteach

Problem-Solving Investigation: Choose the Best Strategy

Four friends posing for a group photo. How many ways can the friends be arranged if they all stand in one row?

Step 1 Understand	**Make sure you understand the problem.** What do you know? ______________________________ What do you need to find out? ______________________________ ______________________________
Step 2 Plan	**Make a plan.** You can use the *make a table* strategy to write each way that the players could be standing.
Step 3 Solve	1	2	3	4 2	3	4	1 3	4	1	2 Continue writing scenarios until there are none left. After finishing, you find that there are 24 possible ways the friends could be standing.
Step 4 Check	Make a list of all possible positions. Since there are 24 items in the list and 24 items in the chart, the answer is correct.

Use any strategy shown below to solve each problem.

- Act it out
- Look for a pattern
- Make a table

Name ______________________________

5–5

Reteach

Problem-Solving Investigation: Choose the Best Strategy (continued)

1. Mayumi is driving home from college. She has 510 miles left to go. Her average speed is 52 miles per hour. How long will it take for her to get there?

____

____

2. Leo goes on a hot air balloon ride. The ride covers 70 miles and takes 4 hours. What was the speed of the balloon?

____

____

3. The number of goals Dana scored in the first three years of playing hockey are shown. At this rate, how many goals should he expect to score at the end of the fourth year?

Year	Goals
1	3
2	5
3	7
4	

4. For a class project, Javier has to create a flag to represent his class. The flag must have 2 solid horizontal stripes (one white and one blue) with a silver diamond in the center of one of the stripes. There are several possibilities for the flag that Javier can create. Find how many different flags Javier can make with two stripes and one diamond.

____

____

5. Kim has to drive a total of 275 miles to visit her grandfather. If she drives 65 miles per hour for the first 160 miles and then 70 miles per hour for the rest of the trip, how long will it take her to make the trip?

____

6. To train for a race, you plan to run 1 mile the first week and double the number of miles each week for five weeks. How many miles will you run the fifth week?

____

Name ______________________________

5–5

Skills Practice

Problem-Solving Investigation: Choose the Best Strategy

Use any strategy shown below to solve each problem.

- Act it out
- Look for a pattern
- Make a table

1. To train for the bicycle race, Dan plans to ride 10 miles per day the first week, adding 3 miles per day each week. How many miles will he ride per day the eighth week?

____

2. A rancher is building a square corral with sides that are 20 feet long. He plans to put a post every 5 feet around the edge of the corral. How many posts will he need?

____

3. At 5:00 P.M., the temperature was 24°C. By 8:00 P.M., the temperature had dropped 6°C. What was the temperature at 8:00 P.M.?

____

4. Write a problem that you can solve using a problem-solving strategy. What strategy would you use to solve the problem? Explain why you chose that strategy.

____

Name ______________________________

5–6

Reteach

Function Tables

A **function rule** describes the relationship between the input and output of a **function.** The inputs and outputs can be organized in a **function table.**

Example 1 **Complete the function table.**

Input (c)	$c - 3$	Output
9	9 − 3	■
8	8 − 3	■
6	6 − 3	■

Input **Output**

9 − 3 → 6

8 − 3 → 5

6 − 3 → 3

→

Input (c)	$c - 3$	Output
9	9 − 3	6
8	8 − 3	5
6	6 − 3	3

The function rule is $c - 3$.
Subtract 3 from each input.

Example 2 **Each person involved in the school play gets four tickets to the play. Find the function rule. Then make a function table to find how many tickets 6, 7, and 8 people would receive.**

Input (p)	$4p$	Output
6	4 × 6	24
7	4 × 7	28
8	4 × 8	32

So, 6, 7, and 8 people would receive 24, 28, and 32 tickets, respectively. Complete each function table.

1.

Input (x)	$2x$	Output
0	2 × 0	
2	2 × 2	
4	2 × 4	

2.

Input (x)	$4 + x$	Output
0	4 + 0	
1	4 + 1	
4	4 + 4	

3. A popcorn machine costs $5 per day to rent. Find the function rule. Then make a function table to find how much the machine would cost for 3, 6, or 9 days.

____

Input (d)		Output

Name ______________________________

5–6

Skills Practice

Function Tables

Use the information below to answer Exercises 1 and 2.

Beth has 7 more model horses than her friend Jasmine.

1. Find the function rule. ____________

2. Make a function table to find how many model horses Beth has if Jasmine has 11, 13, or 15 horses.

Input (*j*)		**Output**

3. Marie is sending books to her cousin. Each book weighs 4 ounces. Find the function rule. Then make a function table to find how many ounces 5, 6, or 7 books would weigh.

Input (*b*)		**Output**

____

4. Steven is ordering puzzles for his friends. Each puzzle costs $12. Find the function rule. Then make a frequency table to find how much 4, 5, or 6 puzzles would cost.

Input (*p*)		**Output**

____

Name ______________________________

5–7

Reteach

Order of Operations

To make fruit baskets, Claudia bought 6 bags of 12 apples and 4 bags of 8 oranges. Write an expression to find how many pieces of fruit she has in all. Evalute the expression.

$f = (6 \times 12) + (4 \times 8)$	Write the expression.
$f = 72 + 32$	Multiply 6 and 12. Multiply 4 and 8.
$f = 104$	Add 72 and 32.

So, there are 104 pieces of fruit in all.

Find the value of each expression.

1. $(36 - 10) + (5 \times 2)$ ______

2. $6 \times (9 - 4)$ ______

3. $7 \times (3 + 9) =$ ______

4. $(12 \times 3) - (3 \times 7) =$ ______

5. $(3 \times 4) + (8 - 5) =$ ______

6. $(100 + 10) \times (6 - 3) =$ ______

7. $36 \times (10 - 3) =$ ______

8. $(5 \times 2) + 4 =$ ______

9. $36 \div (9 - 5) =$ ______

10. $(25 - 2) \times (6 + 16) =$ ______

11. $(9 \times 14) - (3 \div 3) =$ ______

12. $(63 \div 9) + (2 \times 5) =$ ______

5–7

Name ______________________________

Skills Practice

Order of Operations

Find the value of each expression.

1. 44 + (7 × 3) ______

2. 48 ÷ (8 − 2) ______

3. (3 + 4) × 8 ______

4. (18 + 12) ÷ (2 + 3) ______

5. (4 × 2) − 7 ______

6. (6 ÷ 3) + (8 × 5) ______

7. (3 + 2) × 3 ______

8. (24 ÷ 6) × (3 + 52) ______

9. (2 × 5) − (3 × 3) ______

10. 96 ÷ (3 × 4) ______

11. (100 − 8) + (4 ÷ 4) ______

12. (200 − 50) ÷ (12 − 9) ______

13. 47 + (3 × 11) − (36 ÷ 3) ______

14. (7 + 6) × (7 − 3) ______

Solve.

15. Tickets to the school play cost $4 for adults and $2 for students. If 255 adults and 382 students attended the play, write an expression that shows the total amount of money made on ticket sales. Then evaluate the expression.

____

____

16. At the school play, popcorn costs $1 and juice costs $2. Suppose 235 people buy popcorn and 140 people buy juice. Write an expression that shows the total amount of money made by selling refreshments. Then simplify the expression.

____

____

6–1

Name ______________________________

Reteach

Addition and Subtraction Equations

You can use subtraction to solve addition equations.

Solve: $c + 25 = 39$

To find the value of c, subtract 25 from each side of the equation.

$$\begin{array}{r} c + 25 = 39 \\ -\ 25 = -25 \\ \hline c = 14 \end{array}$$

Check your answer by substituting 14 for *c* in the original equation.

$$\begin{array}{r} c + 25 = 39 \\ 14 + 25 = 39 \\ 39 = 39 \leftarrow \text{It checks.} \end{array}$$

You can use addition to solve subtraction equations.

Solve: $f - 24 = 138$

To find the value of f, add 24 to each side of the equation.

$$\begin{array}{r} f - 24 = 38 \\ +\ 24 = +24 \\ \hline f = 62 \end{array}$$

Check your answer by substituting 62 for *f* in the original equation.

$$\begin{array}{r} f - 24 = 38 \\ 62 - 24 = 38 \\ 38 = 38 \leftarrow \text{It checks.} \end{array}$$

Solve each equation. Check your solution.

1. $a + 9 = 75$

$a =$ ________

2. $h - 6 = 43$

$h =$ ________

3. $n - 22 = 70$

$n =$ ________

4. $z + 6 = 14$

$z =$ ________

5. $y + 34 = 42$

$y =$ ________

6. $y - 4 = 3$

$y =$ ________

Name ______________________

6–1

Skills Practice

Addition and Subtraction Equations

Solve each equation. Check your solution.

1. $a + 8 = 23$ ______

2. $s + 9 = 26$ ______

3. $f + 36 = 58$ ______

4. $z + 16 = 59$ ______

5. $v + 14 = 162$ ______

6. $h + 2 = 3$ ______

7. $k + 60 = 84$ ______

8. $t + 30 = 94$ ______

9. $r + 3 = 17$ ______

10. $96 = d + 78$ ______

11. $s + 15 = 32$ ______

12. $100 = c + 42$ ______

13. $a - 7 = 4$ ______

14. $v - 9 = 25$ ______

15. $96 = i - 3$ ______

16. $30 + a = 51$ ______

17. $16 + v = 24$ ______

18. $3 = n - 1$ ______

19. $e - 9 = 23$ ______

20. $9 + b = 18$ ______

21. $6 + a = 13$ ______

22. $c - 0 = 4$ ______

23. $298 = i - 1$ ______

24. $17 = r - 4$ ______

Solve.

25. The high temperature one day in Washington, D.C., was 40°F. That was 14°F greater than the low temperature. Write an addition equation to describe the situation. Use *t* to represent the low temperature. Then solve the equation.

______

______

26. A chapter has 45 pages. Larry has read *n* pages, and has 8 pages left. Write a subtraction equation to represent this situation. Then solve the equation to find the number of pages Larry has left to read.

______

______

6–2

Name ______________________

Reteach

Multiplication Equations

You can use division to solve multiplication equations.

Solve: $12s = 240$

To find the value of *s*, divide each side of the equation by 12.

$$12s = 240$$
$$\frac{12s}{12} = \frac{240}{12}$$
$$s = 20$$

Check your answer by substituting 20 for *s* in the original equation.

$$12s = 240$$
$$12 \times 20 = 240$$
$$240 = 240 \leftarrow \text{It checks.}$$

Solve each equation. Check your solution.

1. $8d = 96$
$d =$ ______

2. $3m = 75$
$m =$ ______

3. $2k = 4$
$k =$ ______

4. $7y = 42$
$y =$ ______

5. $n \times 15 = 60$
$n =$ ______

6. $w \times 7 = 56$
$w =$ ______

7. $a \times 3 = 18$
$a =$ ______

8. $v \times 9 = 72$
$v =$ ______

9. $30b = 600$
$b =$ ______

10. $2a = 26$
$a =$ ______

11. $5b = 25$
$b =$ ______

12. $3z = 51$
$z =$ ______

13. $2x = 10$
$x =$ ______

14. $7y = 49$
$y =$ ______

15. $3a = 15$
$a =$ ______

16. $3b = 45$
$b =$ ______

17. $8x = 64$
$x =$ ______

18. $9z = 27$
$z =$ ______

6–2

Name ____________________

Skills Practice

Multiplication Equations

Solve each equation. Check your solution.

1. $7w = 28$ ______

2. $6q = 108$ ______

3. $20d = 180$ ______

4. $6a = 12$ ______

5. $4e = 276$ ______

6. $15y = 45$ ______

7. $8k = 40$ ______

8. $4p = 16$ ______

9. $3j = 39$ ______

10. $12s = 60$ ______

11. $30h = 60$ ______

12. $8w = 64$ ______

13. $3y = 12$ ______

14. $2c = 120$ ______

15. $10x = 20$ ______

16. $7s = 21$ ______

17. $4x = 12$ ______

18. $32f = 64$ ______

19. $6t = 60$ ______

20. $4w = 24$ ______

Solve.

21. The Martinez family paid $40 for 5 movie passes. Write a multiplication equation to describe the situation. Solve it to find the cost in dollars, *c*, of each movie pass.

____

22. Three friends each bought a gift. Each of the presents cost the same amount. Together, they paid $15. Write a multiplication equation to describe the situation.

____

6–3

Name ____________________

Reteach

Problem-Solving Strategy: Make a Table

A music store kept track of the number of CDs it sold every day. In which week did they sell the most CDs?

Number of CDs Sold			
Day	Week 1	Week 2	Week 3
Mon.	38	28	17
Tues.	36	25	15
Wed.	29	19	18
Thur.	30	23	21
Fri.	31	20	23

Step 1 Understand	**Be sure you understand the problem.** Read carefully. What do you know? • The number of ____________________ What do you need to find? • The week they sold the most CDs. ____________________ ____________________
Step 2 Plan • Draw a Picture • Make a Table • Guess and Check • Solve a Simpler Problem	**Make a plan.** Choose a strategy. You can make a table to help you solve the problem. A table can help you organize the data and make it easier to see the totals for each day.

6–3

Name ____________________

Reteach

Problem-Solving Strategy: Make a Table (continued)

Step 3 Solve	**Carry out your plan.** Make a table. Find the sum for each week. Week / Number Sold 1 — 38 + 36 + 29 + 30 + 31 — 164 2 — 28 + 25 + 19 + 23 + 20 — 115 3 — 17 + 15 + 18 + 21 + 23 — 94 In which week did they sell the most CDs? ____________________
Step 4 Check	**Is the solution reasonable?** Reread the problem. Does your answer make sense? __________ What other methods could you use to check your answer? ____________________

Practice

Use the *make a table* strategy to solve.

A meteorologist records the high temperature, in degrees Fahrenheit, each day.

Day	Temperature	Day	Temperature
1	90	6	79
2	86	7	82
3	91	8	76
4	94	9	83
5	88	10	90

1. Between which two days did the greatest temperature change occur?

____

2. Between which two days did the least temperature change occur?

____

6–3

Name ______________________________

Skills Practice

Problem-Solving Strategy: Make a Table

Use the *make a table* strategy to solve.

A card shop recorded how many packs of trading cards it sold each day.

1. In which week did they sell the most packs of cards?

____

2. In which week did they sell the least amount?

____

Trading Cards Sold			
Day	**Week 1**	**Week 2**	**Week 3**
Mon.	28	48	25
Tue.	32	43	37
Wed.	38	45	42
Thur.	44	41	35
Fri.	36	39	41

3. A bookstore records 8 months of sales of *The Lion, the Witch, and the Wardrobe,* by C.S. Lewis. Did they sell more books in the first four months or the last four months?

____

Bookstore Sales			
Month	**Copies**	**Month**	**Copies**
1	26	5	38
2	24	6	19
3	32	7	15
4	18	8	30

4. Joseph took a survey of his classmates to find their favorite color. The results are shown in the table to the right. How many students chose blue as their favorite color?

____

Favorite Colors			
Blue	Green	Blue	Yellow
Red	Brown	Purple	Pink
Blue	Pink	Red	Green
Purple	Blue	Red	Brown
Blue	Green	Red	Pink

Name ____________________

6–4

Reteach

Geometry: Ordered Pairs

You can find points on a coordinate plane by using ordered pairs. An example of an ordered pair is (4,3).

(4,3)

The first number is the *x*-coordinate and corresponds to the *x*-axis.

The second number is the *y*-coordinate and corresponds to the *y*-axis.

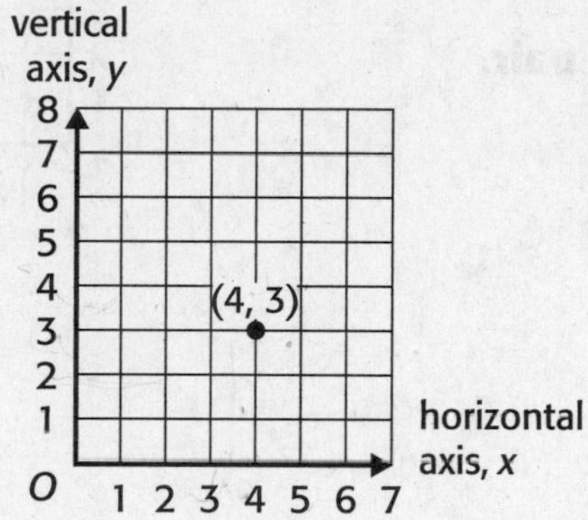

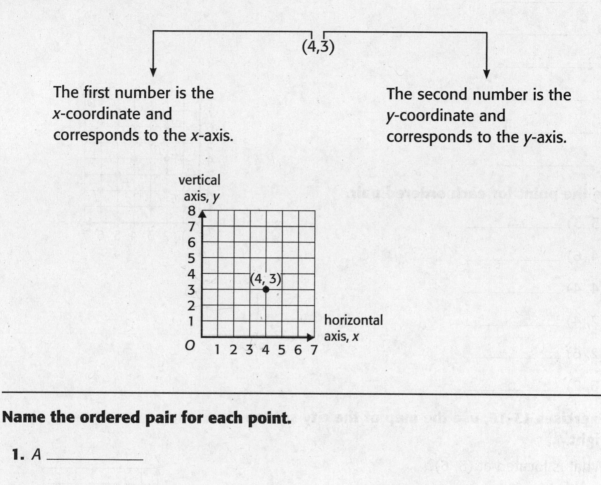

Name the ordered pair for each point.

1. *A* ____________

2. *B* ____________

3. *C* ____________

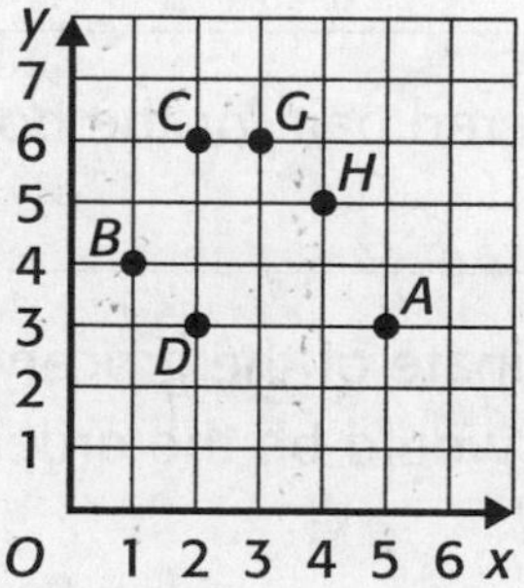

Name the point for each ordered pair.

4. (2, 3) ____________

5. (4, 5) ____________

6. (3, 6) ____________

6–4

Name ______________________________

Skills Practice

Geometry: Ordered Pairs

Name the ordered pair for each point.

1. *A* __________
2. *B* __________
3. *C* __________
4. *D* __________
5. *E* __________
6. *F* __________

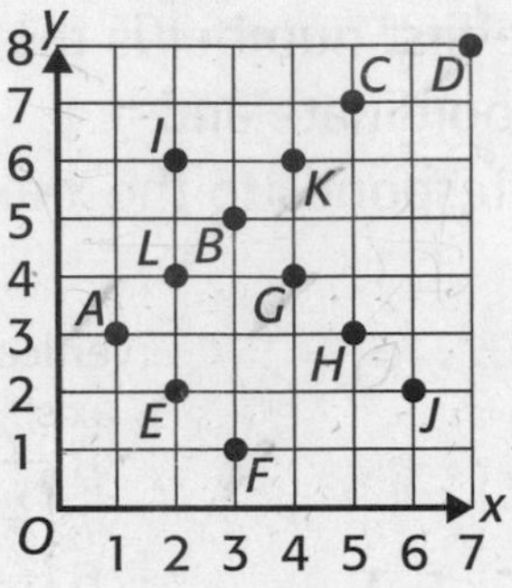

Name the point for each ordered pair.

7. (5, 3) __________
8. (4, 6) __________
9. (4, 4) __________
10. (2, 4) __________
11. (2, 6) __________
12. (6, 2) __________

For Exercises 13-16, use the map of the city square at the right.

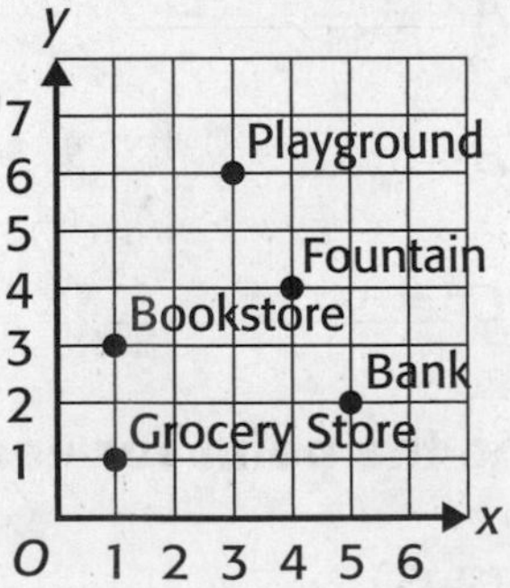

13. What is located at (3, 6)?

____

14. Write the ordered pair for the bookstore.

____

15. If the *y*-coordinate of the grocery store was moved up 4 units, what would be the ordered pair of the grocery store?

____

16. Suppose point (4, 2) was moved 2 units to the left and moved 3 units up. Write the new ordered pair.

____

Name ______________________________

6–5

Reteach

Algebra and Geometry: Graph Functions

Another way to represent a function is to use a graph.

Graph the function represented in the following equation.

$b = 2a + 1$

Make a table to find ordered pairs. Choose several values for a. For each value, evaluate the expression $2a + 1$ to find the corresponding value of b.

a	$2a + 1$	b	Ordered Pair (a, b)
0	$(2 \times 0) + 1$	1	(0, 1)
1	$(2 \times 1) + 1$	3	(1, 3)
2	$(2 \times 2) + 1$	5	(2, 5)
3	$(2 \times 3) + 1$	7	(3, 7)

Graph the ordered pairs.

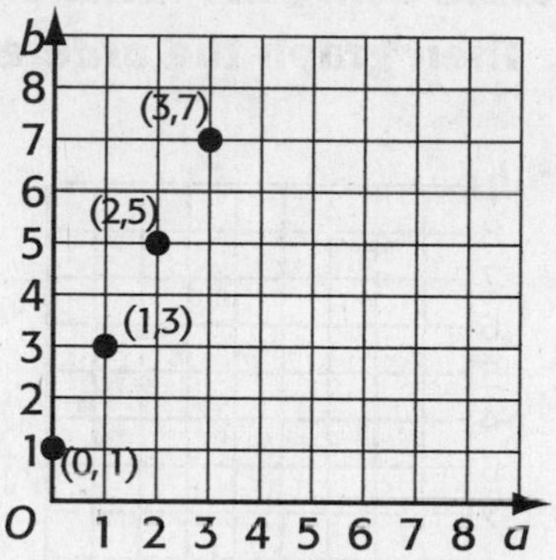

Remember, the first coordinate tells the number of units to the right or left of the origin. The second coordinate tells the number of units above or below the origin.

(3, 7) is (3 units right, 7 units up).

Complete the table for the function represented in each equation. Then graph the ordered pairs.

1. $n = m + 3$

m	$m + 3$	n	Ordered Pair (m, n)
0	$0 + 3$	3	(0, 3)
1	$1 + 3$	4	
2	$2 + 3$		

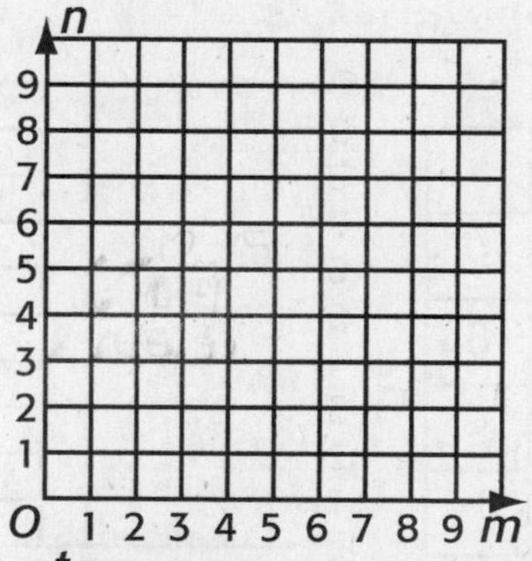

2. $t = 3s - 1$

s	$3s - 1$	t	Ordered Pair (s, t)
1	$(3 \times 1) - 1$	2	(1, 2)
2	$(3 \times 2) - 1$		
3			
4			

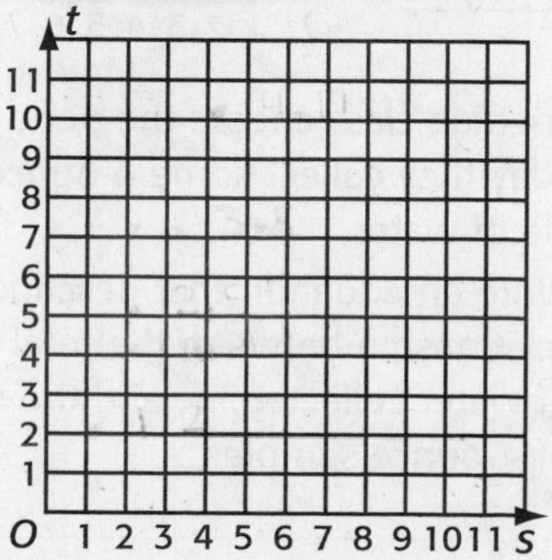

Name ____________________

6–5

Skills Practice

Algebra and Geometry: Graph Functions

Graph and label each point on the coordinate grid.

1. *A* (5, 9) **2.** *I* (7, 2) **3.** *F* (0, 4)

4. *L* (9, 8) **5.** *G* (0, 7) **6.** *D* (6, 6)

7. *H* (8, 5) **8.** *B* (4, 4) **9.** *E* (2, 7)

10. *K* (7, 0) **11.** *C* (3, 9) **12.** *J* (9, 9)

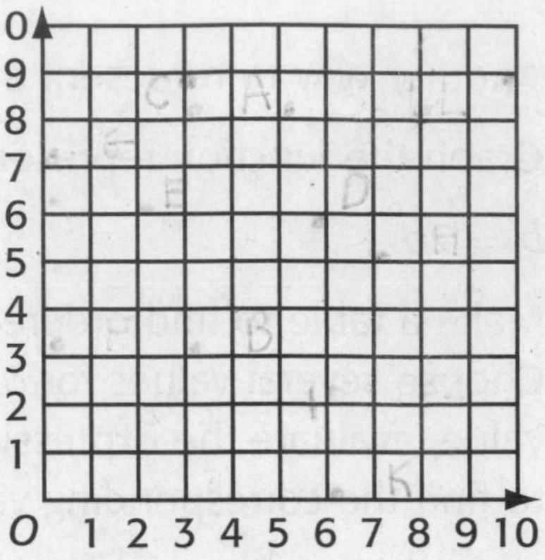

Complete each table using the function represented in the equation. Then graph the ordered pairs.

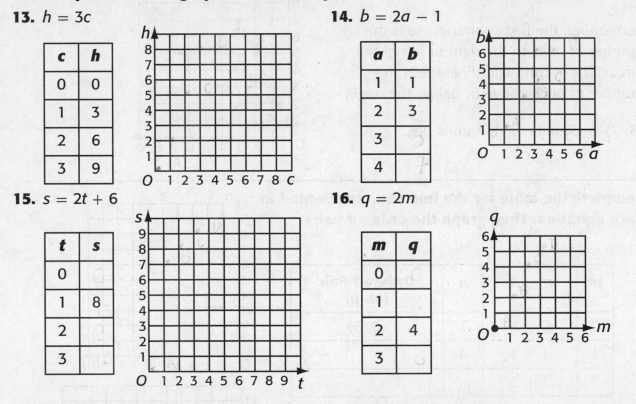

13. $h = 3c$

c	*h*
0	0
1	3
2	6
3	9

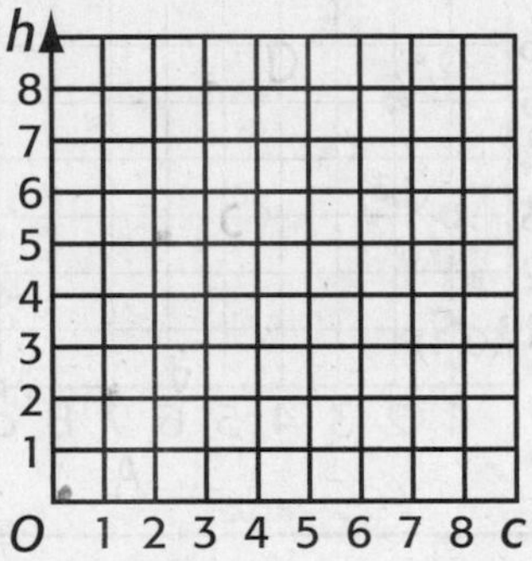

14. $b = 2a - 1$

a	*b*
1	1
2	3
3	
4	

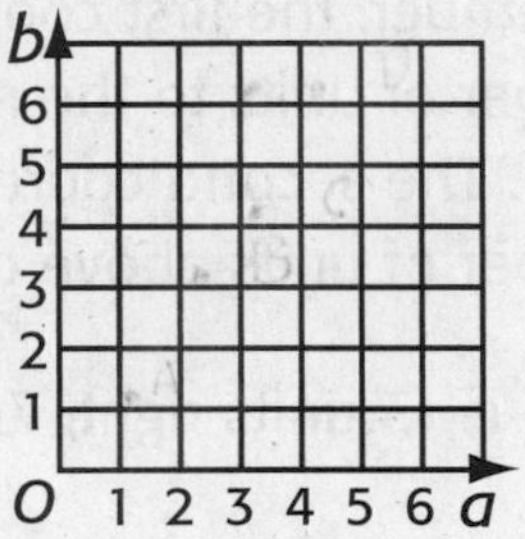

15. $s = 2t + 6$

t	*s*
0	
1	8
2	
3	

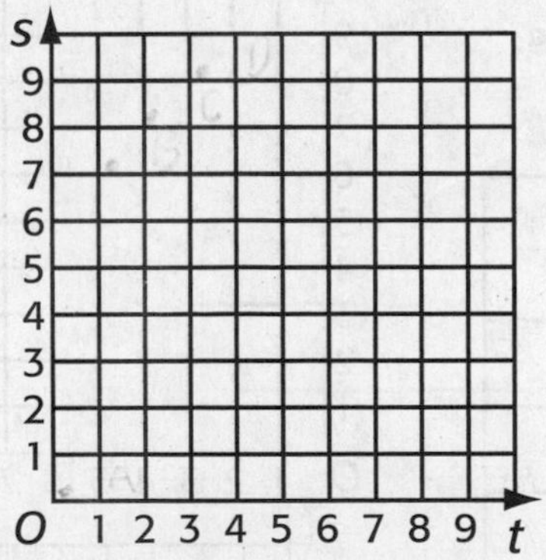

16. $q = 2m$

m	*q*
0	
1	
2	4
3	

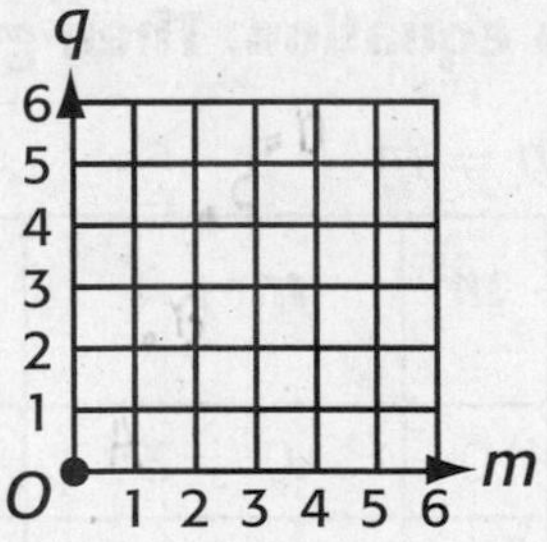

A fifth-grade class checks the pond water in the school's nature center. Each day they collect some 4-ounce samples of water and one 8-ounce sample of water.

17. Write an equation that describes the relationship between the total ounces of water collected, *w*, and the number of 4-ounce samples, *s*.

____

18. What is the total amount of water that will be collected if students collect three 4-ounce samples?

____

Name ______________________________

6–6

Reteach

Functions and Equations

A function is a relationship in which one quantity depends on another quantity. You can use an equation to represent a function. An equation is a mathematical statement that contains an equals sign.

A poster of Lake Tahoe comes in several sizes. However, for every poster, the width is 6 inches more than 3 times its length.

You can make a table to show the function.

Length (inches), ℓ	6	12	18	24	30
Width (inches), w	24	42	60	78	96

You can describe a function in words or you can write an equation.

Words: The width is 6 inches more than 3 times the length.

Equation: Let ℓ represent the length of the rectangle.
Let w represent the width.
Write $w = 3\ell + 6$.

Complete the table for each function.

1. The cost of shipping an item is \$3.00 plus \$2.00 per pound.

Let w *represent* the weight in pounds.

Let c represent the shipping cost in dollars.

$c = 2w + 3$

Weight (pounds), w	1	2	3	4	5
Shipping cost (dollars), c	\$5	\$7			

2. The length of a certain rectangle is 4 inches more than twice its width.

Let ℓ represent the length of the rectangle and w represent its width. $\ell = 2w + 4$

Width (inches), w	2	8	12	15	20
Length (inches), ℓ	8	20			

Name ____________________

6–6

Skills Practice

Functions and Equations

Complete the table. Write an equation to show the relationship.

1.

Input	*x*	0	2	3	4	5
Output	*y*	1	3	5	7	

____

2.

Input	*x*	0	1	2	3	4	5
Output	*y*	3	4	5	6		

____

3.

Input	*x*	0	1	2	3	4	5
Output	*y*	1	4	7	10		

____

4

Input	*x*	0	1	2	3	4	5
Output	*y*	5	7	9	11		

____

Write an equation for the function described in words. Tell what each variable in the equation represents.

5. The width of a certain rectangle is 4 times its length.

____

____

6. The length of a certain rectangle is 2 times its width.

____

____

7. The length in inches of a pencil is equal to 2.54 times its length in centimeters.

____

____

Name ______________________________

6–7

Reteach

Problem-Solving Investigation: Choose the Best Strategy

The high tide at Sunshine Beach on Monday was 7 feet. The low tide on Monday was 3 feet. Molly claimed that the difference in the heights of the tides was 4 feet. Use logical reasoning to find out if Molly's claim is correct.

Step 1 Understand	What do you know? High tide was ______ and low tide was ______ . What do you need to find out? ________________
Step 2 Plan	Which operation should you use to find the difference in the heights of the tides? ________________ What is Molly's claim? ________________ ________________
Step 3 Solve	Complete. Evaluate Molly's claim. Explain. ________________ ________________
Step 4 Check	To check, find the difference. ________________ The difference is ______.

Use any strategy shown below to solve.

- Use logical reasoning
- Work backward
- Guess and check

1. On Thursday, the high tide reached 10 feet. The low tide on Thursday was 7 feet lower than high tide. Glen calculated that the low tide was 3 feet. Is his calculation correct? Explain.

____

2. At 2:00 A.M., the temperature was 3°F. By 6:00 A.M., the temperature had risen 4°F. Carmen calculates the temperature at 6:00 A.M. is 7°F. Is her calculation correct? Explain.

____

Name ______________________________

6–7

Reteach

Problem-Solving Investigation: Choose the Best Strategy (continued)

3. Your parents have given you twice as many dollars as your age on each birthday since your fifth birthday. If you are 10 years old, how much money have you been given over the years?

____

4. Find the missing term in the pattern below.

..... ______, 5, 8, 11, 14

____

5. Sarah needs to arrive at work at 7:45 A.M. It takes her 12 minutes to drive to her office, 15 minutes to make and eat breakfast, and 37 minutes to get ready. What time does she need to set her alarm for to get to work on time?

____

6. On Wednesday, 72 cookbooks were sold at a book sale. This is 9 more than one half the amount sold on Tuesday. How many cookbooks were sold on Tuesday?

____

7. Robert has 39 model cars and his brother, Frank, has 56 model cars. How many more model cars does Robert need to have the same number as his brother?

____

8. The local pet store made a profit of $300 in March, but only made a profit of $150 in April. How much more did the pet store make in March?

____

6–7

Name ______________________________

Skills Practice

Problem-Solving Investigation: Choose the Best Strategy

Use any strategy shown below to solve.

- Use logical reasoning
- Work backward
- Guess and check

1. At 3:00 A.M, the tide was 4 feet. By 9:00 A.M., the tide had risen 6 feet. Andre calculates that the tide reached 10 feet at 9:00 A.M. Is his calculation correct? Explain.

____

2. A scuba diver descended 8 feet below the surface of the water. Then he descended an additional 12 feet. He then ascends 3 feet. How far below the surface is he?

____

3. A croquet ball has a mass of 460 grams. Together, the mass of a golf ball and a croquet ball is the same as the mass of 11 golf balls. What is the mass of one golf ball?

____

4. The temperature recorded at 5:00 A.M. was 25°F. The temperature increased by 2°F every hour for the next four hours. What was the temperature at the end of the four hours?

____

5. In a farmyard, there are 12 horses and ducks altogether. If José counts 42 legs, how many horses and ducks are there?

____

6. The Wiggins family spent a total of $29.00 on tickets to go to a movie. If adult tickets are $7.00 and children's tickets are $5.00, how many adult and children's tickets did they purchase if there are 5 people in the family?

____

____

Name ______________________________

7–1

Reteach

Mean, Median, and Mode

You can use the mean, median, and mode to describe the numbers of E-mail messages Jon sent.

Number of E-mail Messages Jon Sent							
Day	Sun.	Mon.	Tues.	Wed.	Thur.	Fri.	Sat.
Number of Messages	7	4	6	5	7	5	8

Write the numbers of messages in order from least to greatest. 4, 5, 5, 6, 7, 7, 8

What you want to know	**What you find**	**How you find it**
What is the mean number of messages sent?	**mean** the average number for the data set	Add data and divide by 7. The mean is 6.
What is the middle number of messages sent?	**median** the middle number	6 is in the middle. The median is 6 messages.
What is the most common number of messages sent?	**mode** the number that occurs most often	The mode is 5 and 7 messages.

Number of E-mail Messages Jon Received							
Day	Sun.	Mon.	Tues.	Wed.	Thur.	Fri.	Sat.
Number of Messages	3	9	2	5	8	2	6

1. Write the number of messages received in order from least to greatest.

____

2. What is the mean number of messages received? ____________

3. What is the median of messages received? ____________

4. What is the mode of messages received? ____________

7–1

Name ____________________

Skills Practice

Mean, Median, and Mode

Find the mean, median, and mode of each set of data.

1. 1, 2, 0, 5, 8, 2, 9, 2, 7 ____________________

2. 9, 4, 7, 9, 3, 10, 8, 6 ____________________

3. 34, 17, 10, 23, 21, 15 ____________________

4. 67, 67, 98, 49, 98, 89 ____________________

5. 27, 31, 76, 59, 33, 48, 24, 58 ____________________

6. 105, 126, 90, 50, 75, 90, 62, 112 ____________________

7. \$1.50, \$2.50, \$1.50, \$4.00, \$5.00 ____________________

8. 1.4, 1.6, 2.1, 1.7, 3.4, 2.5, 2.9, 1.4 ____________________

9. 20, 12.5, 30, 15.4, 25, 18.6, 17.8 ____________________

10. \$3.35, \$8.50, \$3.35, \$4.35, \$8.25 ____________________

11.

Student	Ann	Ben	Cara	Fran	Ian	Mike	Kim	Lou
Number of Pets	4	6	0	3	1	5	2	3

____

7-2

Name ______________________________

Reteach

Problem–Solving Investigation: Choose the Best Strategy

Choose a Strategy

Farmer Smith has twice as many chickens as cows on his farm. He counts a total of 32 legs among all his cows and chickens. The farm's chicken coop only holds 10 chickens. Does Farmer Smith have enough room to fit all of the chickens in the coop?

Step 1 Understand	**Be sure you understand the problem.** Farmer Smith has twice as many chickens as cows. The animals have a total of 32 legs. Each cow has four legs, and each chicken has two legs.
Step 2 Plan	**Make a plan.** Choose a strategy. You can draw a diagram. You know that Farmer Smith has twice as many chickens as cows, so start by drawing one cow and two chickens.
Step 3 Solve	**Carry out your plan.** Count the number of legs in your diagram. One cow and two chickens have a total of 8 legs. You know that the animals have a total of 32 legs, so add animals, remember that there must be twice as many chickens as cows. 4 cows and 8 chickens have a total of 32 legs. Farmer Smith can fit all 8 chickens in the coop.
Step 4 Check	**Is the solution reasonable?** Reread the problem. Have you answered the question? How can you check your answer?

7–2

Name ___

Reteach

Problem–Solving Investigation: Choose the Best Strategy *(continued)*

Use any strategy shown below to solve each problem.

- Draw a picture
- Guess and check
- Act it out
- Make a table

1. John is the tallest. Jessica is shorter than Paul, but taller than Mary. Put the four friends in order from shortest to tallest.

___

2. Pam and Jim are selling pretzels to raise money for a trip. They make $0.75 for each pretzel that they sell. They need to raise $80 altogether. If Pam sells 56 pretzels and Jim sells 52 pretzels, how much money will they make? Is it enough for the trip?

___

3. Emily is training to run in a race. She runs 10 miles the first week, 12 miles the second week, and 14 miles the third week. If this pattern continues, how many miles will Emily run in the fifth week?

___

4. Jenna is planning a birthday party. She needs to buy a gift, decorate the house, and make some punch. How many different orders can Jenna complete all of the tasks?

___

5. Manny practices the guitar for 60 minutes on Monday, 45 minutes on Tuesday, 60 minutes on Wednesday, and 45 minutes on Thursday. If this pattern continues, how many minutes will he have practiced from Monday through Friday?

___

7–2

Name ______________________________

Skills Practice

Problem–Solving Investigation: Choose the Best Strategy

Solve.

1. Tim is building a wall with plastic bricks. Each row contains 10 bricks. The first row has 2 red bricks and 8 blue bricks. The second row has 3 red bricks and 7 blue bricks. The third row has 4 red bricks and 6 blue bricks. If the pattern continues, how many blue bricks will there be in the sixth row of the wall?

____

2. Bob has cats and ducks as pets. Bob has twice as many cats as ducks. He counts a total of 30 legs among all his cats and ducks. How many cats and ducks does Bob have?

____

3. Michael and Dwight work together. Michael makes twice as much money as Dwight does, and together they make $60,000 per year. How much money does Dwight make?

____

4. Ben, Ray, Don, and Chris are going on a ski trip. The hotel where they want to stay costs $100 per person each night. If they stay at the hotel for four nights, what is the total cost?

____

5. Heidi just started a new job at a restaurant. On her first night, she made $20 in tips. On the second night, she made $25, and on the third night she made $30. If this pattern continues, how much money will she make on the fifth night?

____

7–3

Name ______________________________

Reteach

Line Plots

Students in one fifth grade class recorded how many first cousins each student had. Here are the results:

Number of First Cousins						
6	5	1	7	3	4	4
5	1	5	6	4	7	5
5	6	7	5	4	6	4

Draw and label a number line that includes the least and greatest data values. Place as many Xs above each number as there are responses for that number.

Line Plot

Number of First Cousins

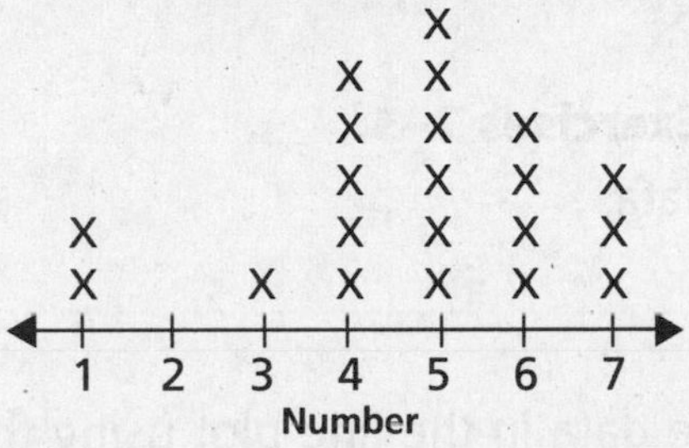

For the next month, the fifth-graders kept a record of how many times they called one of their first cousins on the phone. Here are the results:

2, 0, 2, 1, 1, 3, 4, 2, 2, 3, 4, 3, 6, 0, 3, 2, 1, 2, 3, 1, 2

1. Record the results in the line plot below.

Phone Calls to First Cousins

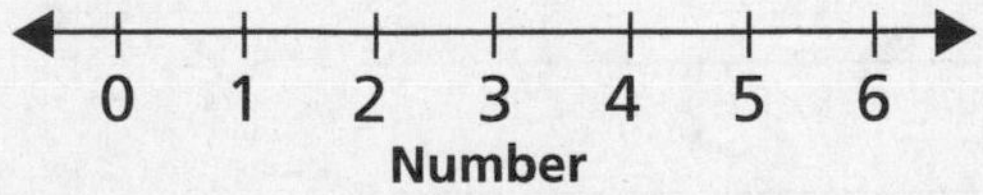

Use the line plot for Exercises 2 and 3.

2. How many students made at least one phone call to a first cousin?

____

3. Find the median, mode, range, and any outliers of the data shown in the line plot.

____

7–3

Name ______________________________

Skills Practice

Line Plots

The Johnson family kept a record of the length of telephone calls they made in one weekend.

8 minutes	**6 minutes**	**4 minutes**	**10 minutes**	**4 minutes**	**8 minutes**
7 minutes	**8 minutes**	**8 minutes**	**7 minutes**	**9 minutes**	**8 minutes**
3 minutes	**9 minutes**	**7 minutes**	**8 minutes**	**4 minutes**	**6 minutes**
9 minutes	**8 minutes**	**7 minutes**	**9 minutes**	**7 minutes**	

1. Make a line plot of the data.

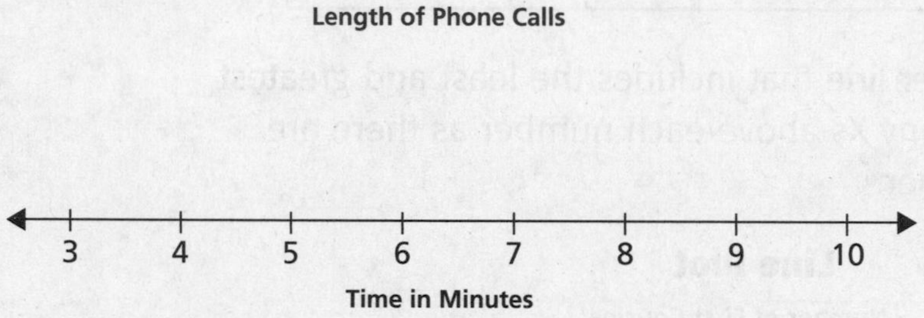

Use the data from your line plot for Exercises 2–5.

2. Find the median and mode of the data.

____

3. Write a few sentences describing the data in the line plot using the median and the mode.

____

____

____

____

4. Find the range and any outliers of the data.

____

5. Write a few sentences describing the data in the line plot using the range and outliers.

____

____

____

Name ______________________________

7–4

Reteach

Frequency Tables

Mario asked his classmates how many pets they have. Here are the results:

Number of Pets							
3	1	2	3	6	4	2	0
0	0	1	2	2	1	3	4
2	1	2	0	5	5	4	0

Make one tally in the frequency table for each time a particular number of pets occurs. Count and record the number of tallies.

Frequency Table

Number of Pets	Tally	Frequency
0		
1		
2		
3		
4		
5		
6		

The number of games won by the school baseball team over the last 15 years are shown below.

10, 8, 11, 7, 9, 12, 13, 9, 7, 8, 10, 10, 9, 8, 8

1. Make a frequency table of the data.

Number of Wins	Tally	Frequency
7		
8		
9		
10		
11		
12		
13		

2. How many times did the team win 10 or more games?

____

3. Find the median, mode, range, and any outliers of the data.

____

7–4

Name ____________________

Skills Practice

Frequency Tables

The table shows the names of several famous artists.

Famous Artists			
Matisse	Monet	Cezanne	Picasso
Manet	Renoir	Rothko	Whistler
Dali	Van Gogh	Magritte	Degas
Miro	Da Vinci	Gauguin	Chagall

1. Make a frequency table to show the number of letters in each name.

Number of Letters	Tally	Frequency

2. Find the median, mode, and range of the data. Identify any outliers.

____

Violet took a survey of her classmates' hobbies. Her results appear in the table.

Classmates' Hobbies					
R	D	S	R	D	R
P	P	S	S	S	P
T	S	T	S	S	D
T	R	S	D	D	S

R = reading
D = drawing
P = photography
S = sports
T = watching TV

3. Make a frequency table of the data.

Hobbies	Tally	Frequency

4. What is the mode of the data?

____

Name ______________________________

7–5

Reteach

Scales and Intervals

The frequency table shows the cost of T-shirts at the mall.

T-Shirt Prices at the Mall		
Price ($)	**Tally**	**Frequency**
10–11.99	~~IIII~~ II	7
12–13.99	~~IIII~~ ~~IIII~~ I	11
14–15.99	II	2
16–17.99	III	3
18–19.99	II	2

The frequency table has a scale from $10 to $19.99. The scale includes the least and greatest values in the data set. The scale is separated into intervals. The interval separates the scale into equal parts. There are 5 intervals in the frequency table. The interval size is $1.99.

Most T-shirts are in the ______________ interval.

The cost of a gallon of orange juice at 20 different supermarkets is shown.

Orange Juice Prices (per gallon)				
$2.11	$2.07	$2.23	$2.25	$2.28
$2.27	$2.26	$2.15	$2.25	$2.47
$2.27	$2.26	$2.25	$2.35	$2.25
$2.35	$2.25	$2.37	$2.49	$2.27

1. Choose an appropriate scale and interval size for a frequency table that will represent the data. Describe the intervals. Then make a frequency table.

____

Orange Juice Prices (per gallon)		
Price ($)	**Tally**	**Frequency**

2. Write a sentence or two to describe how the data are distributed among the intervals.

____

Name ___________________________

7–5

Skills Practice

Scales and Intervals

The table shows the 25 highest mountains in Texas.

Highest Mountains in Texas (ft)				
8,378	7,835	7,031	7,730	8,368
6,781	8,508	8,749	6,894	6,860
8,631	6,814	7,550	8,615	6,398
7,748	8,085	6,521	6,432	7,825
6,717	6,580	6,725	6,350	6,650

Source: Texas State Library

1. Choose an appropriate scale and interval size for a frequency table that will represent the data. Then make a frequency table.

____

25 Highest Mountains in Texas		
Height (ft)	Tally	Frequency

2. Write a sentence or two to describe how the data are distributed among the intervals.

____

____

The table shows race results to the nearest tenth for the school track team.

Track Team Race Times (min.)				
10.3	11.7	10.1	12.8	10.7
11.9	9.5	7.3	9.7	10.8
12.1	13.6	9.3	9.1	14.5

3. Choose an appropriate scale and interval size for a frequency table that will represent the data. Then make a frequency table.

____

Track Team Race Times		
Time (min.)	Tally	Frequency

4. Write a sentence or two to describe how the data are distributed among the intervals.

____

____

Name ______________________________

7–6

Reteach

Bar Graphs

A **bar graph** uses bars to display the number of items in a group.

The table shows the number of fifth grade students in different activities.

Activity	Number of Students
Band	30
Chorus	20
Art Club	25
Computer Club	25

1. Make a bar graph of the data.

2. According to the graph, the most popular activity is ____________.

3. According to the graph, the least popular activity is ____________.

4. What is the mode of the data?

______________________________________.

Name ______________________________

7–6

Skills Practice

Bar Graphs

1. The table shows the times Ken and Pat rode their bikes each day last week. Make a double-bar graph of the data.

Time Spent Riding a Bike (minutes)

Day	Ken	Pat
Sunday	20	25
Monday	30	40
Tuesday	25	20
Wednesday	5	45
Thursday	20	35
Friday	15	35
Saturday	30	20

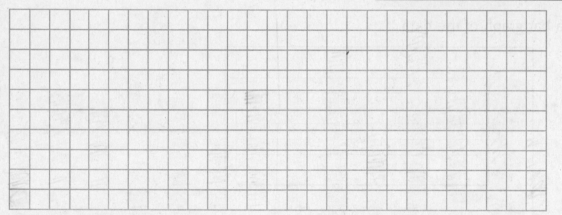

Use data from the graph at the right for Exercises 2–4.

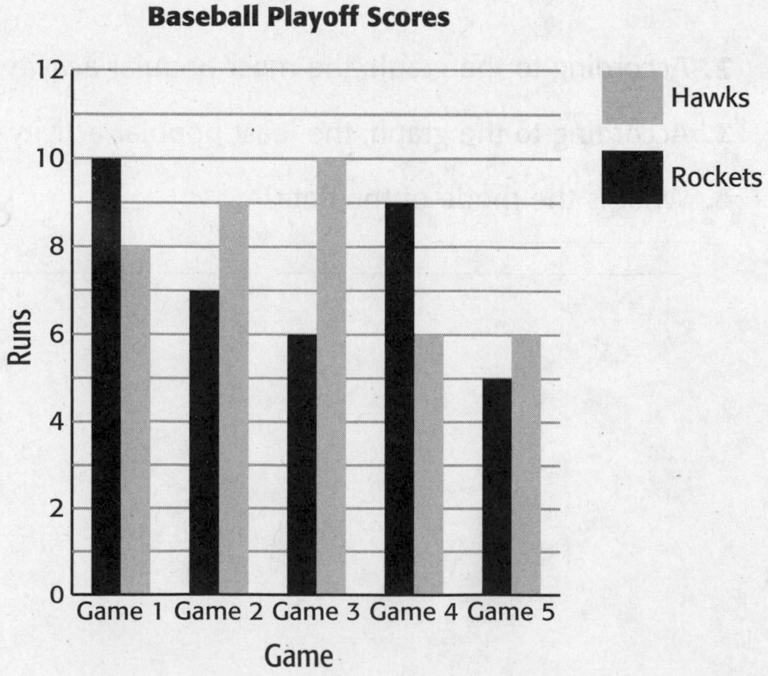

2. What is the mode of the data?

____

3. Who won Game 4? By how many runs?

____

4. The team that wins 3 games wins the playoffs. Who won the playoffs?

____

Name ______________________

7–7

Reteach

Line Graphs

You can use a line graph to show how a quantity changes over time. This graph shows Ricky's height over five years. To make a line graph, plot points to represent the data. Then draw a line to connect the points.

Ricky's Height

Year	Height (in inches)
2004	46
2005	47
2006	49
2007	52
2008	56

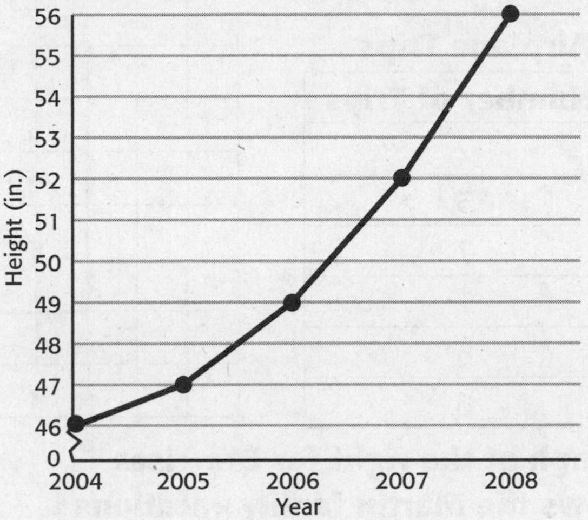

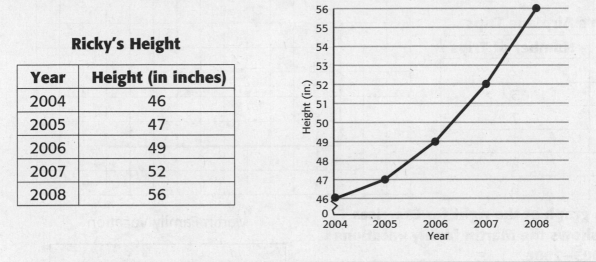

Marie grew a pumpkin. The table shows the weight gain in pounds of her pumpkin. Make a line graph to display the data. Use the line graph to solve the problems.

Marie's Pumpkin

Month	Weight (in pounds)
1	$\frac{1}{2}$
2	1
3	3
4	6
5	$8\frac{1}{2}$
6	9
7	9

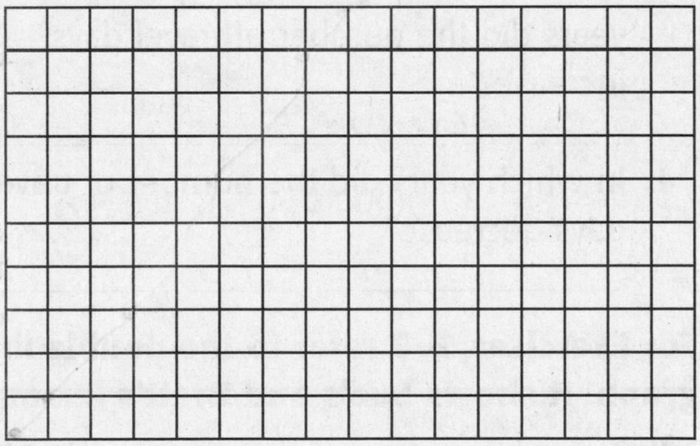

1. On a line graph, a line that rises shows that a quantity is increasing. In which months did Marie's pumpkin gain the most weight?

____

2. On a line graph, a line that is horizontal shows that a quantity stays the same. In which month did the weight of the pumpkin stay the same?

____

Name ______________________________

7–7

Skills Practice

Line Graphs

The table shows Beth's airplane trips from 2003–2008.

1. Make a line graph to display the data in the table.

Beth's Airplane Trips

Year	Number of Trips
2003	2
2004	3
2005	7
2006	7
2007	5
2008	6

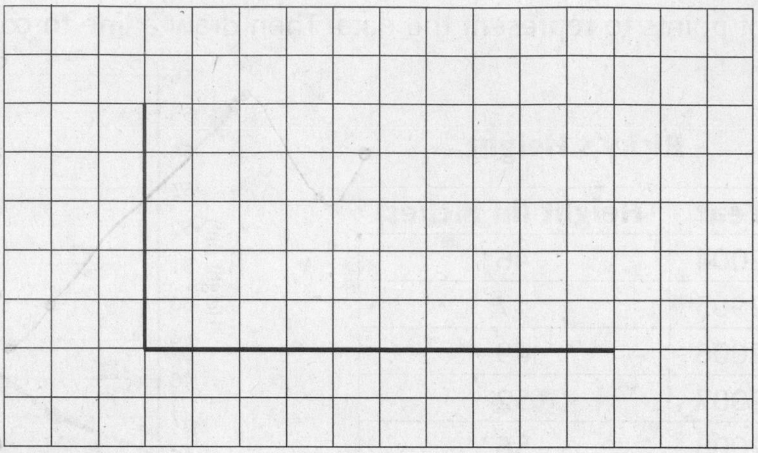

Use the graph at the right for Exercises 2–4. It shows the Martin family vacations from 2003–2008.

Martin Family Vacation

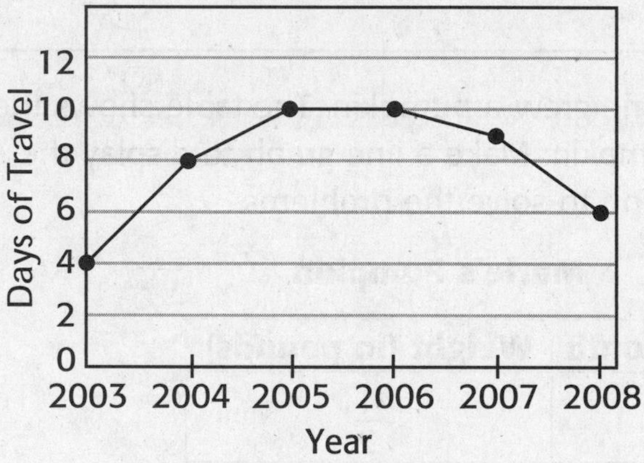

2. In which year(s) did they have the most travel days?

____

3. On a line graph, a line that rises shows that a quantity is increasing. In which years did the number of travel days increase?

____

4. In which years did the number of travel days decrease?

____

For Exercises 5–7 refer to the double line graph. It shows Sue's and Brett's lemonade sales.

Lemonade Sales

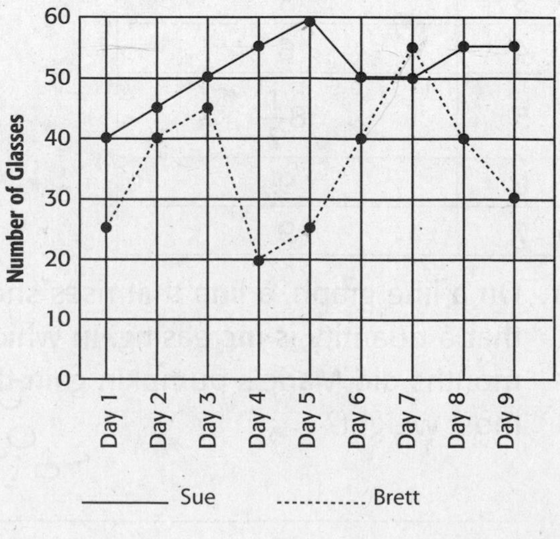

5. Who sold more lemonade in nine days?

____

6. In all, how many glasses did Sue sale?

____

7. What was the difference in cups sold between Sue and Brett?

____

7–8

Name ____________________

Reteach

Use an Appropriate Graph

Students went on a fishing trip. At the end of one week, these were how many fish were caught.

Which type of graph would you use to display the data in the table?

Fish caught	
Day	**Number caught**
Monday	3
Tuesday	2
Wednesday	1
Thursday	1
Friday	0
Saturday	4
Sunday	3

When deciding which kind of graph to use for a set of data, consider the following:

- Is the data shown in frequency intervals?
- Do both axes have numbers?
- Are two sets of data compared?
- Does the data show a change over time?

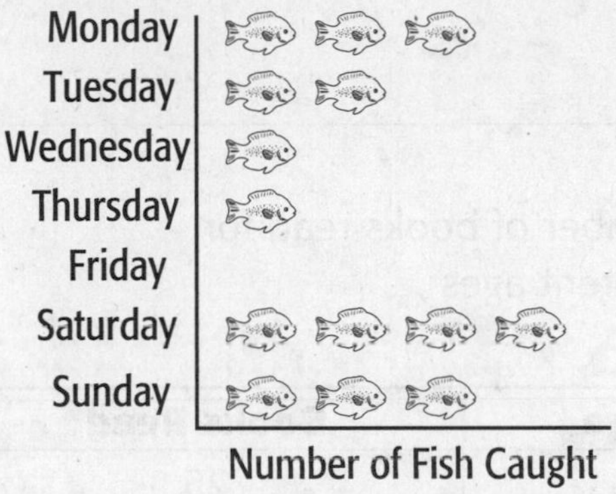

The fish data shows equal intervals. Only one axis on a graph would have numbers.

A pictograph is an appropriate graph for the data.

Which type of graph would you use to display the data in each problem? Explain why. Then make the graph.

1. The following test scores were recorded for a science test in Ms. Martin's class: 88, 79, 89, 92, 90, 95, 87, 89, 95, 94, 85, 83, 91, 80, and 87.

____

____

2. Katie kept a log of the number of sit-ups she did each day from Monday through Friday.

M	T	W	Th	F
52	75	98	80	100

____

____

Name ______________________________

7–8

Skills Practice

Use an Appropriate Graph

Which type of graph would you use to display the data in each table? Explain why. Then make the graph.

1. CDs owned by Patrick

Type of CD	Number of CDs
Country	3
Rock	10
Rap	8
Blues	6
Pop	2

____

2. The number of laps completed by students jogging around Lincoln Park

Number of Laps	Number of Students
1	4
2	3
3	5
4	2

____

3. Number of books read for different ages

Age	Books Read
8	25
9	35
10	50
11	75

____

4. Temperatures at different times

Time	Temperature
1 P.M.	64°F
2 P.M.	68°F
3 P.M.	70°F
4 P.M.	66°F

____

Solve.

5. Write a problem in which you could use a graph to display the data. Share it with others.

____

____

____

Name ______________________________

7–9

Reteach

Problem-Solving Strategy: Make a Graph

Choose the graph that best displays the data: The number of paintings by men and the number of paintings by women at a museum. Explain.

Step 1 Understand	**Be sure you understand the problem** Read carefully. What do you know? • Number of paintings by ______________ at the museum. • ____________________ by women at the museum. What do you need to find? • The graph that ______________________ .
Step 2 Plan	**Make a plan.** Choose a strategy. Making a graph will help you solve the problem. Decide which graph best represents the data. Think of the types of graphs with which you are familiar. Choose a bar graph, double-bar graph, line graph, double-line graph, line plot, or pictograph. Think about how each type of graph is used to display data.

Name ___________________________

7–9

Reteach (continued)

Problem-Solving Strategy: Make a Graph

Step 3 Solve	**Carry out your plan.** What do you know? Since no data exists about dates of the paintings, the data does not show change over time. So, you can't use a ____________. You can't use numbers on both axes, so a ____________ or a ____________ would not be good choices. The data compares one set of data (the number of paintings by men and the number of paintings by women), so you wouldn't use a ____________. A good choice for representing the data is a ____________.
Step 4 Look Back	**Is the solution reasonable?** Reread the problem. What other graph could you use to display the data? ____________

Choose the graph that best displays the data. Explain.

1. Two schools held book fairs recently. Each book fair lasted four days. Attendance at the fairs was recorded each day for both the schools.

   A line plot

   B double-line graph

   ____

   ____

2. A table shows the price of homes in a neighborhood over a span of 15 years.

   C bar graph **D** line graph

   ____

   ____

7–9

Name ______________________________

Skills Practice

Problem-Solving Strategy: Make a Graph

Solve by using a graph.

1. Renee surveyed her classmates to find out how many books they had in their backpacks. What was the most frequent number of books found in a backpack? ______________

Number of Books						
3	2	2	0	1	3	4
2	2	2	3	1	4	2
4	3	1	3	1	3	3

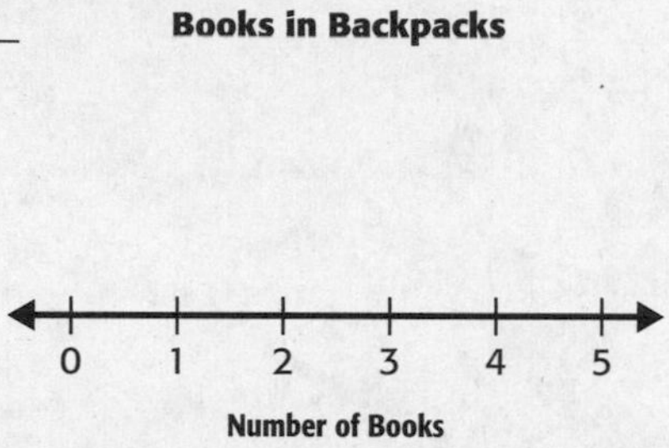

2. In which years was there an increase in the mean math test scores of Mrs. Sprankle's fifth-grade class? ______________

Math Test Scores

Year	Mean Score
2000	86
2001	83
2002	88
2003	87
2004	85
2005	83
2006	86

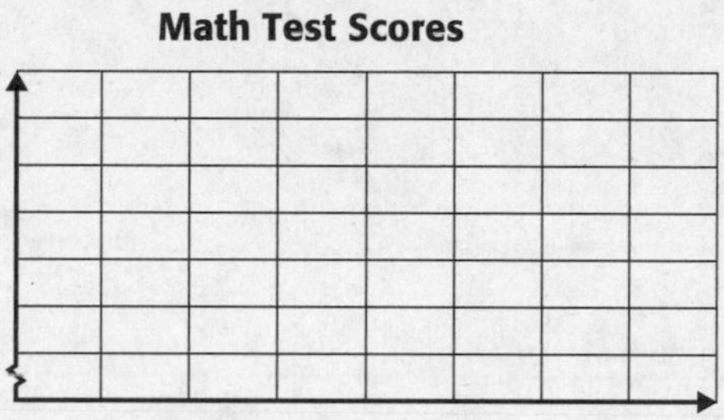

3. The following table shows the kinds of movies favored by students in fourth and fifth grades. What kind of movie is favored most by students in both grades? ______________

Favorite Movies

Movie Type	4th Graders	5th Graders
Comedy	17	19
Drama	5	7
Animation	11	8
Horror	7	10

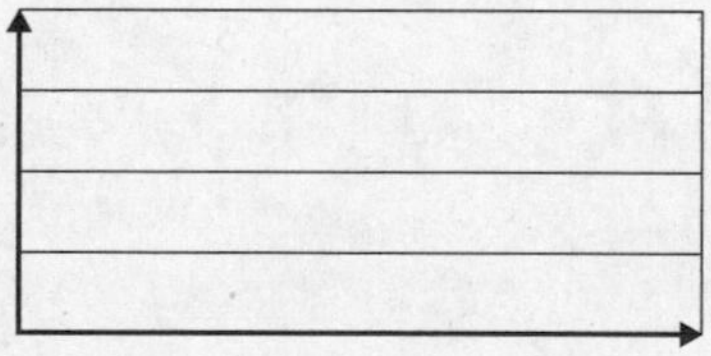

8–1

Name ______________________

Reteach

Fractions and Division

Kelly, Jose, Jason, and Melanie are sharing 1 pizza. How much pizza does each person get?

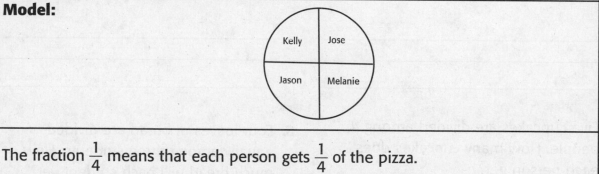

A **fraction** is a number that names equal parts of a whole or parts of a group. A fraction represents division. If 1 is divided into 4 equal parts, one part is $\frac{1}{4}$.
The **numerator** is the number above the bar in a fraction. / The **denominator** is the number below the bar in a fraction.
Words: 1 pizza divided among 4 people **Symbols:** $1 \div 4$
Fraction: 1 pizza → 1 ← numerator 4 people → 4 ← denominator
Model: 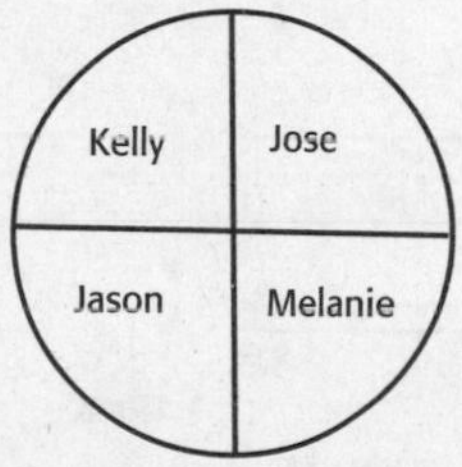
The fraction $\frac{1}{4}$ means that each person gets $\frac{1}{4}$ of the pizza.

Represent each situation using a fraction. Then solve.

1. At the picnic there are 3 pieces of fruit for 4 people. How many pieces of fruit will each person receive?

____

____

____

2. Six bags of trail mix are divided among 17 people. How much of the trail mix did each person receive?

____

____

____

Name ______________________

8–1

Skills Practice

Fractions and Division

Represent each situation using a fraction. Then solve.

1. Mr. Janson has 3 jars of soup to divide among 4 people. How much soup will each person receive?

____

____

2. Andrew shares his suitcase with his two brothers on vacation. How much space in the suitcase will Andrew and his brothers each have?

____

____

3. Two small pizzas are shared by three people. How much pizza does each person get?

____

____

4. One container of paint is used to paint 7 tables. How much paint did each table use?

____

____

5. Five cupcakes are divided among 4 people. How many cupcakes does each person get?

____

____

6. Four loaves of bread are divided equally among three students. How much bread will each student get?

____

____

Name ______________________________

8–2

Reteach

Improper Fractions

An **improper fraction** is a fraction that has a numerator that is greater than or equal to its denominator. **Example:** $\frac{7}{4}$ $\frac{8}{6}$ $\frac{9}{2}$ $\frac{2}{2}$	A **mixed number** has a whole number and a fraction. **Example:** $5\frac{1}{3}$ $3\frac{1}{2}$ $6\frac{2}{5}$

Renaming an Improper Fraction

To write an improper fraction as a mixed number, divide the numerator by the denominator. Write the remainder as a fraction of the divisor.

Example: $\frac{8}{3} = 3\overline{)8}$ → $2\frac{2}{3}$ (2R2; $8 - 6 = 2$)

Example: $\frac{19}{4} = 4\overline{)19}$ → $4\frac{3}{4}$ (4R3; $19 - 16 = 3$)

Write each improper fraction as a mixed number.

1. $\frac{15}{2}$ ________
2. $\frac{18}{5}$ ________
3. $\frac{9}{4}$ ________
4. $\frac{4}{3}$ ________
5. $\frac{7}{2}$ ________
6. $\frac{19}{6}$ ________
7. $\frac{17}{2}$ ________
8. $\frac{9}{8}$ ________
9. $\frac{13}{2}$ ________
10. $\frac{7}{4}$ ________
11. $\frac{27}{7}$ ________
12. $\frac{29}{8}$ ________
13. $\frac{23}{3}$ ________
14. $\frac{33}{5}$ ________
15. $\frac{19}{2}$ ________

Name ___

8–2

Skills Practice

Improper Fractions

Write each improper fraction as a mixed number.

1. $\frac{13}{2}$ ___ **2.** $\frac{5}{3}$ ___ **3.** $\frac{19}{3}$ ___

4. $\frac{3}{2}$ ___ **5.** $\frac{17}{4}$ ___ **6.** $\frac{31}{5}$ ___

7. $\frac{16}{5}$ ___ **8.** $\frac{4}{3}$ ___ **9.** $\frac{13}{9}$ ___

10. $\frac{11}{3}$ ___ **11.** $\frac{49}{8}$ ___ **12.** $\frac{8}{5}$ ___

13. $\frac{44}{9}$ ___ **14.** $\frac{12}{11}$ ___ **15.** $\frac{38}{7}$ ___

16. $\frac{20}{7}$ ___ **17.** $\frac{41}{8}$ ___ **18.** $\frac{10}{7}$ ___

19. $\frac{19}{5}$ ___ **20.** $\frac{7}{3}$ ___ **21.** $\frac{29}{9}$ ___

22. $\frac{51}{8}$ ___ **23.** $\frac{17}{6}$ ___ **24.** $\frac{9}{2}$ ___

25. $\frac{45}{8}$ ___ **26.** $\frac{68}{7}$ ___ **27.** $\frac{12}{5}$ ___

28. $\frac{22}{3}$ ___ **29.** $\frac{49}{6}$ ___ **30.** $\frac{28}{3}$ ___

Name ______________________________

8–3

Reteach

Problem-Solving Strategy: Use Logical Reasoning

Use the logical reasoning strategy to solve problems.

The table shows the times of some women who competed in the Snowboard Cross event in the 2006 Winter Olympics. How much less time did it take Tanja Frieden than Yuka Fujimori?

Athlete	**Time (minutes)**
Lindsey Jacobellis	1 min 29 sec
Tanja Frieden	1 min 30 sec
Katharina Himmler	1 min 43 sec
Yuka Fujimori	1 min 48 sec

Understand	**What facts do you know?** Tanja Frieden's time was 1 minute 30 seconds. Yuka Fujimori's time was 1 minute 48 seconds. **What do you need to find?** How much less time it took Tanja Frieden than it took Yuka Fujimori.
Plan	You can subtract 1 minute 30 seconds from 1 minute 48 seconds to find the answer.
Solve	**Use your plan to solve the problem.** 1 min 48 sec − 1 min 30 sec = 18 sec
Check	Look back. 1 minute 30 seconds + 18 seconds = 1 minute 48 seconds. So, you know the answer is correct.

Solve. Use logical reasoning.

1. Miss Graham's class is buying supplies for a party. They need to buy 3 packs of balloons, 2 rolls of streamers, and 1 set of wall decorations. Use the chart below to find out how much each item costs. How much will their party supplies cost in all?

Item	Cost
Pack of Balloons	$1.37
Roll of Streamers	$0.99
Set of Wall Decorations	$8.50

8–3

Name ________________________________

Reteach

Problem-Solving Strategy: Use Logical Reasoning (continued)

Solve. Use logical reasoning.

2. Barbara can swim four laps in 2 minutes. How long does it take her to swim one lap?

____

3. The park has 3 more maple trees than spruce trees. There are 13 maple and spruce trees in all. How many maple trees are there?

____

4. Leonard can run a mile in 9 minutes. Alicia can run a mile in 7 minutes. If they run together, how long after Alicia finishes will Leonard finish?

____

5. Carl is making a garden. He buys 3 packets of violet seeds for $0.35 each, 2 packets of marigold seeds for $0.50 each, one bag of soil for $1.50, and a new pair of gloves for $4.50. How much money will Carl spend in all?

____

6. Ramona can ride her bike 1 mile in 5 minutes. How long will it take her to ride 4 miles?

____

7. Ronald and his brother are going to visit their grandmother. If their father drives 45 miles an hour, it will take 2 hours to get there. How far do they have to travel?

____

8–3

Name ______________________________

Skills Practice

Problem-Solving Strategy: Use Logical Reasoning

Solve. Use logical reasoning.

1. Julia can make 2 pieces of toast in 3 minutes. How long will it take her to make 8 pieces of toast?

____

2. Jeff has saved $40.50. He wants to buy a new pair of shoes which cost $35.75. The sales tax on these shoes is $2.50. How much money will Jeff have left over after making this purchase?

____

3. In the school choir there are 3 more boys than girls. There are 13 boys and girls in the choir in all. How many boys are there in the choir?

____

4. The following chart shows some of the countries who earned the most gold medals in the 2006 Winter Olympics. How many more medals did Austria win than Estonia?

____

Country	Number of Gold Medals
Germany	11
Austria	9
South Korea	6
Estonia	3

5. Louise, Jacqueline, and Martha ran a one-mile race. Louise finished in 8.47 minutes, Jacqueline finished in 9.32 minutes, and Martha finished in 8.34 minutes. How much time passed between Martha's finish and Jacqueline's finish?

____

6. Shamera and Diana have played 14 games of checkers. Shamera has won 2 more games than Diana. How many games has Diana won?

____

8–4

Name ____________________

Reteach

Mixed Numbers

A **mixed number** is made up of a whole number and a fraction.
An **improper fraction** is a fraction in which the numerator is greater than or equal to the denominator.

Write $2\frac{2}{3}$ as an improper fraction.

Step 1
Multiply the whole number by the denominator.

$2\frac{2}{3} \longrightarrow 2 \times 3 = 6$

Step 2
Add the numerator to the product.

$6 + 2 = 8$

Step 3
Write the sum over the denominator.

$2\frac{2}{3} = \frac{8}{3}$

Write each mixed number as an improper fraction.

1. $2\frac{2}{7}$ __________ **2.** $5\frac{3}{4}$ __________ **3.** $6\frac{5}{8}$ __________

4. $3\frac{4}{10}$ __________ **5.** $9\frac{1}{3}$ __________ **6.** $4\frac{4}{5}$ __________

7. $1\frac{1}{8}$ __________ **8.** $3\frac{1}{2}$ __________ **9.** $2\frac{2}{5}$ __________

10. $2\frac{2}{3}$ __________ **11.** $1\frac{3}{4}$ __________ **12.** $1\frac{1}{5}$ __________

13. $6\frac{2}{3}$ __________ **14.** $3\frac{2}{5}$ __________ **15.** $4\frac{1}{2}$ __________

16. $1\frac{4}{5}$ __________ **17.** $3\frac{5}{8}$ __________ **18.** $2\frac{2}{3}$ __________

Name ______________________________

8–4

Skills Practice

Mixed Numbers

Write each mixed number as an improper fraction.

1. $3\frac{1}{2}$ ________ **2.** $5\frac{3}{4}$ ________ **3.** $6\frac{7}{8}$ ________

4. $5\frac{5}{12}$ ________ **5.** $4\frac{1}{6}$ ________ **6.** $6\frac{2}{3}$ ________

7. $12\frac{2}{3}$ ________ **8.** $10\frac{23}{100}$ ________ **9.** $9\frac{1}{4}$ ________

10. $8\frac{2}{5}$ ________ **11.** $25\frac{1}{4}$ ________ **12.** $22\frac{1}{2}$ ________

13. $6\frac{4}{5}$ ________ **14.** $4\frac{3}{10}$ ________ **15.** $6\frac{1}{100}$ ________

16. $7\frac{5}{8}$ ________ **17.** $6\frac{3}{8}$ ________ **18.** $3\frac{9}{100}$ ________

19. $5\frac{5}{6}$ ________ **20.** $9\frac{3}{17}$ ________ **21.** $25\frac{1}{3}$ ________

22. $5\frac{2}{9}$ ________ **23.** $12\frac{2}{3}$ ________ **24.** $5\frac{3}{7}$ ________

25. $6\frac{4}{9}$ ________ **26.** $10\frac{1}{18}$ ________ **27.** $5\frac{5}{12}$ ________

28. $6\frac{2}{13}$ ________ **29.** $25\frac{4}{5}$ ________ **30.** $20\frac{5}{6}$ ________

Solve.

31. Tina spent $3\frac{1}{3}$ hours practicing the piano. Write this quantity as an improper fraction.

____

32. Suppose you have $2\frac{1}{4}$ oranges. Write this quantity as an improper fraction.

____

Name ______________________________

8-5

Reteach

Fractions on a Number Line

Giselle is making a recipe that calls for $\frac{1}{6}$ cup of brown sugar and $\frac{5}{6}$ cup of flour. Does the recipe have more brown sugar or flour?

You can see from the models that $\frac{1}{6} < \frac{5}{6}$.

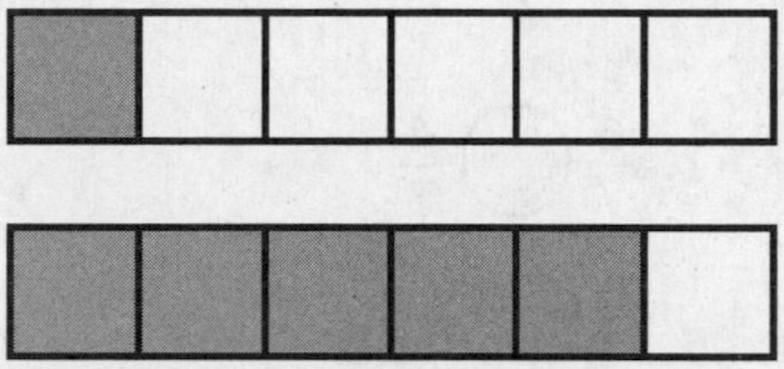

You can also use number lines to compare fractions. There are 6 equal sections between 0 and 1.

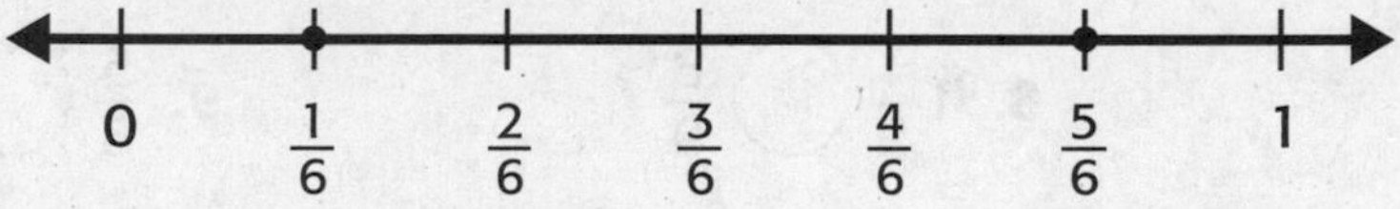

Since $\frac{5}{6}$ is to the right of $\frac{1}{6}$ on the number line, $\frac{5}{6} > \frac{1}{6}$. So, the recipe has more flour than brown sugar.

Use the number line for Exercises 1–6. Replace each ◯ with < or > to make a true statement.

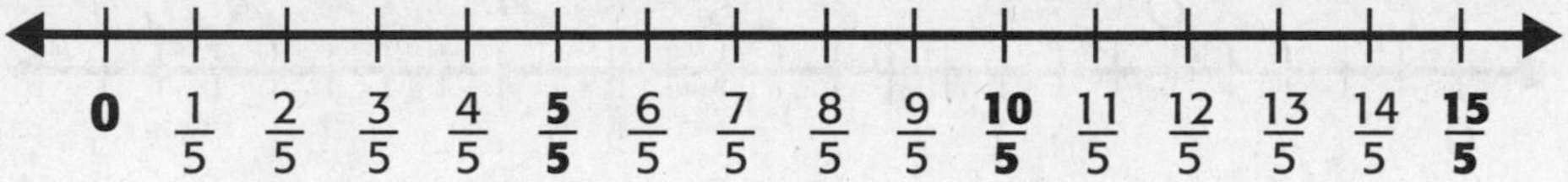

1. $\frac{1}{5}$ ◯ $\frac{3}{5}$

2. $\frac{7}{5}$ ◯ $\frac{2}{5}$

3. $2\frac{1}{5}$ ◯ $\frac{12}{5}$

4. $\frac{6}{5}$ ◯ $\frac{2}{5}$

5. $\frac{13}{5}$ ◯ $2\frac{4}{5}$

6. $1\frac{4}{5}$ ◯ $\frac{7}{5}$

Name ______________________________

8-5

Skills Practice

Fractions on a Number Line

Use the number line for Exercises 1–6. Replace each ◯ with < or > to make a true statement.

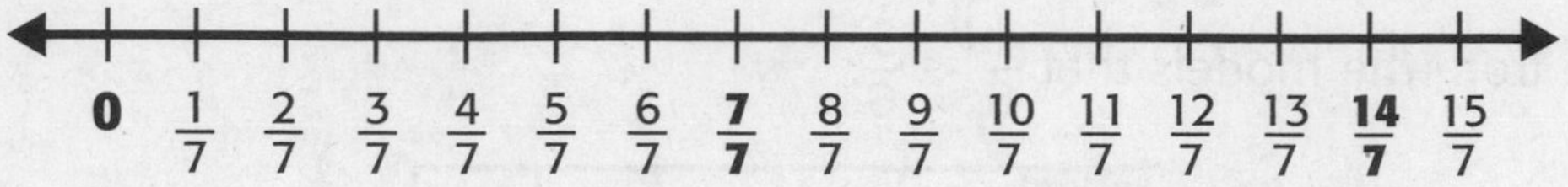

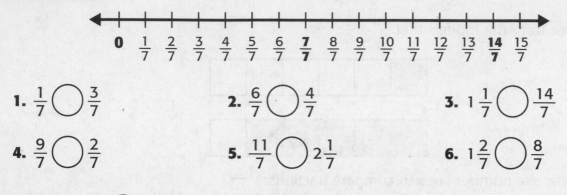

1. $\frac{1}{7}$ ◯ $\frac{3}{7}$ **2.** $\frac{6}{7}$ ◯ $\frac{4}{7}$ **3.** $1\frac{1}{7}$ ◯ $\frac{14}{7}$

4. $\frac{9}{7}$ ◯ $\frac{2}{7}$ **5.** $\frac{11}{7}$ ◯ $2\frac{1}{7}$ **6.** $1\frac{2}{7}$ ◯ $\frac{8}{7}$

Replace each ◯ with < or > to make a true statement.

7. $\frac{2}{4}$ ◯ $\frac{3}{4}$ **8.** $1\frac{1}{9}$ ◯ $\frac{8}{9}$ **9.** $\frac{5}{6}$ ◯ $\frac{2}{6}$

10. $\frac{9}{10}$ ◯ $\frac{2}{10}$ **11.** $1\frac{2}{8}$ ◯ $\frac{11}{8}$ **12.** $\frac{14}{7}$ ◯ $2\frac{3}{7}$

13. $\frac{9}{5}$ ◯ $1\frac{3}{5}$ **14.** $\frac{7}{11}$ ◯ $\frac{6}{11}$ **15.** $\frac{10}{4}$ ◯ $2\frac{1}{4}$

Write the fraction or mixed number that is represented by each point.

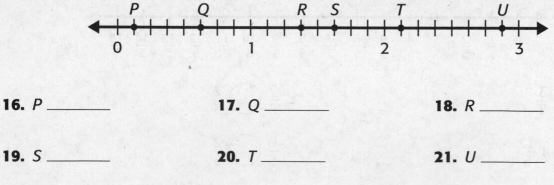

16. *P* ________ **17.** *Q* ________ **18.** *R* ________

19. *S* ________ **20.** *T* ________ **21.** *U* ________

Solve.

22. Amelia's bookshelf is $\frac{3}{5}$ full of books and $\frac{1}{5}$ full of magazines. Does her bookshelf have more books or magazines? Explain.

____

Name ____________________

8–6

Reteach

Round Fractions

Round Up

If the numerator is almost as large as the denominator, round the number up to the next whole number.

Example: $\frac{9}{10}$ rounds to 1.

9 is almost as large as 10.

Round to $\frac{1}{2}$

If the numerator is about half of the denominator, round the fraction to $\frac{1}{2}$.

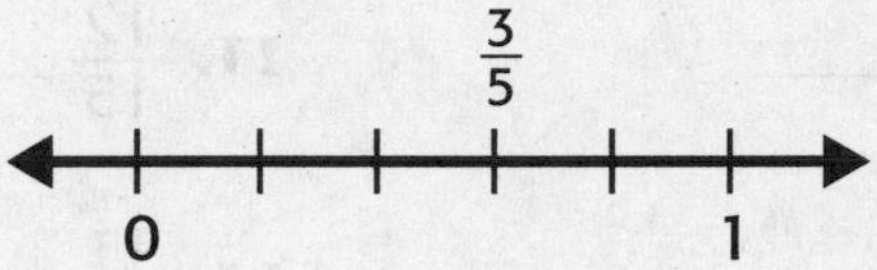

Example: $\frac{3}{5}$ rounds to $\frac{1}{2}$.

3 is about half of 5.

Round Down

If the numerator is much smaller than the denominator, round the number down to the previous whole number.

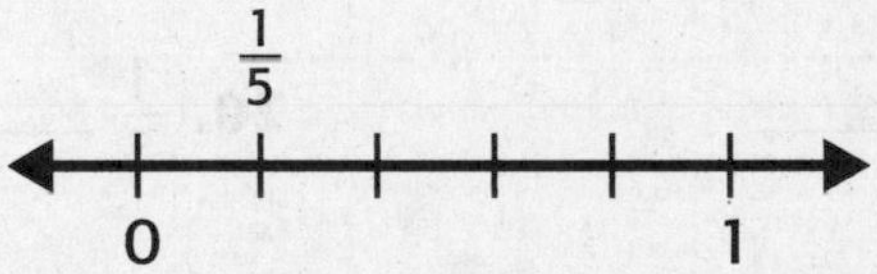

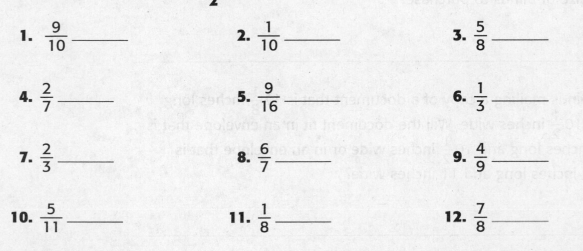

Example: $\frac{1}{5}$ rounds to 0.

1 is much smaller than 5.

Round each number to 0, $\frac{1}{2}$, or 1.

1. $\frac{9}{10}$ ______ **2.** $\frac{1}{10}$ ______ **3.** $\frac{5}{8}$ ______

4. $\frac{2}{7}$ ______ **5.** $\frac{9}{16}$ ______ **6.** $\frac{1}{3}$ ______

7. $\frac{2}{3}$ ______ **8.** $\frac{6}{7}$ ______ **9.** $\frac{4}{9}$ ______

10. $\frac{5}{11}$ ______ **11.** $\frac{1}{8}$ ______ **12.** $\frac{7}{8}$ ______

8–6

Name ____________________

Skills Practice

Round Fractions

Round each number to 0, $\frac{1}{2}$ or 1.

1. $\frac{1}{12}$ ______ **2.** $\frac{12}{13}$ ______ **3.** $\frac{9}{18}$ ______

4. $\frac{3}{4}$ ______ **5.** $\frac{2}{9}$ ______ **6.** $\frac{2}{3}$ ______

7. $\frac{1}{2}$ ______ **8.** $\frac{3}{8}$ ______ **9.** $\frac{7}{8}$ ______

10. $\frac{1}{8}$ ______ **11.** $\frac{12}{15}$ ______ **12.** $\frac{2}{9}$ ______

13. $\frac{1}{4}$ ______ **14.** $\frac{11}{12}$ ______ **15.** $\frac{5}{6}$ ______

16. $\frac{2}{16}$ ______ **17.** $\frac{1}{3}$ ______ **18.** $\frac{4}{5}$ ______

19. $\frac{1}{8}$ ______ **20.** $\frac{1}{5}$ ______ **21.** $\frac{8}{9}$ ______

Solve.

22. Mrs. Jones is putting up blinds to fit in a window opening that is $\frac{7}{8}$ yard wide. Should she round $\frac{7}{8}$ up or down when deciding on the size of blinds to purchase?

____

23. Marvin is mailing a copy of a document that is $12\frac{1}{8}$ inches long and $10\frac{1}{2}$ inches wide. Will the document fit in an envelope that is 12 inches long and $10\frac{1}{2}$ inches wide or in an envelope that is $12\frac{1}{2}$ inches long and 11 inches wide?

____

Name ______________________________

8–7

Reteach

Problem-Solving Investigation: Choose the Best Strategy

Fina did a survey of how much time students spend on homework each night. Out of 16 people interviewed, $\frac{1}{2}$ spend about 1 hour on homework and $\frac{1}{4}$ spend about 45 minutes on homework. The rest spend about 30 minutes on homework. How many students spend 30 minutes on homework?

Understand	$\frac{1}{2}$ of 16 students spend 1 hour on homework. $\frac{1}{4}$ of 16 students spend 45 minutes on homework. You need to know how many people spend 30 minutes on homework.
Plan	You can use the *act it out* strategy. Draw 16 students. Cross out the students who spend 1 hour and the students who spend 45 minutes on homework. You will be left with the students who spend 30 minutes on homework.
Solve	$\frac{1}{2}$ of 16 is 8. Cross out 8 students.  $\frac{1}{4}$ of 16 is 4. Cross out 4 more students. Count the students that are left. 4 students spend about 30 minutes on homework.
Check	Use math to check your work. $16 - 8 - 4 = 4$ Your answer is correct.

8–7

Name ______________________________

Reteach

Problem-Solving Investigation: Choose the Best Strategy (continued)

Use any strategy shown below to solve.

- Act it out
- Make a table
- Use logical reasoning
- Guess and check
- Work backward
- Solve a simpler problem

1. Out of the 200 students at Groves High, 50 spend 2 hours a night on homework, 25 spend 1 hour on homework, and 75 spend 45 minutes on homework. The rest spend 30 minutes on homework. How many students spend 30 minutes on homework?

____

2. Mrs. Jones told her class of 30 students that 8 people scored 90 or above on a math test, 7 people scored between 80 and 89 and 10 people scored between 70 and 79. How many people scored lower than 70?

____

3. If square tables are arranged in a restaurant so that only one person can sit on any side of the table, how many tables will it take to seat 40 people?

____

4. Alan bought a computer that was on sale for $568. If the computer originally cost $647, how much money did Alan save?

____

5. Forty people in a restaurant spend a total of $500. $\frac{1}{2}$ of the 40 people spend $20 each. What is the least amount of money each of the rest of the people spend?

____

Name ______________________________

8–7

Skills Practice

Problem-Solving Investigation: Choose the Best Strategy

Use any strategy shown below to solve.

- Guess and check
- Make a table
- Work backward
- Use logical reasoning
- Solve a simpler problem
- Act it out

1. In how many ways can 5 people stand in line if one of the people always has to be first in line?

____

2. The teacher told the class of 30 students that $\frac{1}{2}$ of them scored above an 80 on their math test. An additional $\frac{1}{3}$ of them scored at least a 70. How many of them scored below 70?

____

3. Alicia bought a CD player for $10 less than the regular price. If she paid $58 for the CD player, what was the regular price?

____

4. Miguel bought boxes of chocolates. The first box weighed $4\frac{1}{4}$ pounds, the second, $2\frac{3}{4}$, and the third, $1\frac{1}{3}$. What is the total amount of chocolate that Miguel bought?

____

5. After Miguel shared the chocolate with his friends, he had $3\frac{5}{8}$ pounds left. Then, he gave $2\frac{3}{4}$ pounds to his mother. Now, how much does he have?

____

6. The first $\frac{1}{5}$ mile of a $\frac{3}{4}$-mile path through a rose garden is paved with bricks. How much of the path is not paved with bricks?

____

9–1

Name ______________________ Date ______________

Reteach

Common Factors

A common factor is a number that is a factor of two or more numbers. The GCF(greatest common factor) of two numbers is the greatest number that is a factor of both.

Find the GCF of 12 and 16.
Factors of 12: 1, 2, 3, 4, 6, 12
Factors of 16: 1, 2, 4, 8, 16
The GCF of 12 and 16 is 4.

Find the GCF of 20 and 24.
Factors of 20: 1, 2, 4, 5, 10, 20
Factors of 24: 1, 2, 3, 4, 6, 8, 12, and 24
The GCF of 20 and 24 is 4.

List all the factors of each number. Circle each set of common factors. Then identify the GCF.

1. 8: ______, ______, ______, ______

32: ______, ______, ______, ______, ______, ______

GCF: ______

2. 9: ______, ______, ______

15: ______, ______, ______, ______

GCF: ______

3. 6: ______, ______, ______, ______

42: ______, ______, ______, ______, ______, ______, ______, ______

GCF: ______

Find the greatest common factor (GCF) of each set of numbers.

4. 28 and 40 ______ **5.** 10 and 25 ______ **6.** 18 and 24 ______

7. 14 and 21 ______ **8.** 35 and 42 ______ **9.** 15, 25, 30 ______

Name ______________________ Date ______________

9–1

Skills Practice

Common Factors

Find the GCF of each set of numbers.

1. 10 and 15 ______

2. 6 and 24 ______

3. 16 and 36 ______

4. 24 and 30 ______

5. 9 and 21 ______

6. 12 and 40 ______

7. 8 and 28 ______

8. 18 and 27 ______

9. 12 and 60 ______

10. 14 and 18 ______

11. 20 and 30 ______

12. 24 and 45 ______

13. 27 and 30 ______

14. 10 and 22 ______

15. 12 and 36 ______

16. 11 and 15 ______

17. 18 and 45 ______

18. 21 and 27 ______

19. 13 and 25 ______

20. 8 and 48 ______

21. 16 and 18 ______

22. 24 and 36 ______

23. 4, 12, and 30 ______

24. 12, 18, and 36 ______

25. 9, 16, and 25 ______

26. 9, 15, and 21 ______

27. 12, 15, and 21 ______

28. 9, 36, and 45 ______

29. 3, 9, and 31 ______

30. 15, 30, and 50 ______

31. 16, 24, and 30 ______

32. 30, 50, and 100 ______

Solve.

33. Thirty people at the nature center signed up for hiking, and 18 signed up for bird watching. They will be divided into smaller groups. What is the greatest number of people that can be in each group and have all groups the same size?

____

34. Rosa found 8 different wildflowers and 20 different leaves on her hike. She plans to display them in 7 equal rows on a poster. What is the greatest number of flowers or leaves she can put in each row?

____

Name ______________________ Date ____________

9–2

Reteach

Prime and Composite Numbers

- A number is **prime** if it is a whole number that has exactly two factors, 1 and the number itself.

  Example: $7 = 1 \times 7$

- A number is **composite** if it is greater than 1 and has more than two factors.

  Example: $4 = 2 \times 2$, 1×4

You can use models and factor pairs to identify prime and composite numbers.

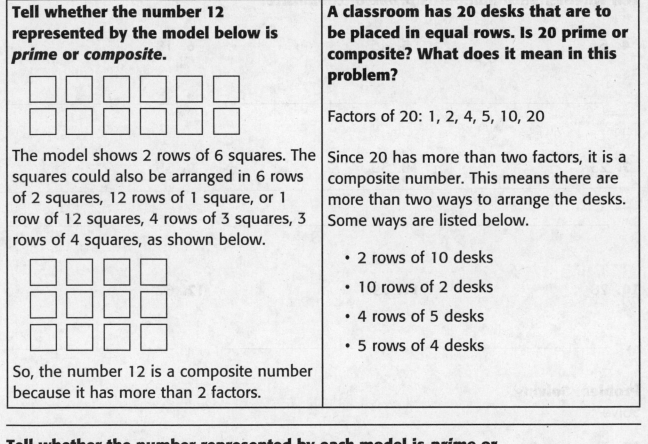

Tell whether the number 12 represented by the model below is *prime* or *composite*.

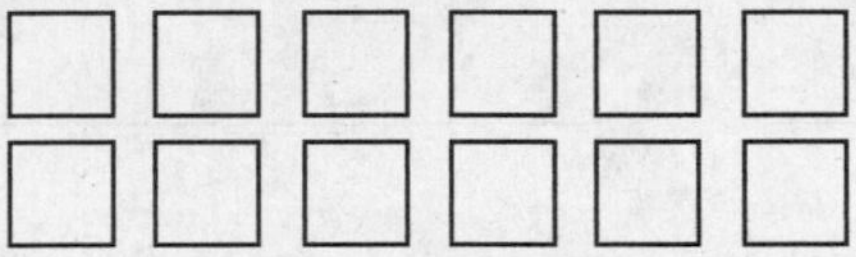

The model shows 2 rows of 6 squares. The squares could also be arranged in 6 rows of 2 squares, 12 rows of 1 square, or 1 row of 12 squares, 4 rows of 3 squares, 3 rows of 4 squares, as shown below.

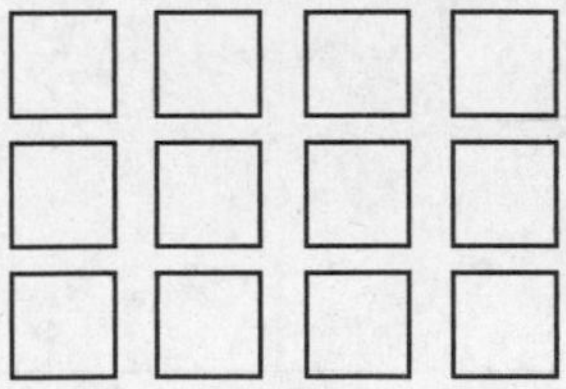

So, the number 12 is a composite number because it has more than 2 factors.

A classroom has 20 desks that are to be placed in equal rows. Is 20 prime or composite? What does it mean in this problem?

Factors of 20: 1, 2, 4, 5, 10, 20

Since 20 has more than two factors, it is a composite number. This means there are more than two ways to arrange the desks. Some ways are listed below.

- 2 rows of 10 desks
- 10 rows of 2 desks
- 4 rows of 5 desks
- 5 rows of 4 desks

Tell whether the number represented by each model is *prime* or *composite*.

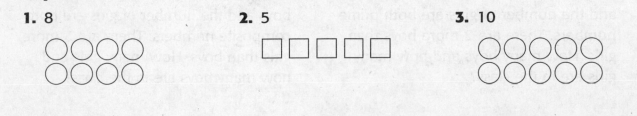

1. 8

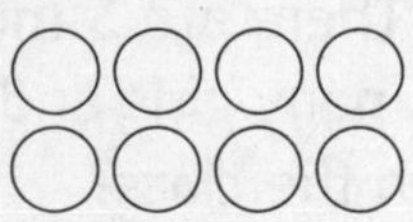

____

2. 5

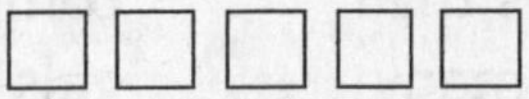

____

3. 10

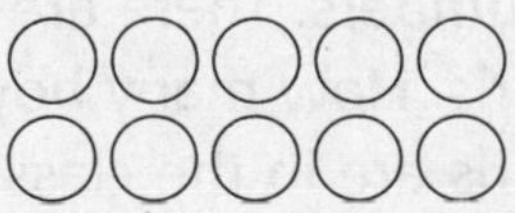

____

Name ______________________ Date ____________

9–2

Skills Practice

Prime and Composite Numbers

Tell whether the number represented by each model is *prime* or *composite*.

1. 6

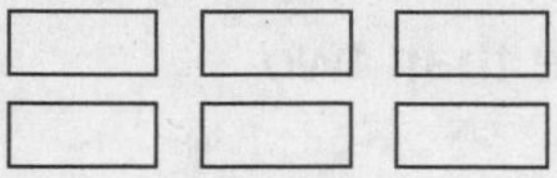

____

2. 12

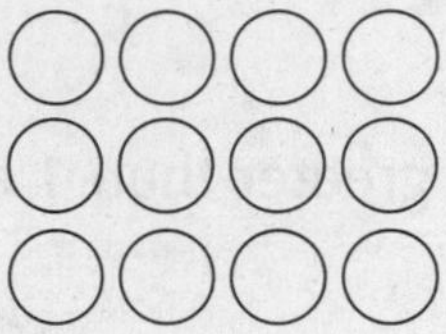

____

3. 7

____

Tell whether each number is *prime* or *composite*.

4. 64 ______________

5. 45 ______________

6. 18 ______________

7. 23 ______________

8. 39 ______________

9. 55 ______________

10. 28 ______________

11. 79 ______________

12. 62 ______________

Problem Solving.

Solve.

13. There are 24 students in Mrs. Blackwell's class. The number of boys and the number of girls are both prime numbers. There are 2 more boys than girls. How many boys and how many girls are in the class?

____

14. There are 27 students in Mr. Rodriguez's class. The number of boys and the number of girls are both composite numbers. There are 3 more girls than boys. How many girls and how many boys are in the class?

____

9–3

Name ______________________ Date __________

Reteach

Equivalent Fractions

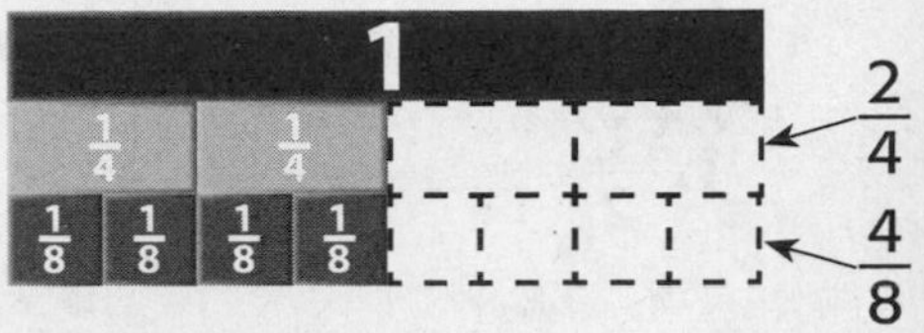

Two fractions that have the same value are called **equivalent fractions**.

One way to find equivalent fractions is to use fraction strips. The fraction strips show that $\frac{2}{4}$ and $\frac{4}{8}$ are equivalent fractions.

You can also use multiplication or division to find an equivalent fraction. You can multiply the numerator and the denominator by the same number. Or, you can divide the numerator and the denominator by the same number.

Complete: $\frac{6}{8} = \frac{\square}{24}$

Look at the denominators.

8 < 24, so multiply.

Think: $8 \times ? = 24$

$8 \times 3 = 24$

$\frac{6}{8} = \frac{6 \times 3}{8 \times 3} = \frac{18}{24}$

Complete: $\frac{6}{8} = \frac{3}{\square}$

Look at the numerators.

6 , 3, so divide.

Think: $6 \div ? = 3$

$6 \div 2 = 3$

$\frac{6}{8} = \frac{6 \div 2}{8 \div 2} = \frac{3}{4}$

Write two equivalent fractions shown by the models.

1.

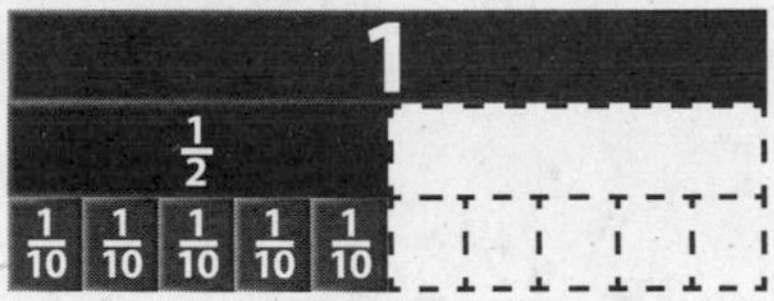

____

2.

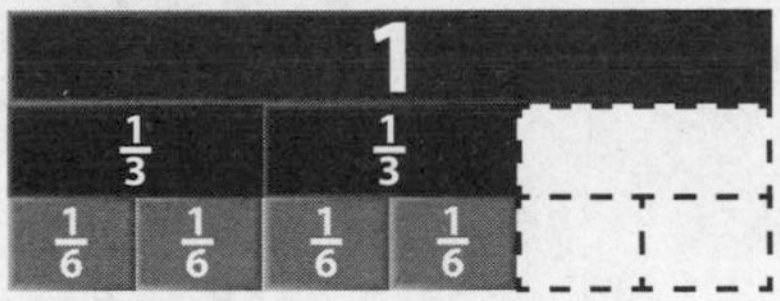

____

Find the number for $\square$ that makes the fractions equivalent.

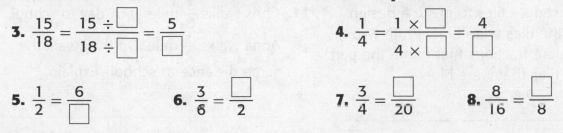

3. $\frac{15}{18} = \frac{15 \div \square}{18 \div \square} = \frac{5}{\square}$

4. $\frac{1}{4} = \frac{1 \times \square}{4 \times \square} = \frac{4}{\square}$

5. $\frac{1}{2} = \frac{6}{\square}$

6. $\frac{3}{6} = \frac{\square}{2}$

7. $\frac{3}{4} = \frac{\square}{20}$

8. $\frac{8}{16} = \frac{\square}{8}$

Name ______________________ Date ______________

9–3

Skills Practice

Equivalent Fractions

Find two fractions that are equivalent to each fraction.

1. $\frac{1}{2}$ ______

2. $\frac{1}{4}$ ______

3. $\frac{2}{5}$ ______

4. $\frac{5}{6}$ ______

5. $\frac{7}{8}$ ______

6. $\frac{2}{3}$ ______

7. $\frac{8}{10}$ ______

8. $\frac{3}{8}$ ______

9. $\frac{4}{12}$ ______

10. $\frac{4}{16}$ ______

Algebra Find the number for $\square$ that makes the fractions equivalent.

11. $\frac{1}{4} = \frac{\square}{12}$

12. $\frac{3}{5} = \frac{\square}{10}$

13. $\frac{7}{10} = \frac{\square}{20}$

14. $\frac{8}{12} = \frac{\square}{3}$

15. $\frac{10}{12} = \frac{\square}{6}$

16. $\frac{4}{10} = \frac{\square}{5}$

17. $\frac{3}{5} = \frac{\square}{20}$

18. $\frac{2}{3} = \frac{6}{\square}$

19. $\frac{12}{16} = \frac{\square}{4}$

Problem Solving.

Solve.

20. Nina used 24 tiles to make a design. Six of the tiles were blue. Write two equivalent fractions that name the part of the tiles that were blue.

____

21. Chris walks $\frac{3}{8}$ mile each day to school. Anna walks $\frac{1}{2}$ mile. Do they walk the same distance to school? Explain.

____

Name ______________________ Date ____________

9–4

Reteach

Simplest Form

When a fraction is in simplest form, the GCF of its numerator and denominator is 1.
Write $\frac{16}{40}$ in simplest form.

Step 1
Find the GCF of the numerator and the denominator.

Factors of 16: 1, 2, 4, **8**, 16
Factors of 40: 1, 2, 4, 5, **8**, 10, 20, 40
GCF: 8

Step 2
Divide the numerator and the denominator by their GCF.

$$\frac{16}{40} = \frac{16 \div 8}{40 \div 8} = \frac{2}{5}$$

Check that $\frac{2}{5}$ is in simplest form.

Factors of 2: 1, 2
Factors of 5: 1, 5

The only common factor of 2 and 5 is 1, so $\frac{2}{5}$ is in simplest form.

Write each fraction in simplest form.

1. $\frac{6}{10}$

Factors of 6: ____________

Factors of 10: ____________

Simplest Form: ____________

2. $\frac{9}{36}$

Factors of 9: ____________

Factors of 36: ____________

Simplest Form: ____________

3. $\frac{12}{30}$

Factors of 12: ____________

Factors of 30: ____________

Simplest Form: ____________

4. $\frac{20}{25}$

Factors of 20: ____________

Factors of 25: ____________

Simplest Form: ____________

5. $\frac{6}{18}$ ______ **6.** $\frac{15}{40}$ ______ **7.** $\frac{8}{30}$ ______ **8.** $\frac{24}{27}$ ______

9. $\frac{16}{28}$ ______ **10.** $\frac{30}{48}$ ______ **11.** $\frac{20}{24}$ ______ **12.** $\frac{21}{28}$ ______

Name ______________________ Date ______________

9–4

Skills Practice

Simplest Form

Write each fraction in simplest form.

1. $\frac{4}{28}$ ______
2. $\frac{15}{20}$ ______
3. $\frac{6}{21}$ ______
4. $\frac{30}{35}$ ______
5. $\frac{3}{30}$ ______
4. $\frac{12}{14}$ ______
7. $\frac{9}{24}$ ______
8. $\frac{14}{42}$ ______
9. $\frac{20}{25}$ ______
10. $\frac{14}{21}$ ______
11. $\frac{16}{18}$ ______
12. $\frac{4}{36}$ ______
13. $\frac{8}{14}$ ______
14. $\frac{14}{35}$ ______
15. $\frac{10}{12}$ ______
16. $\frac{24}{40}$ ______
17. $\frac{12}{30}$ ______
18. $\frac{4}{32}$ ______

Write each fraction in simplest form. If the fraction is already in simplest form, write *simplified*.

19. $\frac{16}{20}$ ______
20. $\frac{1}{2}$ ______
21. $\frac{3}{12}$ ______
22. $\frac{2}{5}$ ______
23. $\frac{3}{7}$ ______
24. $\frac{28}{32}$ ______
25. $\frac{40}{48}$ ______
26. $\frac{12}{18}$ ______
27. $\frac{5}{8}$ ______
28. $\frac{15}{36}$ ______
29. $\frac{2}{3}$ ______
30. $\frac{3}{24}$ ______

Solve.

31. Of the 27 students in Jarrod's class, 18 receive an allowance each week. What fraction of the students, in simplest form, receive an allowance?

____

32. Of the 18 students who receive an allowance, 14 do chores around the house. What fraction of these students, in simplest form, do chores around the house?

____

Name ______________________ Date ____________

9–5

Reteach

Decimals and Fractions

You can write a decimal as a fraction. Think of place value. Then simplify the fraction if necessary.

Write 0.12 as a fraction. Think: 12 hundredths

Write: $\frac{12}{100}$

Simplify: $\frac{12}{100} = \frac{12 \div 4}{100 \div 4} = \frac{3}{25}$ So, $0.12 = \frac{3}{25}$.

Write 0.25 as a fraction. Think: 25 hundredths

Write: $\frac{25}{100} = \frac{25 \div 25}{100 \div 25} = \frac{1}{4}$

Write each decimal as a fraction in simplest form.

1. 0.65

Think: 65 ____________

Write: $\frac{65}{\quad}$

Simplify: $\frac{65}{\quad} = \frac{65 \div \quad}{\quad \div \quad} =$

2. 0.6

Think: ____________

Write:

Simplify: $\frac{\quad}{\quad} = \frac{6 \div \quad}{\quad \div \quad} =$

3. 0.86 ______ **4.** 0.57 ______ **5.** 0.5 ______ **6.** 0.68 ______

7. 0.25 ______ **8.** 0.15 ______ **9.** 0.40 ______ **10.** 0.9 ______

11. 0.33 ______ **12.** 0.10 ______ **13.** 0.75 ______ **14.** 0.98 ______

15. 0.20 ______ **16.** 0.50 ______ **17.** 0.12 ______ **18.** 0.78 ______

19. 0.4 ______ **20.** 0.70 ______ **21.** 0.05 ______ **22.** 0.65 ______

23. 0.3 ______ **24.** 0.11 ______

Name ______________________ Date __________

9–5

Skills Practice

Decimals and Fractions

Write each decimal as a fraction in simplest form.

1. 0.3 ______ **2.** 0.49 ______ **3.** 0.7 ______ **4.** 0.50 ______

5. 0.94 ______ **6.** 0.80 ______ **7.** 0.72 ______ **8.** 0.2 ______

9. 0.55 ______ **10.** 0.1 ______ **11.** 0.25 ______ **12.** 0.03 ______

13. 0.77 ______ **14.** 0.6 ______ **15.** 0.26 ______ **16.** 0.99 ______

17. 0.36 ______ **18.** 0.75 ______ **19.** 0.70 ______ **20.** 0.4 ______

Write each decimal as a mixed number in simplest form.

21. 8.9 ______ **22.** 12.1 ______ **23.** 14.5 ______ **24.** 17.03 ______

25. 9.35 ______ **26.** 42.96 ______ **27.** 7.425 ______ **28.** 50.60 ______

29. 8.43 ______ **30.** 3.25 ______ **31.** 2.25 ______ **32.** 1.33 ______

33. 4.10 ______ **34.** 7.75 ______ **35.** 8.60 ______ **36.** 16.03 ______

Solve.

37. The largest butterfly in the world is found in Papua, New Guinea. The female of the species weighs about 0.9 ounce. Use a fraction to write the female's weight.

____

38. The shortest recorded fish is the dwarf goby found in the Indo-Pacific. The female of this species is about thirty-five hundredths inch long. Use a decimal to write the female's length.

____

Name ______________________ Date ____________

9–6 Reteach

Problem-Solving Strategy: Look for a Pattern

Look for a Pattern

Measure the length of the sides of the four squares with a centimeter ruler. If you were going to add another square after the largest one, what would be the length of the sides?

Step 1 Understand	**Be sure you understand the problem** Read carefully. What do you know? • The ______________ of the ______ squares. What do you need to find? • The ______________ of the next largest square.
Step 2 Plan • Logical Reasoning • Draw a Picture or Diagram • Make a Graph • Make a Table or List • Look for a Pattern • Guess and Check • Work Backward • Solve a Simpler Problem	**Make a plan.** Choose a strategy. You can look for a pattern to solve the problem. Find the pattern between the lengths of the sides of the squares. Then extend the pattern to find the length of a side of the next largest square.

Name ______________________ Date ______________

9–6

Reteach

Problem-Solving Strategy: Look for a Pattern (continued)

Look for a Pattern

Step 3 Solve	**Carry out your plan.** Measure the length of one side of each square. Record the data in a table to help you see the pattern. Square: 1, 2, 3, 4 Side length: ___, ___, ___, ___ Look at the data in the table. What pattern do you see? Use the pattern to find the length of a side of the next square.
Step 4 Check	**Is the solution reasonable?** Reread the problem. Have you answered the question? Is your answer reasonable? Explain. How can you check your answer?

Square	1	2	3	4
Side length				

Solve.

1. Paige uses different size squares to make a quilt. The smallest square is 2 inches on a side. The next three squares have sides of 5, 8, and 11 inches. If the pattern continues, what are the lengths of the sides of the next two squares?

____

2. There are 64 cans used in the first row of a display. The second row uses 49 cans and the third row uses 36 cans. If the pattern continues, how many cans are used in the fifth row of the display? What is the pattern?

____

9–6

Name ______________________ Date ______________

Skills Practice

Problem Solving Strategy: Look for a Pattern

Solve. Use the *look for a pattern* strategy.

1. Martina is designing chains. The diagram shows the number of rings she uses in each chain. If she continues the pattern, how many rings will be in the next chain?

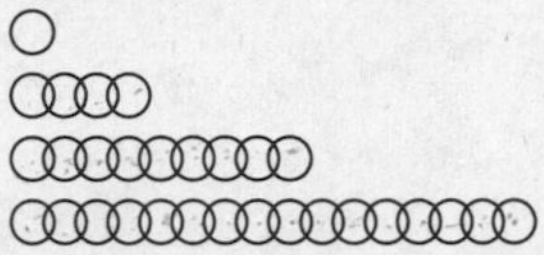

____

2. A sculptor is using a pattern of glass cubes to create a sculpture with 5 sections. The first section has 4 cubes, the second section has 8 cubes, and the third section has 16 cubes. If the pattern continues, how many cubes are in the fifth section?

____

3. Mika is making a pattern of circles. The smallest circle has a diameter of 8 centimeters. The next circle has a diameter of 12 centimeters and the circle after that has a diameter of 16 centimeters. What is the diameter of the sixth circle?

____

4. The bottom layer of a pyramid has 150 blocks. The layer above the bottom has 120 blocks. The third layer from the bottom has 90 blocks. If the pattern continues, how many blocks will be in the next two layers?

____

5. In a set of bowls, the diameters of the bowls increase in a pattern. The smallest bowl has a diameter of 15 centimeters, the next bowl has a diameter of 21 centimeters. If the largest bowl has a diameter of 45 centimeters, what are the diameters of the other three bowls?

____

6. The price of apples at a farm market is shown in the table. How much will 12 apples cost?

Number of Apples	Cost ($)
3	$1.50
6	$3.00
9	$4.50
12	■

____

9–7

Name ____________________ Date ____________

Reteach

Multiples

A **multiple** of a number is the product of the number and any whole number. A whole number that is a multiple of two or more whole numbers is a **common multiple**. The least common multiple is the least multiple, other than 0, common to sets of multiples.

Find the **least common multiple** (LCM) of 12 and 18.
List the multiples of each number.

Multiples of 12: 12, 24, **36**, 48, 60, 72, 84,...
Multiples of 18: 18, **36**, 54,...

Name the least common multiple (LCM): 36

List the multiples of each number. Then find the least common multiple (LCM) of each set of numbers.

1. 10 and 15 ____________

2. 14 and 21 ____________

3. 12 and 13 ____________

4. 15 and 25 ____________

5. 15 and 18 ____________

6. 9 and 21 ____________

Find the least common multiple (LCM) of each set of numbers.

7. 2 and 12 ____________

8. 4 and 9 ____________

9. 6 and 10 ____________

10. 3 and 5 ____________

11. 12 and 15 ____________

12. 12 and 20 ____________

13. 3, 6, and 8 ____________

14. 5, 6, and 10 ____________

Name ______________________ Date __________

9–7

Skills Practice

Multiples

Find the least common multiple (LCM) of the numbers.

1. 5 and 15 ______ **2.** 2 and 9 ______ **3.** 2 and 11 ______

4. 6 and 9 ______ **5.** 4 and 5 ______ **6.** 8 and 12 ______

7. 4 and 8 ______ **8.** 10 and 25 ______ **9.** 3 and 4 ______

10. 2 and 3 ______ **11.** 8 and 9 ______ **12.** 4 and 10 ______

13. 2, 4, and 16 ______ **14.** 3, 5, and 6 ______ **15.** 3, 6, and 8 ______

Identify the first three common multiples of each set of numbers.

16. 2, 5 ______________

17. 1, 6 ______________

18. 2, 3, 4 ______________

19. 7, 14 ______________

Solve.

20. José and Sara are walking around the track at the same time. José walks one lap every 8 minutes. Sara walks a lap every 6 minutes. What is the least amount of time they would both have to walk for them to cross the starting point together?

____

21. Pamela and David walk on the same track. It takes Pamela 9 minutes and David 6 minutes to walk one lap. If they start walking at the same time, how many laps will each have walked when they cross the starting point together for the first time?

____

Name ______________________________ Date ____________

9–8

Reteach

Problem-Solving Investigation: Choose the Best Strategy

Choose a Strategy

On Saturday, the Stevensons went shopping and spent a total of $40 on meat for dinners for the week. They purchased chicken for $3 per pound and some hamburger for $2 per pound. They spent three times as much money on chicken as on hamburger. How many pounds of chicken and how many pounds of hamburger did the family purchase?

Step 1 Understand	**What do you know?** You know the Stevensons spent $40 on meat. You know chicken costs $3 per pound and hamburger costs $2 per pound. You also know the family spent three times as much on chicken as on hamburger. **What do you need to find?** How many pounds of chicken and hamburger the family purchased.
Step 2 Plan	Choose a strategy. Will it help to make a table, list, or number line so you can see how numbers change? You may need to guess and check a few times to find the information that you need. A table would help you compare the amount spent on chicken to the amount spent on hamburger.
Step 3 Solve	Use a ____ for the number that's missing. $3 × ____ + $2 × ____ = $40 ($3 × ____) + ($2 × ____) = $40
Step 4 Check	($3 × 10) + ($2 × 5) = $40 $30 + $10 = $40

Name ______________________ Date ______________

9–8

Reteach

Problem-Solving Investigation: Choose the Best Strategy (continued)

Use any strategy shown below to solve each problem.

- Guess and check
- Act it out
- Make a table

1. Marcie wants to sit by her three sisters at the school assembly. How many different ways can they sit together along one row?

____

2. A department store has the following options for jackets:

Jacket	Color
rain slicker	blue
windbreaker	black
spring jacket	green
jean jacket	

How many combinations of style and color are possible?

____

3. The Parson family spent a total of $24.00 on tickets to go to a museum. An adult ticket costs $6.00 and a student ticket costs $3.00. If there are six people in the family, how many of each kind of tickets were purchased?

____

4. Selena is making a pizza for dinner. She has mushrooms, onions, and pineapple to put on the pizza. How many different pizzas can Selena make with toppings?

____

5. Tyrone enjoys swimming laps in the pool. His goal by the end of the summer is to be able to swim 50 laps. He starts by swimming five laps the first week. Each week, he adds five laps to the number of laps he swam the previous week. How many weeks will it take him to swim 50 laps?

____

9–8

Name ______________________ Date ______________

Skills Practice

Problem-Solving Investigation: Choose the Best Strategy

Choose any strategy shown below to solve each problem.

- Guess and check
- Act it out
- Make a table

1. In a farmyard, there are 10 cows and chickens altogether. If Sondra counts 26 total legs, how many cows and chickens are there?

____

2. Maria is reading a book. Each day, she reads three more pages than the day before. If she read 22 pages the first day, how many pages will she have read altogether after the sixth day?

____

3. Jerry's team played 12 games, and during that time he made 42 baskets. If he played in 2 games out of every 4 that the team played and he made an equal number of baskets each of these games, how many baskets did he make each game?

____

4. Patty's goal was to make 40 bracelets. She made 5 bracelets the first week, 5 bracelets the second week, and 10 bracelets the third week. What fraction of her goal did she make?

____

5. At the end of basketball season, the player with the most points wins a basketball. Davina scored one point in the first game and one more each game than she had in the previous game for 5 games. Sally got 3 points each game for 4 games. Who had the most total points?

____

Name ______________________ Date ____________

9–9

Reteach

Compare Fractions

To order fractions, rewrite them with a common denominator. Then compare the numerators, two at a time, to order the numerators.

Compare: $\frac{4}{9}$ and $\frac{5}{6}$

Step 1

Find the LCD of 9, 6, and 18.

Multiples of 9: 9, 18, 27, 36
Multiples of 6: 6, 12, 18
LCD: 18

Step 2

Find equivalent fractions with a denominator of 18.

$\frac{4}{9} = \frac{4 \times 2}{9 \times 2} = \frac{8}{18}$

$\frac{5}{6} = \frac{5 \times 3}{6 \times 3} = \frac{15}{18}$

Step 3

Compare the numerators.

Since $8 < 15$ then $\frac{8}{18} < \frac{15}{18}$.

Compare each pair of fractions using the LCD.

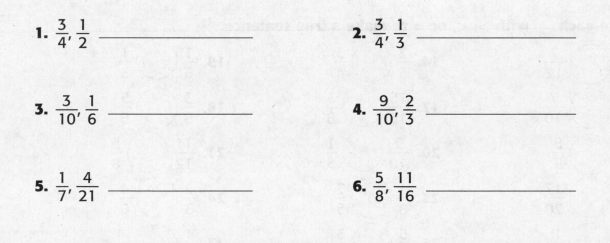

1. $\frac{3}{4}, \frac{1}{2}$ ______________

2. $\frac{3}{4}, \frac{1}{3}$ ______________

3. $\frac{3}{10}, \frac{1}{6}$ ______________

4. $\frac{9}{10}, \frac{2}{3}$ ______________

5. $\frac{1}{7}, \frac{4}{21}$ ______________

6. $\frac{5}{8}, \frac{11}{16}$ ______________

9–9

Name ______________________ Date ____________

Skills Practice

Compare Fractions

Compare each pair of fractions using the LCD.

1. $\frac{2}{5}, \frac{1}{10}$ ____________

2. $\frac{1}{9}, \frac{1}{12}$ ____________

3. $\frac{3}{8}, \frac{1}{12}$ ____________

4. $\frac{2}{5}, \frac{7}{8}$ ____________

5. $\frac{5}{9}, \frac{5}{8}$ ____________

6. $\frac{5}{8}, \frac{7}{10}$ ____________

7. $\frac{2}{5}, \frac{1}{4}$ ____________

8. $\frac{1}{5}, \frac{2}{15}$ ____________

9. $\frac{7}{12}, \frac{1}{10}$ ____________

10. $\frac{3}{4}, \frac{1}{8}$ ____________

11. $\frac{2}{9}, \frac{1}{2}$ ____________

12. $\frac{3}{15}, \frac{3}{10}$ ____________

Replace each ◯ with >, <, or = to make a true sentence.

13. $\frac{3}{4}$ ◯ $\frac{7}{12}$

14. $\frac{2}{5}$ ◯ $\frac{3}{4}$

15. $\frac{1}{6}$ ◯ $\frac{1}{3}$

16. $\frac{1}{2}$ ◯ $\frac{7}{10}$

17. $\frac{15}{16}$ ◯ $\frac{3}{8}$

18. $\frac{3}{8}$ ◯ $\frac{5}{6}$

19. $\frac{7}{8}$ ◯ $\frac{8}{9}$

20. $\frac{2}{10}$ ◯ $\frac{1}{5}$

21. $\frac{11}{12}$ ◯ $\frac{5}{8}$

22. $\frac{4}{5}$ ◯ $\frac{17}{20}$

23. $\frac{1}{8}$ ◯ $\frac{2}{5}$

24. $\frac{2}{3}$ ◯ $\frac{4}{6}$

25. $\frac{1}{5}$ ◯ $\frac{1}{4}$

26. $\frac{5}{8}$ ◯ $\frac{3}{5}$

27. $\frac{1}{6}$ ◯ $\frac{4}{18}$

Solve.

28. Visitors to an art museum were asked to name a favorite type of art. Pottery was named by $\frac{9}{40}$ of the visitors, painting was named by $\frac{2}{5}$, and sculpture was named by $\frac{3}{8}$. What was the favorite type of art of most visitors?

____

10–1

Name ______________________ Date ____________

Reteach

Add Like Fractions

Follow these steps to add fractions with like denominators.

Add $\frac{3}{8} + \frac{1}{8}$

Step 1

Add the numerators.
Use the like denominator.

$\frac{3}{8} + \frac{1}{8} = \frac{4}{8}$

So, $\frac{3}{8} + \frac{1}{8} = \frac{4}{8}$.

Step 2

Write the sum in simplest form.
Divide the numerator and denominator by their greatest common factor.

$\frac{4}{8} = \frac{4 \div 4}{8 \div 4} = \frac{1}{2}$

Add. Write each sum in simplest form.

1. $\frac{5}{7} + \frac{4}{7} =$ ______

2. $\frac{1}{4} + \frac{1}{4} =$ ______

3. $\frac{3}{10} + \frac{1}{10} =$ ______

4. $\frac{7}{8} + \frac{5}{8} =$ ______

5. $\frac{11}{12} + \frac{7}{12} =$ ______

6. $\frac{3}{10} + \frac{2}{10} =$ ______

7. $\frac{1}{3} + \frac{3}{3} =$ ______

8. $\frac{1}{2} + \frac{3}{2} =$ ______

9. $\frac{1}{9} + \frac{3}{9} =$ ______

10. $\frac{1}{7} + \frac{4}{7} =$ ______

11. $\frac{2}{10} + \frac{3}{10} =$ ______

12. $\frac{1}{6} + \frac{3}{6} =$ ______

Name ______________________ Date ______________

10–1

Skills Practice

Add Like Fractions

Add. Write each in simplest form.

1. $\frac{7}{10} + \frac{1}{10} =$ ______

2. $\frac{13}{16} + \frac{7}{16} =$ ______

3. $\frac{4}{5} + \frac{1}{5} =$ ______

4. $\frac{7}{12} + \frac{5}{12} =$ ______

5. $\frac{4}{5} + \frac{3}{5} =$ ______

6. $\frac{5}{6} + \frac{5}{6} =$ ______

7. $\frac{7}{15} + \frac{2}{15} =$ ______

8. $\frac{9}{20} + \frac{3}{20} =$ ______

9. $\frac{1}{4} + \frac{1}{4} =$ ______

10. $\frac{3}{8} + \frac{1}{8} =$ ______

11. $\frac{2}{3} + \frac{1}{3} =$ ______

12. $\frac{5}{6} + \frac{1}{6} =$ ______

13. $\frac{7}{16} + \frac{3}{16} =$ ______

14. $\frac{3}{10} + \frac{9}{10} =$ ______

15. $\frac{7}{8} + \frac{7}{8} =$ ______

16. $\frac{7}{12} + \frac{11}{12} =$ ______

17. $\frac{19}{20} + \frac{5}{20} =$ ______

18. $\frac{11}{20} + \frac{7}{20} =$ ______

19. $\frac{9}{16} + \frac{7}{16} =$ ______

20. $\frac{4}{5} + \frac{3}{5} =$ ______

21. $\frac{7}{9} + \frac{4}{9} =$ ______

Replace each ◯ with >, <, or = to make a true sentence.

22. $\frac{7}{8} + \frac{5}{8}$ ◯ $\frac{3}{4} + \frac{3}{4}$

23. $\frac{7}{10} + \frac{9}{10}$ ◯ $\frac{3}{5} + \frac{4}{5}$

24. $\frac{2}{3} + \frac{2}{3}$ ◯ $\frac{5}{12} + \frac{7}{12}$

25. $\frac{3}{8} + \frac{3}{8}$ ◯ $\frac{9}{16} + \frac{5}{16}$

26. $\frac{3}{5} + \frac{3}{5}$ ◯ $\frac{7}{10} + \frac{7}{10}$

27. $\frac{5}{8} + \frac{7}{8}$ ◯ $\frac{13}{16} + \frac{11}{16}$

Name ______________________ Date ____________

10–2

Reteach

Subtract Like Fractions

Follow these steps to subtract fractions with like denominators.

Subtract $\frac{8}{9} - \frac{2}{9}$.

Step 1

Subtract the numerators.
Use the like denominator.

$\frac{8}{9} - \frac{2}{9} = \frac{6}{9}$

So, $\frac{8}{9} - \frac{2}{9} = \frac{6}{9} = \frac{2}{3}$.

Step 2

Write the difference in simplest form.
Divide the numerator and denominator by their greatest common factor.

$\frac{6}{9} = \frac{6 \div 3}{9 \div 3} = \frac{2}{3}$

Subtract. Write each difference in simplest form.

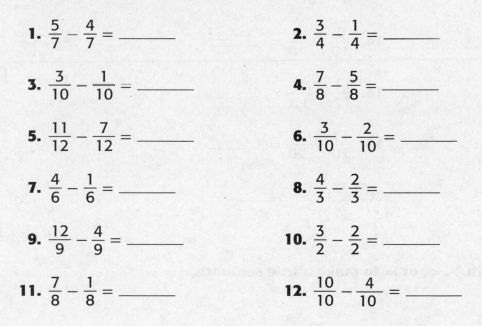

1. $\frac{5}{7} - \frac{4}{7} =$ ______
2. $\frac{3}{4} - \frac{1}{4} =$ ______
3. $\frac{3}{10} - \frac{1}{10} =$ ______
4. $\frac{7}{8} - \frac{5}{8} =$ ______
5. $\frac{11}{12} - \frac{7}{12} =$ ______
6. $\frac{3}{10} - \frac{2}{10} =$ ______
7. $\frac{4}{6} - \frac{1}{6} =$ ______
8. $\frac{4}{3} - \frac{2}{3} =$ ______
9. $\frac{12}{9} - \frac{4}{9} =$ ______
10. $\frac{3}{2} - \frac{2}{2} =$ ______
11. $\frac{7}{8} - \frac{1}{8} =$ ______
12. $\frac{10}{10} - \frac{4}{10} =$ ______

Name ______________________ Date ______________

10–2

Skills Practice

Subtract Like Fractions

Subtract. Write each difference in simplest form.

1. $\frac{7}{10} - \frac{1}{10} =$ ______ **2.** $\frac{13}{16} - \frac{7}{16} =$ ______

3. $\frac{4}{5} - \frac{1}{5} =$ ______ **4.** $\frac{7}{12} - \frac{5}{12} =$ ______

5. $\frac{4}{5} - \frac{3}{5} =$ ______ **6.** $\frac{5}{6} - \frac{4}{6} =$ ______

7. $\frac{7}{15} - \frac{2}{15} =$ ______ **8.** $\frac{9}{20} - \frac{3}{20} =$ ______

9. $\frac{3}{8} - \frac{1}{8} =$ ______ **10.** $\frac{3}{8} - \frac{1}{8} =$ ______

11. $\frac{2}{3} - \frac{1}{3} =$ ______ **12.** $\frac{5}{6} - \frac{1}{6} =$ ______

13. $\frac{7}{16} - \frac{3}{16} =$ ______ **14.** $\frac{9}{10} - \frac{3}{10} =$ ______

15. $\frac{7}{8} - \frac{7}{8} =$ ______ **16.** $\frac{11}{12} - \frac{7}{12} =$ ______

17. $\frac{19}{20} - \frac{5}{20} =$ ______ **18.** $\frac{11}{20} - \frac{7}{20} =$ ______

19. $\frac{9}{16} - \frac{7}{16} =$ ______ **20.** $\frac{4}{5} - \frac{3}{5} =$ ______

Replace each ◯ with >, <, or = to make a true sentence.

21. $\frac{7}{8} - \frac{5}{8}$ ◯ $\frac{3}{4} - \frac{3}{4}$ **22.** $\frac{9}{10} - \frac{7}{10}$ ◯ $\frac{4}{5} - \frac{3}{5}$

23. $\frac{2}{3} - \frac{1}{3}$ ◯ $\frac{7}{12} - \frac{5}{12}$ **24.** $\frac{3}{8} - \frac{3}{8}$ ◯ $\frac{9}{16} - \frac{5}{16}$

25. $\frac{5}{5} - \frac{3}{5}$ ◯ $\frac{10}{10} - \frac{7}{10}$ **26.** $\frac{7}{8} - \frac{5}{8}$ ◯ $\frac{13}{16} - \frac{11}{16}$

10–3

Name ________________________ Date ____________

Reteach

Add Unlike Fractions

When adding fractions with unlike denominators, it helps to write the problems in vertical form.

Add $\frac{7}{8} + \frac{2}{3}$.

Step 1

Find the least common denominator (LCD).

Multiples of 3: 3, 6, 9, 12, 15, 18, 21, **24**, . . .

Multiples of 8: 8, 16, **24**, . . .

The LCD is 24.

Step 2

Rename each fraction using the LCD.

$\frac{7}{8} = \frac{21}{24}$

$\frac{2}{3} = \frac{16}{24}$

Step 3

Write the problems in vertical form.

Add.

$$\begin{array}{rcr} \frac{7}{8} & = & \frac{21}{24} \\ +\frac{2}{3} & = & +\frac{16}{24} \\ \hline & & \frac{37}{24} = 1\frac{13}{24} \end{array}$$

Add. Write your answer in simplest form.

1. $\frac{3}{8} + \frac{5}{6}$

Multiples of 8: ____________

Multiples of 6: ____________

LCD: ______

So, $\frac{3}{8} + \frac{5}{6} =$ ____________

2. $\frac{11}{12} + \frac{3}{4}$

Multiples of 12: ____________

Multiples of 4: ____________

LCD: ______

So, $\frac{11}{12} + \frac{3}{4} =$ ____________

3. $\frac{4}{5} + \frac{2}{3} =$ ______

4. $\frac{3}{5} + \frac{9}{10} =$ ______

5. $\frac{9}{10} + \frac{5}{6} =$ ______

6. $\frac{7}{10} + \frac{3}{4} =$ ______

7. $\frac{5}{8} + \frac{2}{5} =$ ______

8. $\frac{3}{4} + \frac{5}{6} =$ ______

9. $\frac{1}{2} + \frac{3}{8} =$ ______

10. $\frac{1}{4} + \frac{3}{8} =$ ______

11. $\frac{3}{5} + \frac{3}{4} =$ ______

12. $\frac{7}{12} + \frac{1}{3} =$ ______

13. $\frac{5}{6} + \frac{5}{8} =$ ______

14. $\frac{7}{10} + \frac{2}{5} =$ ______

Name ______________________ Date ____________

10–3

Skills Practice

Add Unlike Fractions

Add. Write your answer in simplest form.

1. $\frac{1}{2} + \frac{1}{5}$

2. $\frac{2}{5} + \frac{7}{10}$

3. $\frac{5}{8} + \frac{3}{16}$

4. $\frac{3}{5} + \frac{3}{20}$

5. $\frac{9}{10} + \frac{7}{10}$

6. $\frac{7}{12} + \frac{1}{3}$

7. $\frac{9}{10} + \frac{2}{5}$

8. $\frac{3}{16} + \frac{3}{8}$

9. $\frac{3}{4} + \frac{2}{5}$

10. $\frac{7}{12} + \frac{3}{4}$

11. $\frac{2}{3} + \frac{3}{8}$

12. $\frac{9}{20} + \frac{3}{5}$

13. $\frac{7}{16} + \frac{3}{8} =$ ______

14. $\frac{5}{6} + \frac{7}{12} =$ ______

15. $\frac{15}{16} + \frac{5}{8} =$ ______

16. $\frac{17}{20} + \frac{3}{4} =$ ______

17. $\frac{1}{4} + \frac{4}{5} =$ ______

18. $\frac{1}{2} + \frac{1}{5} =$ ______

19. $\frac{5}{8} + \frac{2}{5} =$ ______

20. $\frac{7}{10} + \frac{1}{2} =$ ______

21. $\frac{5}{6} + \frac{5}{8} =$ ______

22. $\frac{5}{8} + \frac{3}{10} =$ ______

23. $\frac{3}{5} + \frac{1}{4} =$ ______

24. $\frac{5}{6} + \frac{7}{9} =$ ______

25. $\frac{9}{10} + \frac{7}{20} =$ ______

26. $\frac{3}{5} + \frac{5}{6} =$ ______

27. $\frac{5}{8} + \frac{35}{12} =$ ______

Problem Solving

Solve.

28. After school, Michael walks $\frac{3}{5}$ mile to the park and then walks $\frac{3}{4}$ mile to his house. How far does Michael walk from school to his house?

____

29. When Rachel walks to school on the sidewalk, she walks $\frac{7}{10}$ mile. When she takes the shortcut across the field, she walks $\frac{1}{4}$ mile less. How long is the shorter route?

____

Name ______________________ Date ______________

10–4 Reteach

Subtract Unlike Fractions

You can draw models to help subtract fractions with unlike denominators.

Subtract $\frac{3}{4} - \frac{1}{3}$.

Show models for $\frac{3}{4}$ and $\frac{1}{3}$.

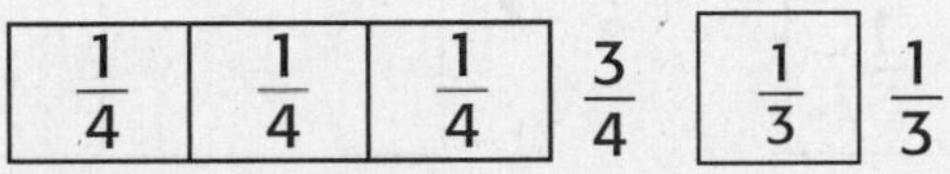

Find the LCD of $\frac{3}{4}$ and $\frac{1}{3}$.

Multiples of 4: 4, 8, 12,...

Multiples of 3: 3, 6, 9, 12,...

The LCD of $\frac{3}{4}$ and $\frac{1}{3}$ is 12

Use models to show how many twelfths are in $\frac{3}{4}$, and how many twelfths are in $\frac{1}{3}$.

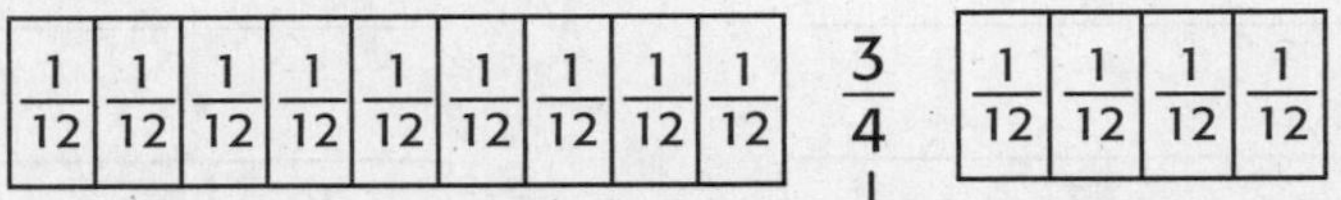

$\frac{3}{4} \rightarrow \frac{9}{12}$ $\qquad$ $\frac{1}{3} \rightarrow \frac{4}{12}$

Take away models to subtract $\frac{4}{12}$.

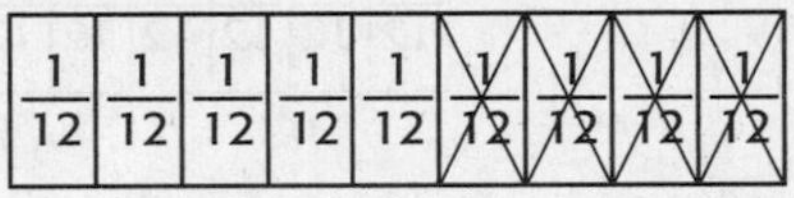

$\frac{3}{4} - \frac{1}{3}$

$\downarrow \quad \downarrow$

So, $\frac{3}{4} - \frac{1}{3} = \frac{5}{12}$. $\qquad$ $\frac{9}{12} - \frac{4}{12} = \frac{5}{12}$

Use the fraction models to subtract the fractions.
Write your answer in simplest form.

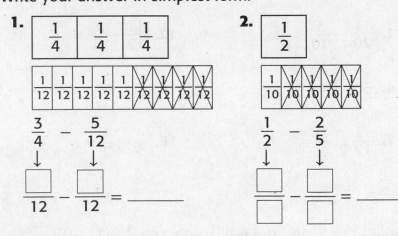

1.

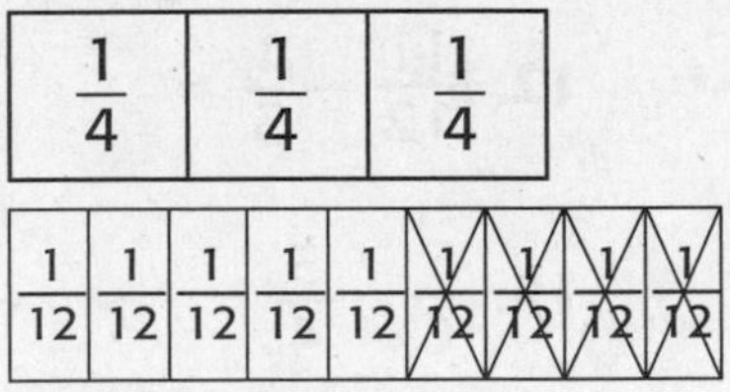

$\frac{3}{4} - \frac{5}{12}$

$\frac{\square}{12} - \frac{\square}{12} =$ ________

2.

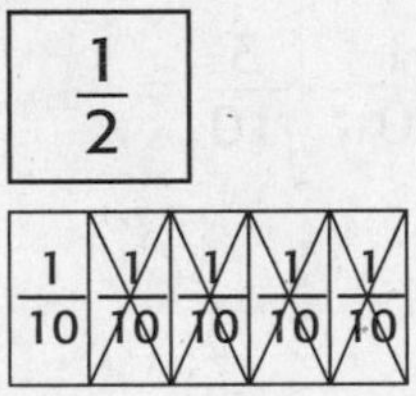

$\frac{1}{2} - \frac{2}{5}$

$\frac{\square}{\square} - \frac{\square}{\square} =$ ________

3.

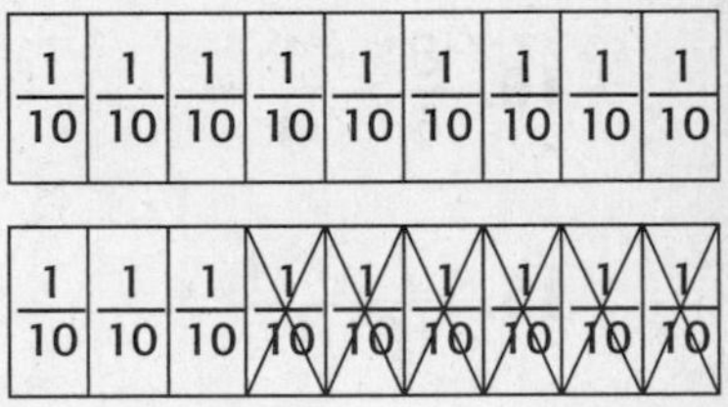

$\frac{9}{10} - \frac{3}{5}$

$\frac{\square}{\square} - \frac{\square}{\square} =$ ________

Subtract. You may use models. Write your answer in simplest form.

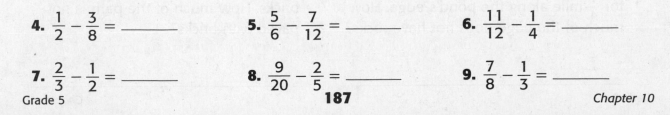

4. $\frac{1}{2} - \frac{3}{8} =$ ________ $\qquad$ **5.** $\frac{5}{6} - \frac{7}{12} =$ ________ $\qquad$ **6.** $\frac{11}{12} - \frac{1}{4} =$ ________

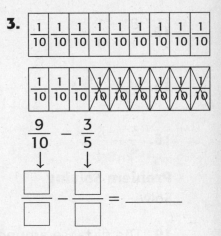

7. $\frac{2}{3} - \frac{1}{2} =$ ________ $\qquad$ **8.** $\frac{9}{20} - \frac{2}{5} =$ ________ $\qquad$ **9.** $\frac{7}{8} - \frac{1}{3} =$ ________

Name ______________________ Date __________

10–4

Skills Practice

Subtract Unlike Fractions

Write the subtraction sentence shown by each model.
Write the difference in simplest form.

1.

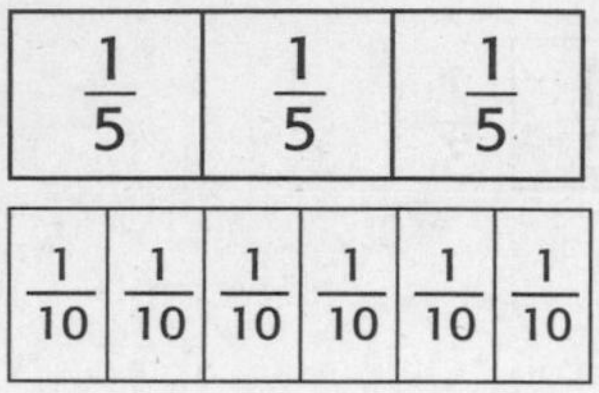

____

2.

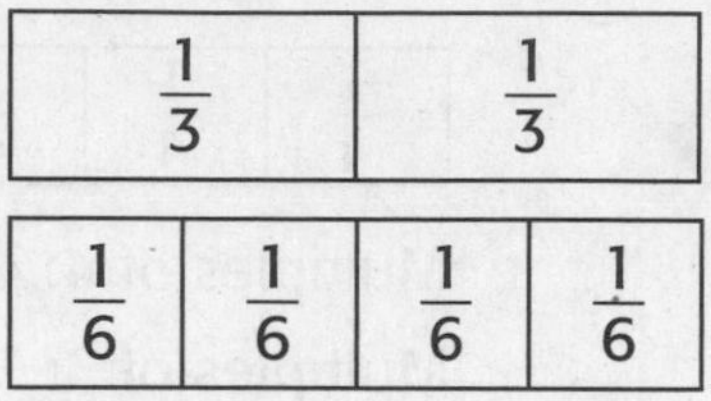

____

3.

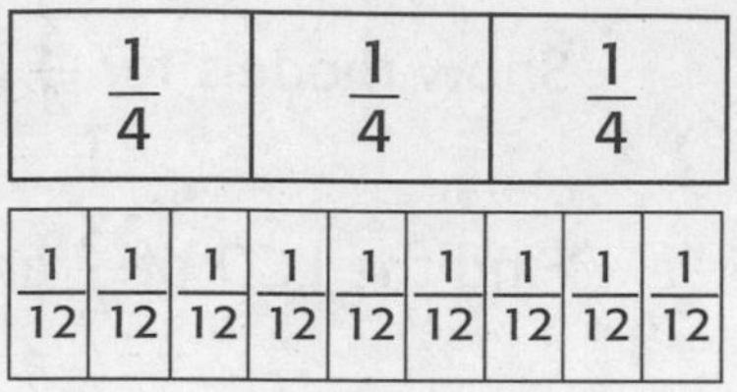

____

4.

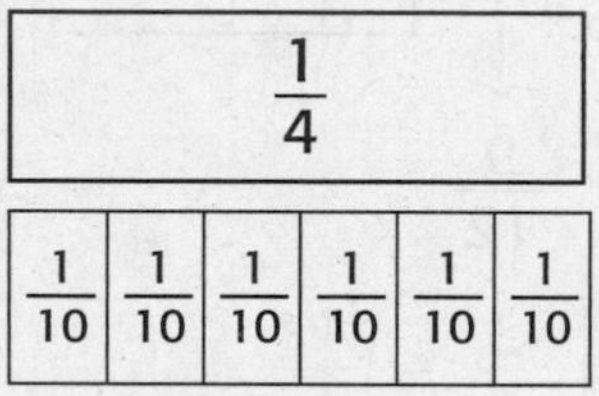

____

5.

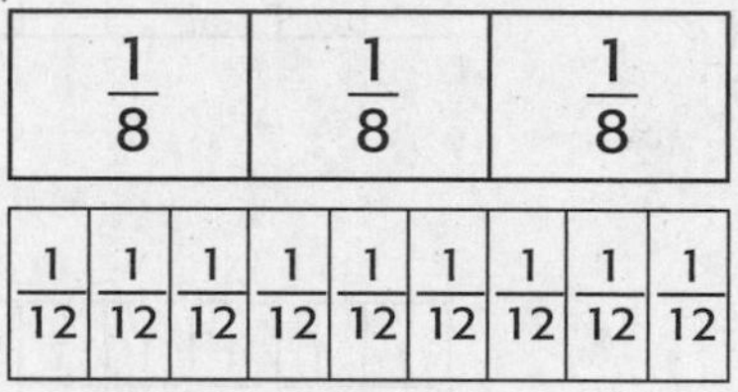

____

6.

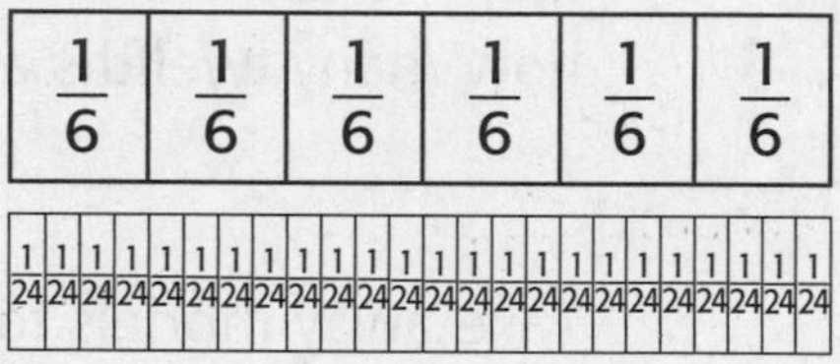

____

Subtract. Write your answer in simplest form.

7. $\frac{7}{12} - \frac{1}{4} =$

8. $\frac{1}{2} - \frac{1}{3} =$

9. $\frac{9}{10} - \frac{2}{5} =$

10. $\frac{8}{5} - \frac{1}{4} =$

11. $\frac{11}{20} - \frac{3}{10} =$

12. $\frac{11}{12} - \frac{1}{3} =$

13. $\frac{7}{10} - \frac{1}{2} =$

14. $\frac{3}{4} - \frac{2}{3} =$

15. $\frac{5}{6} - \frac{3}{4} =$

16. $\frac{3}{4} - \frac{3}{5} =$

17. $\frac{11}{12} - \frac{1}{4} =$

18. $\frac{4}{5} - \frac{1}{2} =$

Problem Solving

Solve.

19. The distance around a lily pound is $\frac{7}{10}$ mile. Rocks have been placed for $\frac{1}{4}$ mile along the pond's edge. How much of the edge does not have rocks?

____

20. The first $\frac{1}{5}$ mile of a $\frac{3}{4}$ mile path through a rose garden is paved with bricks. How much of the path is not paved with bricks?

____

Name ______________________ Date ____________

10–5

Reteach

Problem-Solving Strategy: Determine Reasonable Answers

Linden buys $1\frac{3}{4}$ pounds of cashew nuts and $1\frac{1}{4}$ pounds of peanuts. He mixes the nuts together. About how many pounds of nuts are there altogether?

Step 1 Understand	**What do you know?** • You know the amount of cashew nuts and the amount of peanuts. **What do you need to find?** You need to find about how many pounds of nuts there are altogether.
Step 2 Plan	You can use estimation to find a reasonable answer.
Step 3 Solve	Round each amount to the nearest whole number. Then add. $1\frac{3}{4} \rightarrow 2$ $1\frac{1}{4} \rightarrow 1$ Linden bought about 2 + 1 or 3 pounds of nuts.
Step 4 Check	**Is the answer reasonable?** Yes, because $1\frac{3}{4} + 1\frac{1}{4} = 3$.

10–5

Name ______________________ Date ______________

Reteach

Problem-Solving Strategy: Determine Reasonable Answers (continued)

Solve. Determine which answer is reasonable.

1. Renata bought 0.85 pound of pine nuts and 0.9 pound of macadamia nuts. Is 1.5 pounds, 2 pounds, or 2.5 pounds a more reasonable estimate for how many pounds of nuts she purchased altogether?

____

2. One container has $2\frac{5}{8}$ pounds of pineapple and another has $1\frac{7}{8}$ pounds of pineapple. Sam buys both containers. Which is a more reasonable estimate for how many pounds of pineapple he bought in all: 4 pounds, 5 pounds, or 6 pounds?

____

3. From the beginning of a trail, Claire hiked $4\frac{3}{8}$ miles to the lake. Then she hiked $2\frac{5}{8}$ miles to the nature center. Is 5 miles, 6 miles, or 7 miles a more reasonable estimate for how far Claire hiked altogether?

____

4. At the beginning of the week there were 2.85 pounds of jelly beans in a jar. By the end of the week, there were 1.7 pounds of jelly beans in the jar. Which is a more reasonable estimate for how many jelly beans were eaten during the week: 1 pound, 2 pounds, or 2.5 pounds?

____

5. In the morning, Kevin feeds his cat $\frac{1}{2}$ of a can of cat food, in the afternoon, the cat eats $\frac{1}{4}$ of a can of food, and in the evening, the cat eats $\frac{3}{4}$ of a can of food. Which is a more reasonable estimate for the amount of food the cat eats throughout the day: 1 can, 2 cans, or 3 cans?

____

6. A DVD player costs $154.98. A portable digital music player costs $174.49. Is $15, $20, or $25 a more reasonable estimate for how much more the digital music player costs?

____

10–5

Name ______________________ Date ______________

Skills Practice

Problem-Solving Strategy: Determine Reasonable Answers

Solve. Determine which answer is reasonable.

1. Ms. Montoya makes $2\frac{3}{4}$ pounds of goat cheese in the morning. In the afternoon, she makes $1\frac{1}{4}$ pounds of goat cheese. Is 3 pounds, 4 pounds, or 5 pounds a more reasonable estimate for how much goat cheese Ms. Montoya makes in one day?

   ____

2. The Wilsons decide to churn butter for a family project. The boys in the family make 2.5 pounds of butter. The girls in the family make 4.7 pounds of butter. Which is a more reasonable estimate for how much more butter the girls made than the boys: 2 pounds, 3 pounds, or 4 pounds?

   ____

3. Clara picks 5.75 bushels of apples. Franz picks 3.25 bushels of apples. Is 2 bushels, 3 bushels, or 4 bushels a more reasonable estimate for how many more bushels Clara picked than Franz?

   ____

4. On Monday, Tina makes 4.7 pounds of raisins from grapes. On Tuesday, she makes 3.8 pounds of raisins. Which is a more reasonable estimate for about how many pounds of raisins she made in all: 7 pounds, 8 pounds, or 9 pounds?

   ____

5. Miguel picked 3.68 pounds of grapes last week. This week, he picks 2.27 pounds of grapes. Is 5 pounds, 6 pounds, or 7 pounds a more reasonable estimate for how many pounds Miguel picked altogether?

   ____

Name ______________________________ Date ________________

10–6

Reteach

Estimate Sums and Differences

You can round mixed numbers to the nearest whole number to estimate sums and differences of mixed numbers. Use number lines to help you.

Estimate $5\frac{5}{8} - 2\frac{1}{5}$.

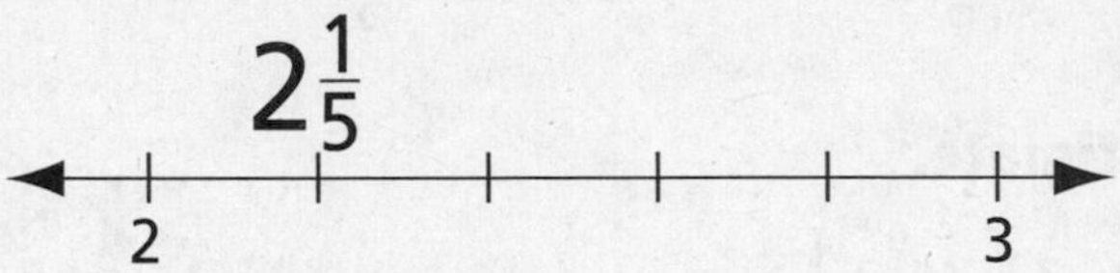

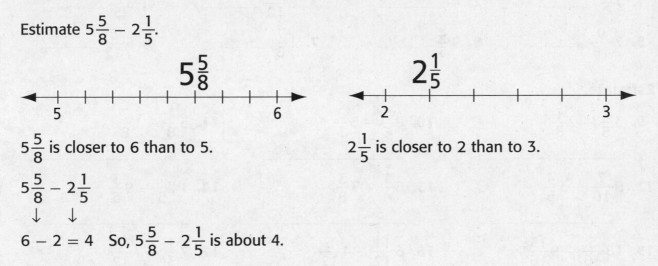

$5\frac{5}{8}$ is closer to 6 than to 5. $2\frac{1}{5}$ is closer to 2 than to 3.

$5\frac{5}{8} - 2\frac{1}{5}$

↓ ↓

$6 - 2 = 4$ So, $5\frac{5}{8} - 2\frac{1}{5}$ is about 4.

Show each mixed number on a number line and round it to the nearest whole number. Then estimate the sum or difference.

1. $3\frac{2}{5} + 4\frac{9}{10}$

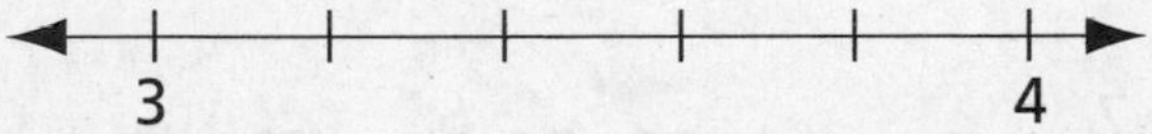

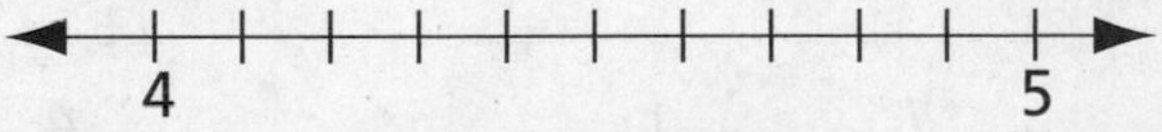

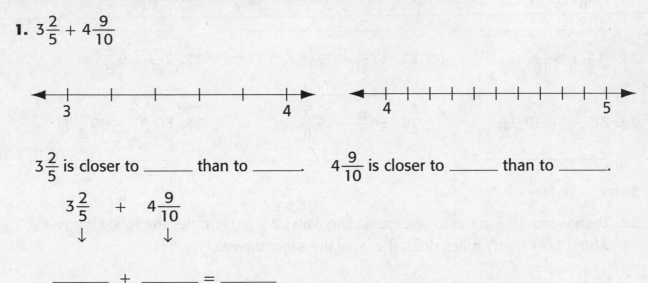

$3\frac{2}{5}$ is closer to ______ than to ______. $4\frac{9}{10}$ is closer to ______ than to ______.

$3\frac{2}{5}$ + $4\frac{9}{10}$

↓ ↓

______ + ______ = ______

Estimate by rounding each mixed number to the nearest whole number.

2. $8\frac{9}{16} - 4\frac{1}{6}$

↓ ↓

____ − ____ = ____

3. $7\frac{9}{10} + 6\frac{7}{10}$

↓ ↓

____ + ____ = ____

4. $9\frac{7}{12} - 1\frac{3}{8}$

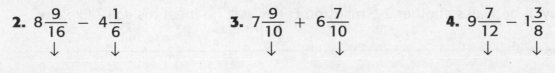

↓ ↓

____ − ____ = ____

Name ______________________ Date ____________

10–6

Skills Practice

Estimate Sums and Differences

Round each mixed number to the nearest whole number.

1. $7\frac{3}{4}$ ______ **2.** $4\frac{1}{6}$ ______ **3.** $8\frac{4}{10}$ ______ **4.** $3\frac{4}{5}$ ______

5. $2\frac{9}{16}$ ______ **6.** $9\frac{4}{5}$ ______ **7.** $1\frac{7}{8}$ ______ **8.** $5\frac{5}{12}$ ______

Estimate.

9. $3\frac{7}{8} + 2\frac{1}{6}$ ______

10. $8\frac{5}{6} - 3\frac{2}{3}$ ______

11. $5\frac{1}{8} - 1\frac{7}{8}$ ______

12. $9\frac{7}{10} + 3\frac{4}{5}$ ______

13. $6\frac{1}{4} + 7\frac{3}{8}$ ______

14. $14\frac{1}{5} - 9\frac{3}{5}$ ______

15. $18\frac{5}{16} - 9\frac{13}{16}$ ______

16. $6\frac{11}{12} + 4\frac{5}{12}$ ______

17. $7\frac{1}{3} + 7\frac{7}{12}$ ______

18. $15\frac{3}{8} - 7\frac{7}{16}$ ______

19. $9\frac{4}{5} + 6\frac{2}{3}$ ______

20. $6\frac{11}{12} - 6\frac{1}{5}$ ______

21. $8\frac{2}{5} + 8\frac{11}{16}$ ______

22. $17\frac{7}{10} - 9\frac{1}{3}$ ______

23. $7\frac{1}{3} + 9\frac{3}{8}$ ______

24. $30\frac{7}{12} + 30\frac{1}{12}$ ______

25. $58\frac{4}{5} - 29\frac{7}{8}$ ______

26. $50\frac{5}{16} - 30\frac{1}{3}$ ______

Solve.

27. Beth walks $10\frac{7}{8}$ miles in one week. She walks $2\frac{1}{4}$ fewer miles the following week. About how many miles does she walk the second week?

____

28. Jon wants to walk at least 8 miles by the end of the week. He walks $5\frac{3}{4}$ miles by Thursday. If he walks another $2\frac{5}{8}$ miles on Friday, will he meet his goal? Explain.

____

Name ______________________ Date ______________

10–7

Reteach

Add Mixed Numbers

Add $2\frac{4}{6} + 4\frac{3}{6}$.

Step 1 Add the whole numbers.

$$\begin{array}{r} \mathbf{2}\frac{4}{6} \\ +\ \mathbf{4}\frac{3}{6} \\ \hline \mathbf{6} \end{array}$$

Step 2 Add the fractions.

$$\begin{array}{r} 2\frac{\mathbf{4}}{\mathbf{6}} \\ +\ 4\frac{\mathbf{3}}{\mathbf{6}} \\ \hline 6\frac{\mathbf{7}}{\mathbf{6}} \end{array}$$

Step 3 Simplify if possible.

$$6\frac{7}{6} = 7\frac{1}{6}$$

So, $2\frac{4}{6} + 4\frac{3}{6} = 7\frac{1}{6}$.

Add. Write each sum in simplest form.

1. $3\frac{5}{9} + 4\frac{2}{9}$ = ______

2. $4\frac{1}{5} + 5\frac{11}{15}$ = ______

3. $2\frac{1}{2} + 4$ = ______

4. $8\frac{2}{5} + 4\frac{1}{10}$ = ______

5. $7\frac{6}{8} + 2\frac{1}{8}$ = ______

6. $2\frac{7}{10} + 3\frac{2}{10} =$ ______

7. $7\frac{2}{9} + 1\frac{4}{9} =$ ______

8. $8\frac{3}{14} + 2\frac{1}{7} =$ ______

9. $9\frac{3}{8} + 2\frac{1}{2} =$ ______

10. $1\frac{3}{4} + 4\frac{7}{8} =$ ______

11. $7\frac{4}{6} + 8\frac{5}{6} =$ ______

12. $1\frac{6}{15} + 9\frac{10}{15} =$ ______

13. $6\frac{3}{4} + 8\frac{4}{5} =$ ______

14. $3\frac{4}{6} + 5\frac{5}{6} =$ ______

15. $4\frac{4}{10} + 6\frac{7}{10} =$ ______

16. $8\frac{1}{16} + 4\frac{10}{16} =$ ______

17. $2\frac{6}{8} + 1\frac{5}{8} =$ ______

18. $8\frac{6}{9} + 1\frac{5}{9} =$ ______

19. $4\frac{12}{20} + 4\frac{15}{20} =$ ______

20. $5\frac{8}{12} + 2\frac{1}{4} =$ ______

10–7

Name ______________________ Date ______________

Skills Practice

Add Mixed Numbers

Add. Write each sum in simplest form.

1. $5\frac{8}{12} + 3\frac{9}{12}$

2. $12\frac{7}{8} + 4\frac{2}{8}$

3. $13\frac{5}{10} + 4\frac{6}{10}$

4. $21\frac{8}{24} + 5\frac{7}{24}$

5. $8\frac{5}{10} + 6\frac{8}{10}$

6. $5\frac{9}{24} + 6\frac{22}{24}$

7. $5\frac{1}{5} + 2\frac{5}{15}$

8. $9\frac{4}{8} + 8\frac{1}{2}$

9. $4\frac{2}{12} + 11\frac{3}{6}$

10. $7\frac{9}{15} + 1\frac{1}{5}$

11. $4\frac{3}{10} + 5\frac{4}{10} =$ ______

12. $3\frac{7}{8} + 2\frac{4}{8} =$ ______

13. $5\frac{2}{12} + 3\frac{3}{12} =$ ______

14. $6\frac{3}{4} + 2\frac{2}{4} =$ ______

15. $1\frac{1}{12} + 3\frac{2}{12} =$ ______

16. $9\frac{4}{10} + 10\frac{3}{10} =$ ______

17. $7\frac{4}{12} + 5\frac{11}{12} =$ ______

18. $11\frac{7}{10} + 4 =$ ______

19. $2\frac{8}{12} + 4\frac{9}{12} =$ ______

20. $7\frac{6}{8} + 2\frac{7}{8} =$ ______

21. $4\frac{3}{6} + 3\frac{5}{6} =$ ______

22. $7\frac{4}{6} + 1\frac{5}{6} =$ ______

23. $2\frac{1}{4} + 4\frac{15}{20} =$ ______

24. $5\frac{3}{8} + 7\frac{4}{16} =$ ______

25. $14\frac{5}{16} + 8\frac{3}{8} =$ ______

26. $15\frac{6}{8} + 12\frac{10}{16} =$ ______

27. $9\frac{2}{12} + 4\frac{15}{18} =$ ______

28. $12\frac{1}{3} + 6\frac{2}{6} =$ ______

Solve.

29. A cave is $5\frac{2}{4}$ miles west of a waterfall. A group of hikers is $2\frac{1}{4}$ miles east of the waterfall. How far is the group of hikers from the cave?

____

30. A mark on the side of a pier shows that the water is $4\frac{7}{8}$ ft deep. When the tide is high, the depth increases by $2\frac{3}{4}$ ft. What is the depth of the water when the tide is high?

____

Name ______________________ Date ____________

10–8 Reteach

Subtract Mixed Numbers

Step 1 Subtract the fractions. Regroup if necessary.

Step 2 Subtract the whole numbers.

Step 3 Simplify if possible.

$$\begin{array}{r} 6\frac{2}{4} \\ -\,2\frac{3}{4} \\ \hline \end{array} \rightarrow \begin{array}{r} 5\frac{\mathbf{6}}{\mathbf{4}} \\ -\,2\frac{\mathbf{3}}{\mathbf{4}} \\ \hline \frac{\mathbf{3}}{\mathbf{4}} \end{array}$$

$$\begin{array}{r} \mathbf{5}\frac{6}{4} \\ -\,\mathbf{2}\frac{3}{4} \\ \hline \mathbf{3}\frac{3}{4} \end{array}$$

$3\frac{3}{4}$ is in simplest form.

So, $6\frac{2}{4} - 2\frac{3}{4} = 3\frac{3}{4}$.

Subtract. Write each difference in simplest form.

1. $\begin{array}{r} 7\frac{6}{8} \\ -\,3\frac{3}{8} \\ \hline \end{array}$

2. $\begin{array}{r} 2\frac{5}{16} \\ -\,1\frac{4}{16} \\ \hline \end{array}$

3. $\begin{array}{r} 9\frac{4}{5} \\ -\,4\frac{3}{5} \\ \hline \end{array}$

4. $\begin{array}{r} 21\frac{2}{16} \\ -\,11\frac{1}{16} \\ \hline \end{array}$

5. $\begin{array}{r} 15\frac{11}{12} \\ -\,11\frac{6}{12} \\ \hline \end{array}$

6. $12\frac{1}{4} - 4\frac{1}{8} =$ ______

7. $3\frac{2}{3} - 1\frac{1}{6} =$ ______

8. $6\frac{16}{20} - 2\frac{1}{4} =$ ______

9. $41\frac{11}{12} - 27\frac{10}{12} =$ ______

10. $70\frac{9}{10} - 45\frac{4}{5} =$ ______

11. $10\frac{3}{5} - 3\frac{2}{5} =$ ______

12. $3\frac{3}{8} - 1\frac{3}{4} =$ ______

13. $4\frac{6}{12} - 1\frac{1}{2} =$ ______

14. $6\frac{3}{4} - 2\frac{2}{8} =$ ______

15. $3\frac{3}{4} - 1\frac{8}{12} =$ ______

16. $18\frac{3}{6} - 1\frac{1}{6} =$ ______

17. $4\frac{3}{8} - 1\frac{1}{8} =$ ______

18. $3\frac{3}{6} - 2\frac{1}{2} =$ ______

19. $4\frac{2}{3} - 1\frac{1}{3} =$ ______

20. $25\frac{5}{8} - 17\frac{3}{8} =$ ______

10–8

Name ____________________ Date ____________

Skills Practice

Subtract Mixed Numbers

Subtract. Write each difference in simplest form.

1. $10\frac{11}{16} - 3\frac{14}{16}$

2. $8\frac{5}{8} - 2\frac{3}{8}$

3. $9\frac{3}{5} - 3\frac{2}{5}$

4. $5\frac{6}{8} - 2\frac{1}{4}$

5. $8\frac{3}{5} - 3\frac{2}{5}$

6. $7\frac{1}{2} - 3\frac{3}{6}$

7. $2\frac{3}{4} - 1\frac{1}{8}$

8. $4\frac{2}{16} - 2\frac{1}{16}$

9. $9\frac{2}{3} - 3\frac{1}{3}$

10. $2\frac{4}{5} - 1\frac{4}{10}$

11. $15\frac{7}{12} - 8\frac{1}{2} =$ _____

12. $6\frac{7}{8} - 2\frac{7}{8} =$ _____

13. $27\frac{7}{12} - 13\frac{1}{12} =$ _____

14. $5\frac{8}{20} - 1\frac{1}{4} =$ _____

15. $10\frac{2}{3} - 7\frac{1}{3} =$ _____

16. $7\frac{1}{3} - 2\frac{1}{9} =$ _____

17. $8\frac{3}{5} - 1\frac{2}{5} =$ _____

18. $10\frac{9}{10} - 2\frac{1}{5} =$ _____

19. $12\frac{3}{10} - 6\frac{1}{10} =$ _____

20. $5\frac{9}{12} - 3\frac{9}{12} =$ _____

21. $15\frac{5}{8} - 7\frac{1}{8} =$ _____

22. $11\frac{6}{8} - 6\frac{5}{8} =$ _____

Solve.

23. Anna has $3\frac{1}{2}$ yd of fabric. She plans to use $2\frac{1}{4}$ yd for curtains. Does she have enough left to make 2 pillows that each use $1\frac{1}{2}$ yd of fabric? Explain.

____

____

24. Paula has 2 yd of elastic. One project needs a $\frac{3}{4}$-yd piece. Does she have enough for another project that needs $1\frac{1}{3}$ yd? Explain.

____

____

Name ______________________ Date ____________

10–9

Reteach

Problem-Solving Investigation: Choose the Best Strategy

Look for a Pattern

Gregory is practicing the high jump. If he starts the bar at 3 feet 4 inches and raises it 0.5 inch after each jump, how high will the bar be on the sixth jump?

Step 1
Understand

What facts do you know?

- Gregory starts the bar at ______________.
- Gregory raises the bar ____________ after each jump.

What do you need to find?

- You need to find how high ______________.

Step 2
Plan

Make a plan.

Using a pattern will help you solve the problem.

Organize the information in a chart.

Step 3
Solve

Carry out your plan.

Make a chart. Look for a pattern in the chart.

Jump Number	1	2	3	4	5	6
Bar Height	3 feet 4 inches	3 feet 4.5 inches	3 feet 5 inches	3 feet 5.5 inches	3 feet 6 inches	

Look at the chart to find the pattern.

What is the pattern?

Continue the pattern to predict the height for the sixth jump.

Jump 6: 3 feet 6 inches + 0.5 inch = ____________

Using the pattern, you can expect that the bar will be set at ____________ for the sixth jump.

Name ______________________ Date ____________

10–9

Reteach

Problem-Solving Strategy: Choose the Best Strategy (continued)

Step 4 Check	**Is the solution reasonable?**
	Look back at the problem.
	Have you answered the question? ________
	Does your answer make sense? ________
	Did you find a pattern and continue it? ________

Use any strategy to solve each problem.

1. On the first day of the crafts fair, 200 people show up. Each day after that, the number of people who attend the fair increases by 150. The craft fair runs for five days. How many people attend the fair on the last day?

____

2. Find the next three numbers in the pattern below. Then describe the pattern.

−5, 0, 5, 10, __, __, __

____

____

3. Jamal, Diego, and Megan went shopping together and each bought a different type of clothing: a hat, a shirt, and a pair of shoes. Jamal did not buy something to put on his feet. Diego bought his item before the person bought the shoes. Either Megan or Diego bought the hat. What item did each person buy?

____

4. A yellow, a green, and a blue marble are placed in a bag. If you take one marble out of the bag at a time, in how many different orders can all three marbles be removed from the bag? List all possibilities.

____

5. Mrs. Reynolds is buying sandwiches for the 10 students in her class as a reward. If she bought at least one of each type of sandwich and spent a total of $34.00, how many of each sandwich did she buy?

____

Sandwiches

Type	Price
Italian	$4.00
Roast Beef	$3.50
Veggie	$3.00

Name ______________________ Date ______________

10–9

Skills Practice

Problem-Solving Investigation: Choose the Best Strategy

Use any strategy to solve each problem.

1. Describe the pattern below. Then find the missing number.

10, 20, 30, ______, 50

____

2. Fifty five families that own pets were asked what type of pets they own. Of the families surveyed, 24 have dogs, 14 have cats, and 5 have both dogs and cats. How many have neither a dog nor cat?

____

3. A designer is making a tile mosaic. The first row of the mosaic has 1 red tile in the center. If the designer increases the number of red tiles in the center of each row by 4, how many red tiles will be in the center of the fifth row?

____

4. Six students are sitting at a lunch table. Two more students arrive, and at the same time, three students leave. Then, four students leave, and two more arrive. How many students are at the table now?

____

5. The sum of two whole numbers between 20 and 40 is 58. The difference of the two numbers is 12. What are the two numbers?

____

6. Ramon has $3.50. He buys two pens that cost $0.75 each and a pencil that costs $0.40. How much money does Ramon have left?

____

Name ______________________ Date __________

10–10

Reteach

Subtraction with Renaming

Sometimes you need to rename fractions in order to subtract them.

Subtract $6\frac{2}{4} - 2\frac{3}{4}$.

Step 1 Regroup $6\frac{2}{4}$ as $5\frac{6}{4}$.	**Step 2** Subtract the fractions.
$\begin{array}{r} 6\frac{2}{4} \\ -\ 2\frac{3}{4} \\ \hline \end{array} \rightarrow \begin{array}{r} 5\frac{6}{4} \\ -\ 2\frac{3}{4} \\ \hline \end{array}$	$\begin{array}{r} 5\frac{6}{4} \\ -\ 2\frac{3}{4} \\ \hline \frac{3}{4} \end{array}$
Step 3 Subtract the whole numbers.	**Step 4** Simplify if possible.
$\begin{array}{r} 5\frac{6}{4} \\ -\ 2\frac{3}{4} \\ \hline 3\frac{3}{4} \end{array}$	$3\frac{3}{4}$ is in simplest form.

So, $6\frac{1}{2} - 2\frac{3}{4} = 3\frac{3}{4}$.

Subtract. Write each difference in simplest form.

1. $\begin{array}{r} 7\frac{3}{8} \\ -\ 3\frac{5}{8} \\ \hline \end{array}$

2. $\begin{array}{r} 2\frac{3}{16} \\ -1\frac{9}{16} \\ \hline \end{array}$

3. $\begin{array}{r} 9\frac{2}{5} \\ -\ 4\frac{4}{5} \\ \hline \end{array}$

4. $\begin{array}{r} 21\frac{7}{12} \\ -11\frac{5}{6} \\ \hline \end{array}$

5. $\begin{array}{r} 15\frac{1}{4} \\ -11\frac{3}{4} \\ \hline \end{array}$

6. $12\frac{1}{4} - 4\frac{6}{8} =$ ______
7. $3\frac{1}{6} - 1\frac{4}{6} =$ ______
8. $6\frac{1}{5} - 2\frac{4}{5} =$ ______
9. $41\frac{2}{3} - 27\frac{11}{12} =$ ______
10. $70\frac{4}{10} - 45\frac{3}{5} =$ ______
11. $10\frac{4}{9} - 3\frac{7}{9} =$ ______
12. $3\frac{2}{8} - 1\frac{7}{8} =$ ______
13. $4\frac{5}{12} - 1\frac{3}{4} =$ ______
14. $6\frac{3}{5} - 2\frac{4}{5} =$ ______
15. $3\frac{10}{16} - 1\frac{7}{8} =$ ______
16. $18\frac{1}{3} - 13\frac{2}{3} =$ ______
17. $4\frac{3}{8} - 1\frac{7}{8} =$ ______

Name ______________________ Date ____________

10–10

Skills Practice

Subtraction with Renaming

Subtract. Write each difference in simplest form.

1. $\begin{array}{r} 10\frac{6}{16} \\ -\ 3\frac{11}{16} \\ \hline \end{array}$

2. $\begin{array}{r} 8\frac{1}{3} \\ -\ 2\frac{2}{3} \\ \hline \end{array}$

3. $\begin{array}{r} 9\frac{2}{5} \\ -\ 3\frac{4}{5} \\ \hline \end{array}$

4. $\begin{array}{r} 5\frac{3}{16} \\ -\ 2\frac{1}{2} \\ \hline \end{array}$

5. $\begin{array}{r} 8\frac{1}{3} \\ -\ 3\frac{4}{6} \\ \hline \end{array}$

6. $\begin{array}{r} 7\frac{5}{9} \\ -\ 3\frac{8}{9} \\ \hline \end{array}$

7. $\begin{array}{r} 2\frac{1}{4} \\ -\ 1\frac{3}{4} \\ \hline \end{array}$

8. $\begin{array}{r} 4\frac{1}{4} \\ -\ 2\frac{5}{8} \\ \hline \end{array}$

9. $5\frac{2}{5} - 1\frac{4}{5} =$ ______

10. $10\frac{1}{3} - 7\frac{2}{3} =$ ______

11. $7\frac{1}{4} - 2\frac{3}{4} =$ ______

12. $8\frac{2}{6} - 1\frac{5}{6} =$ ______

13. $10\frac{1}{3} - 2\frac{5}{9} =$ ______

14. $12\frac{2}{7} - 6\frac{6}{7} =$ ______

15. $5\frac{7}{12} - 3\frac{5}{6} =$ ______

16. $15\frac{1}{8} - 7\frac{5}{8} =$ ______

17. $11\frac{1}{4} - 6\frac{1}{2} =$ ______

Find each missing number.

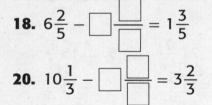

18. $6\frac{2}{5} - \square\frac{\square}{\square} = 1\frac{3}{5}$

19. $15\frac{3}{12} - \square\frac{\square}{\square} = 6\frac{8}{12}$

20. $10\frac{1}{3} - \square\frac{\square}{\square} = 3\frac{2}{3}$

21. $6\frac{5}{9} - \square\frac{\square}{\square} = 3\frac{6}{9}$

Solve.

22. Anna has $3\frac{1}{4}$ yd of fabric. She uses $2\frac{3}{4}$ yd for curtains. How much fabric is left over?

____

____

23. Paula has $2\frac{3}{6}$ yard of elastic. One project needs a $1\frac{4}{6}$ yard piece. Will she have enough elastic to make another project that uses the same amount? Explain.

____

____

Name _________________________ Date ____________

11–1 Reteach

Units of Length

Customary Units of Length	
1 foot (ft) = 12 inches (in.)	1 mile (mi) = 5,280 ft
1 yard (yd) = 36 in.	1 mile (mi) = 1,760 yd
1 yard (yd) = 3 ft	

Multiply to change larger units to smaller units.

9 yd = □ ft

Yards are larger units than feet.

1 yard = 3 feet

So multiply by 3.

9 × 3 = 27

9 yd = 27 ft

Divide to change smaller units to larger units.

37 ft = □ yd □ ft

Feet are smaller units than yards.

3 feet = 1 yard

So divide by 3.

37 ÷ 3 = 12 R1

37 ft = 12 yd 1 ft

Complete.

1. 7 ft = □ in.

1 foot = ________ inches

So multiply by ________.

7 × ________ = ________

7 ft = ________ in.

2. 80 in. = □ ft □ in.

________ inches = 1 foot

So divide by ________.

80 ÷ ________ = ________

80 in. = ________ ft ________ in.

3. 72 in. = ________ yd

4. 60 yd = ________ ft

5. 96 in. = ________ ft

6. 3 yd = ________ in.

7. 10 ft = ________ in.

8. 60 in. = ________ ft

9. 52 in. = ________ yd ________ in.

10. 79 in. = ________ ft ________ in.

11. 17 ft = ________ yd ________ ft

12. 8 ft = ________ yd ________ ft

Choose an appropriate unit to measure the length of each. Write *inch, foot, yard,* or *mile.*

13. distance a football is thrown ________

14. length of a train ride ________

15. height of your school ________

16. width of your math book ________

Name ______________________ Date __________

11–1 Skills Practice

Units of Length

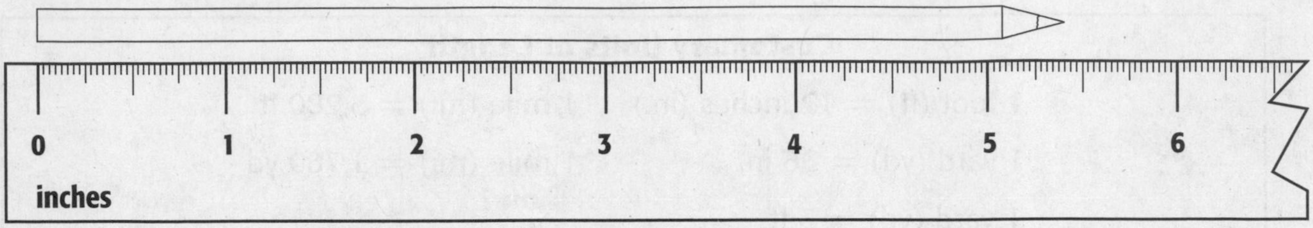

Measure the length of the pencil to the nearest:

1. inch ____ **2.** half inch ____ **3.** quarter inch ____ **4.** eighth inch ____

Choose an appropriate unit to measure the length of each. Write *inch, foot, yard,* or *mile.*

5. distance from Boston to Dallas

____

6. height of a giraffe

____

7. length of an aircraft carrier

____

8. width of a computer diskette

____

Complete.

9. 900 in. = ____ yd **10.** 46 yd = ____ ft **11.** 948 in. = ____ ft

12. 1,218 ft = ____ yd **13.** 19 yd = ____ in. **14.** 62 ft = ____ in.

15. 1,332 in. = ____ yd **16.** 792 ft = ____ yd **17.** 127 ft = ____ in.

18. 153 in. = ____ yd ____ in. **19.** 26 ft = ____ yd ____ ft

20. 113 in. = ____ ft ____ in. **21.** 263 in. = ____ yd ____ in.

22. 519 in. = ____ ft ____ in. **23.** 178 ft = ____ yd ____ ft

Solve.

24. A piece of red ribbon is $4\frac{1}{2}$ ft long. A piece of blue ribbon is 1 yd long. How many feet longer is the piece of red ribbon than the piece of blue ribbon? How many inches longer?

____

25. A bookcase is 6 ft wide and a table is 30 in. wide. Will both fit along a wall that is 3 yd long? Why or why not?

____

11–2

Name ______________________ Date ______________

Reteach

Problem-Solving Strategy: Draw a Diagram

Dominick has 5 posters that he wants to hang in his room. He wants the basketball poster on the left end of the wall and the music poster on the right end of the wall. How many ways can he arrange the posters on the wall?

Understand	**What facts do you know?** • Dominick has 5 posters • The basketball posters needs to be on the left and the music poster needs to be on the right. **What do you need to find?** • The number of ways he can arrange the posters on the wall.
Plan	Solve the problem by drawing a diagram.
Solve	**Use your plan to solve the problem.** Draw a diagram to show how many ways Dominick can arrange the posters on the wall. 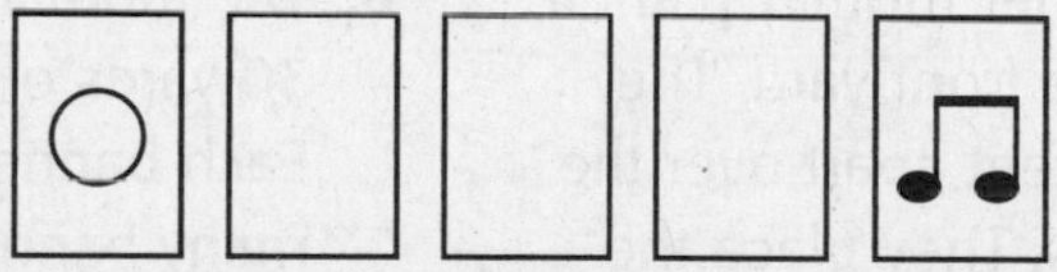 While the basketball poster needs to stay on the left and the music poster needs to stay on the right, the order of the middle posters can be arranged 6 different ways.
Check	Look back at the problem. Make sure you have counted all of the poster arrangements.

Solve.

1. Leah left her house and walked 3 blocks west and 1 block north to volleyball practice. After practice she walked 2 blocks east and 1 block north to her aunt's house. What direction is her house from her aunt's house? ______________

2. A deli has $2\frac{1}{4}$ pounds of tuna salad left at the end of the day. How many pounds of tuna salad did it sell if it started with 12 pounds? ______________

Name ______________________ Date __________

11–2 Reteach

Problem-Solving Strategy: Draw a Diagram (continued)

Solve. Use the *draw a diagram* strategy.

3. An Italian restaurant offers a dinner special on Friday nights. Customers can choose one entrée, one side dish, and one drink from the table shown. How many different dinner combinations can be purchased?

Entrée	Side dish	Drink
Lasagna	Salad	Water
Spaghetti	Fruit	Juice
Fettuccini	Bread	

____

4. There are four shelves of movies next to each other at the library. The comedy movies are on the far right shelf. The mystery movies are on the shelf in between the adventure movies and the children's movies. The adventure movies only have one neighbor. List the order of the movie shelves from left to right.

____

5. Caroline is helping her mother plant a row of shrubs in the front yard. They place the shrubs 3 feet apart over the distance of 12 yards. They place the first at the edge of the yard. How many shrubs do they plant?

____

6. The football booster club buys 30 yards of material to make banners. Each banner will be 5 feet long. How many banners will be made?

____

7. Liam is building a fence around his backyard. The backyard is 24 feet wide and 60 feet long. If Liam uses sections of fencing that are 12 feet long, how many sections does he use?

____

8. Maria uses a pattern to display her swimming trophies. The first row has 2 trophies, the second row has 6 trophies, the third row has 10 trophies, and the fourth row has 14. How many trophies are in the fifth row?

____

11–2

Name ______________________ Date ______________

Skills Practice

Problem-Solving Strategy: Draw a Diagram

1. Michael ate $\frac{3}{8}$ of a pizza. Kenneth ate $\frac{1}{2}$ of a pizza that was the exact same size as Michael's pizza. Who ate more pizza?

____

____

2. Dominic's house, his school, and the park are on the same road. He lives $2\frac{1}{2}$ miles from the school, which is $\frac{1}{2}$ mile farther from his house than the park. How far is it from Dominic's house to the park?

____

3. Mrs. Pintos is planting flowers around the outside edge of a square garden. There will be 10 plants on each side of the garden. What is the least number of flowers she needs to plant?

____

4. **Measurement** A carpenter has a piece of wood 12 feet long. After he cuts the wood into pieces, $3\frac{5}{8}$ feet are left. How much of the wood does the carpenter use?

____

5. Five students are lined up in the cafeteria. Beth is first in line. Jeff is 2 places behind Ernesto. Leah is ahead of Peter, who is fifth in line. Who is third in line?

____

6. For lunch, the corner deli has a special where they sell a sandwich and drink combo for $4.95.

Sandwiches	**Drinks**
Ham	Soda
Turkey	Milk
Roast Beef	Juice
Veggie	
BLT	

How many different sandwich and drink combos are available at the deli?

____

Name ____________________ Date __________

11–3 Reteach

Units of Weight

Customary Units of Weight
1 pound (lb) = 16 ounces (oz)
1 ton (T) = 2,000 lb

Multiply to change larger units to smaller units.

8 T = □ lb

Tons are larger units than pounds.

1 Ton = 2,000 lb

So, multiply by 2,000

8 × 2,000 = 16,000

8 T = 16,000 lb

Divide to change smaller units to larger units.

50 oz = □ lb □ oz

Ounces are smaller units than pounds.

16 ounces = 1 pound

So, divide by 16.

50 ÷ 16 = 3 R2

50 oz = 3 lb 2 oz

Complete.

1. 9 T = □ lb

1 ton = __________ pounds

So, multiply by __________.

9 × __________ = __________

9 T = __________ lb

2. 35 oz = □ lb □ oz

__________ ounces = 1 pound

So, divide by __________.

35 ÷ __________ = __________

35 oz = __________ lb __________ oz

3. 64 oz = ____ lb

4. 12 T = ____ lb

5. 6 lb = ____ oz

6. 16,000 lb = ____ T

7. 32 oz = ____ lb

8. 40 oz = ____ lb ____ oz

Choose an appropriate unit to measure the weight of each. Write *ounce, pound,* or *ton.*

9. horse __________

10. blue whale __________

11. robin __________

11–3

Name ______________________ Date ____________

Skills Practice

Units of Weight

Choose an appropriate unit to measure the weight of each. Write *ounce, pound,* or *ton.*

1. bowling ball ________ **2.** compact disc ________ **3.** ocean liner ________

Complete.

4. 5 lb = ________ oz **5.** 12 lb = ________ oz **6.** $4\frac{1}{2}$ T = ________ lb

7. 400 oz = ________ lb **8.** 64 oz = ________ lb **9.** 8,000 lb = ________ T

10. 42 oz = ________ lb ________ oz **11.** 2,450 lb = ________ T ________ lb

12. 3,500 lb = ________ T ________ lb **13.** 89 oz = ________ lb ________ oz

14. 6,500 lb = ________ T ________ lb **15.** 115 oz = ________ lb ________ oz

Replace each ◯ with >, <, or = to make a true sentence.

16. 6 lb ◯ 100 oz **17.** 5 lb ◯ 50 oz **18.** 1 T ◯ 2,000 oz

19. 7,000 lb ◯ 3 T **20.** 98 oz ◯ 8 lb **21.** 3 T ◯ 6,000 lb

22. 15 lb ◯ 300 oz **23.** 55 oz ◯ 3 lb 10 oz **24.** 130 lb ◯ 1,920 oz

25. Alfonso mails a package that weighs 9 pounds. How many ounces is the package?

____

26. Mr. Hill's truck weighs $1\frac{1}{2}$ tons. His car weighs 1,600 pounds. Which vehicle weighs more? How much more?

____

Name ______________________ Date ______________

11–4

Reteach

Units of Capacity

You can use these charts to help you convert between customary units of measurement.

Customary Units of Capacity
1 cup (c) = 8 fluid ounces (fl oz)
1 pint (pt) = 2 c or 16 fl oz
1 quart (qt) = 2 pt or 4 c or 32 fl oz
1 gallon (gal) = 4 qt

Complete. 4 qt = ■ pt

You are changing from a larger unit to a smaller unit, so multiply.

1 qt = 2 pt

4 qt = 4 × 2 pt = 8 pt

So, 4 qt = 8 pt.

Complete. 64 fl oz = ■ qt

You are changing from a smaller unit to a larger unit, so divide.

1 qt = 32 fl oz

64 fl oz ÷ 32 fl oz = 2 qt

So, 64 fl oz = 2 qt.

Complete.

1. 10 gal = ■ qt

1 gal = ______ qt

10 gal = 10 × ______ qt = ______ qt

2. 52 fl oz = ■ c

1 c = ______ fl oz

52 fl oz ÷ ______ fl oz = ______ c

3. 42 pt = ______ qt **4.** 12 pt = ______ qt **5.** 8 qt = ______ c

6. 12 gal = ______ qt **7.** $1\frac{1}{2}$ qt = ______ pt **8.** 4 c = ______ fl oz

9. 6 gal = ______ qt **10.** 3 qt = ______ pt **11.** 96 fl oz = ______ qt

12. $4\frac{1}{2}$ qt = ______ c **13.** 8 qt = ______ pt **14.** 20 fl oz = ______ c

15. 24 pt = ______ c **16.** 5 pt 1 c = ______ c **17.** 3 gal 3 qt = ______ qt

Name ______________________ Date ____________

11–4 Skills Practice

Units of Capacity

Complete.

1. 38 pt = ______ qt

2. 3 qt = ______ pt

3. 9 c = ______ fl oz

4. 4 c = ______ fl oz

5. 15 pt = ______ c

6. $5\frac{1}{2}$ qt = ______ pt

7. 48 fl oz = ______ pt

8. 36 qt = ______ gal

9. 4 qt = ______ fl oz

10. 12 qt = ______ gal

11. 40 fl oz = ______ c

12. 64 fl oz = ______ pt

13. 3 c = ______ fl oz

14. 6 gal = ______ qt

15. 72 fl oz = ______ c

16. 21 fl oz = ______ c ______ fl oz

17. 70 fl oz = ______ qt ______ fl oz

18. 26 qt = ______ gal ______ qt

19. 34 pt = ______ gal ______ qt

Replace each ◯ with >, < or = to make a true sentence.

20. 20 qt ◯ 4 gal 2 pt

21. 8 pt 1 c ◯ 2 gal

22. 50 fl oz ◯ $1\frac{1}{2}$ qt

23. 63 c ◯ 129 pt

24. 60 fl oz ◯ 10 c

25. 65 gal ◯ 256 qt

Solve.

26. Robert needs 3 pints of milk to make a casserole. He has 5 cups of milk. How many more cups of milk does Robert need?

____

27. Shannon combines 3 quarts of cranberry juice with 3 pints of apple juice. Does Shannon now have at least one gallon of cranberry juice? Why or why not?

____

11–5

Name ______________________ Date __________

Reteach

Units of Time

You can multiply or divide to change units of time.

Multiply to change larger units to smaller units.

13 wk = ☐ d

Weeks are larger units than days.

1 week = 7 days

So, multiply by 7.

$13 \times 7 = 91$

13 wk = 91 d

Divide to change smaller units to larger units.

250 s = ☐ min ☐ s

Seconds are smaller units than minutes.

60 seconds = 1 minute

So, divide by 60.

$250 \div 60 = 4$ R10

250 s = 4 min 10 s

Complete.

1. 600 min = ______ h

2. 4 y 7 mo = ______ mo

3. 8 min = ______ s

4. 139 d = ______ wk ______ d

5. 4 h 53 min = ______ min

6. 73 mo = ______ y ______ mo

Name ______________________ Date ______________

11–5

Skills Practice

Units of Time

Complete.

1. 9 min = ______ s

2. 96 h = ______ d

3. 90 mo = ____ y ____ mo

4. 15 wk = ______ d

5. 12 h = ______ min

6. 730 d = ______ y

7. 7 years = ______ mo

8. 350 s = ____ min ____ s

9. 58 h = ____ d ____ h

10. 72 mo = ______ y

11. 6 d 9 h = ______ h

12. 60 d = ____ wk ____ d

13. A non-stop flight from Boston, Massachusetts, to Chicago, Illinois, takes 2 hours and 50 minutes. What is this time in minutes?

____

14. Germaine entered a walk for charity. He completed the walk in 48 minutes and 35 seconds. What is this time in seconds?

____

15. It took the Johnson family 2 days and 13 hours to drive from Minneapolis, Minnesota to Charlotte, South Carolina. What is this time in hours?

____

16. Muriel completed her math test in 2,100 seconds. What is this time in minutes?

____

11–6

Name ______________________ Date ____________

Reteach

Problem-Solving Investigation: Choose the Best Strategy

On the first day of the month, Jacob puts 2 pennies in a jar on his dresser. On the second day, he puts 2 more pennies in the jar, bringing the total to 4. On the third day, he puts 4 more pennies in the jar, bringing the total to 8. Each day he doubles the amount of pennies in the jar. How many pennies will he have in the jar on the eighth day of the month?

Understand	**What facts do you know?** Jacob doubles the amount of total pennies each day. **What do you need to find?** How many pennies were in the jar on day 8.
Plan	Make a table to show how many pennies are added to the jar, and what the total is each day.
Solve	Use your plan to solve the problem. (see table below) There will be 256 pennies in the jar on the eighth day.
Check	Look back over your table and check to make sure you added correctly.

Day	Number of pennies added	Total number of pennies
1	2	2
2	2	4
3	4	8
4	8	16
5	16	32
6	32	64
7	64	128
8	128	256

Solve.

1. Pablo walked 2 blocks east and 4 blocks south to school. After school he walked 2 blocks west and 1 block north to a friend's house. How far south was Pablo from his house?

   ____

2. James is 4 inches taller than Rashad. Rashad is 5 inches shorter than Tony. Tony is 3 inches taller than Camron. Camron is 58 inches tall. How tall is James?

   ____

Name ______________________ Date ____________

11–6

Reteach

Problem-Solving Investigation: Choose the Best Strategy *(continued)*

Use any strategy to solve each problem.

3. Mrs. George takes a box to the post office. She finds out it will cost $3.43 to mail the box. There are $0.27 stamps, $0.39 stamps, and $0.86 stamps at the post office. What stamps should Mrs. George select to make exact postage for the box?

____

4. Stephen's favorite CD has 4 songs on it. He decides to put his CD player on random, so that the songs can play in any order. How many different orders can the songs play in?

____

5. In the pizza parlor, there are 5 toppings available: pepperoni, green peppers, mushrooms, onions, and broccoli. Each pizza must have at least 1 topping, and as many as 5. How many different topping combinations are possible?

____

6. A number is divided by 4. Next, the number is multiplied by 3. Then 5 is added to the product. If the result is 20, what is the original number?

____

7. How many pounds does a 56 ounce bag of pretzels weigh?

____

8. Juan's family drove to his uncle's house. On the first day they drove 72 miles. On the second day they drove 480 miles. On the third day they drove 315 miles. And on the final day they drove 110 miles. Estimate the total number of miles Juan's family drove during these 4 days.

____

11–6

Name ______________________________ Date ____________________

Skills Practice

Problem-Solving Investigation: Choose the Best Strategy

Use any strategy to solve each problem.

1. Courtney rode her bike 3 miles east to the library. She then rode 2 miles north to the park. Finally, she rode 1 mile west, and 1 mile south. How far east of her original position was Courtney at the end?

____

2. Siri has one box of crayons that weighs 7 ounces, one box of crayons that weighs 23 ounces, and 2 boxes of crayons that weigh 15 ounces. Estimate how many pounds of crayons Siri has.

____

3. Melissa and Jack are putting pencils into boxes. For every 6 yellow pencils, they put half as many red pencils. If they put 18 pencils into a box altogether, how many are red?

____

4. Jonas needs to bring 38 pints of water on his camping trip. He plans to bring this water in gallon jugs. How many jugs will he need?

____

5. Marco works on the computer for 28 minutes on Monday, 37 minutes on Tuesday, and 46 minutes on Wednesday. If he continues this pattern, how many minutes will he work on the computer for on Saturday?

____

6. Jasmine is baking banana bread. Her recipe says that she can make 2 loaves with one pint of milk. How many loaves can she make with a gallon of milk?

____

11–7

Name ______________________ Date __________

Reteach

Elapsed Time

Andrew started volunteering at 2:15 P.M. He finished at 6:35 P.M. How long did Andrew volunteer?

Step 1 Write the time in units of hours and minutes.

Ending time: 6:35 P.M. → 6 hours 35 minutes
Starting time: 2:15 P.M. → 2 hours 15 minutes

Step 2 Subtract the starting time from the ending time. Be sure to subtract hours from hours and minutes from minutes.

6 hours 35 minutes
− 2 hours 15 minutes
Elapsed time: 4 hours 20 minutes

So, Andrew volunteered for 4 hours and 20 minutes.

Find the elapsed time from 9:15 A.M. to 5:45 P.M.

9:15 A.M. + 45 min → 10:00 A.M.

10:00 A.M. + 2 h → 12:00 P.M.

12:00 P.M. + 5 h 45 min → 5:45 P.M.

7 h 90 min or 8 h 30 min

90 min = 60 min + 30 min
= 1h 30 min

So, 9:15 A.M. to 5:45 P.M. is 8 hours 30 minutes.

Find each elapsed time.

1. 1:15 P.M. to 9:30 P.M. ____________

2. 4:30 P.M. to 10:55 P.M. ____________

3. 6:15 A.M. to 12:20 P.M. ____________

4. 11:45 P.M. to 3:30 A.M. ____________

5. 5:24 A.M. to 10:40 A.M. ____________

6. 7:12 P.M. to 8:55 P.M. ____________

Name ______________________ Date ____________

11–7

Skills Practice

Elapsed Time

Find each elapsed time.

1. 3:15 P.M. to 8:30 P.M. ______

2. 5:55 P.M. to 11:58 P.M. ______

3. 6:24 A.M. to 10:30 A.M. ______

4. 9:12 P.M. to 10:55 P.M. ______

5. 2:13 P.M. to 7:45 P.M. ______

6. 1:15 P.M. to 4:29 P.M. ______

7. 7:30 P.M. to 9:55 P.M. ______

8. 2:15 A.M. to 2:20 P.M. ______

9. 5:45 P.M. to 12:30 A.M. ______

10. 6:10 A.M. to 11:05 A.M. ______

11. 1:12 P.M.to 10:45 P.M. ______

12. 8:10 P.M. to 12:50 A.M. ______

13. 3:24 A.M. to 8:19 A.M. ______

14. 1:19 P.M. to 5:35 P.M. ______

15. 4:07 P.M. to 6:10 P.M. ______

16. 6:30 P.M. to 10:55 P.M. ______

17. 5:15 A.M. to 12:20 P.M. ______

18. 7:45 P.M. to 11:45 P.M. ______

19. 9:15 A.M. to 5:30 P.M. ______

20. 8:16 P.M. to 4:00 A.M. ______

21. 9:55 P.M. to 1:55 A.M. ______

22. 10:24 A.M. to 11:40 A.M. ______

23. 4:12 P.M. to 5:55 P.M. ______

24. 9:49 P.M. to 11:39 P.M. ______

25. Eric finished his homework at 7:48 P.M. and Marcus finished at 9:25 P.M. How many minutes faster was Eric than Marcus?

____

26. Erin started exercising at 4:45 P.M. She finished exercising 80 minutes later. At what time did she finish exercising?

____

Name ______________________ Date ____________

12–1

Reteach

Units of Length

The meter (m) is the basic unit of length in the metric system.

Metric Units of Length

1 kilometer (km) = 1,000 meters (m)

1 meter = 100 centimeters (cm) = 1,000 millimeters (mm)

1 centimeter = 10 millimetes (mm)

A compact disc is about 1 millimeter thick.

A doorknob is about 1 meter above the floor.

Complete. 6 m = ■ mm

You are changing from a larger unit to a smaller unit, so multiply.

6 m = 6 × 1,000 mm = 6,000 m

Complete. 200 cm = ■ m

You are changing from a smaller unit to a larger unit, so divide.

200 cm ÷ 100 cm = 2 m

Select an appropriate unit to measure the length of each of the following. Write *millimeter, centimeter, meter,* or *kilometer.*

1. the width of a TV screen ______

2. the height of a building ______

3. the length of the book ______

4. the distance from Miami to Boston ______

Complete.

5. 4 m = ■ cm

1 m = ______ cm

4 m = 4 × ______ cm = ______ cm

6. 7,000 m = ■ km

1 km = ______ m

7,000 m ÷ ______ m = ______ km

7. 3 km = ______ m

8. 90 mm = ______ cm

9. 450 mm = ______ cm

10. 6 m = ______ cm

11. 400 cm = ______ m

12. 1,000 m = ______ km

13. 5,200 cm = ______ m

14. 11 m = ______ cm

15. 720 mm = ______ cm

16. 7 m = ______ cm

17. 8,000 mm = ______ m

18. 20 m = ______ mm

19. 560 mm = ______ cm

20. 2,240 mm = ______ cm

21. 4,000 m = ______ km

Name ______________________ Date ______________

12–1

Skills Practice

Units of Length

Select an appropriate unit to measure the length of each of the following. Write *millimeter, centimeter, meter,* or *kilometer.*

1. length of your arm ________

2. thickness of a penny ________

3. length of a bus ________

4. height of a mountain ________

5. distance from your home to school ________

6. length of a shoelace ________

7. length of a canoe ________

8. height of a diving board ________

Complete.

9. 40 mm = ________ cm

10. 10 km = ________ m

11. 50 mm = ________ cm

12. 21,000 m = ________ km

13. 8,000 mm = ________ m

14. 3,000 m = ________ km

15. 5 km = ________ m

16. 7 km = ________ m

17. 60 mm = ________ cm

18. 45 m = ________ cm

19. 5,000 m = ________ km

20. 18 m = ________ mm

21. 60 mm = ________ cm

22. 90 mm = ________ cm

23. 7,000 m = ________ km

24. 200 cm = ________ m

25. 49,000 m = ________ km

26. 8 m = ________ cm

Solve.

27. Kay is reading a book. Is the book's thickness more likely to be 19 mm or 19 km?

____

28. Scott kicked a football. Is the distance he kicked it more likely to be 35 m or 35 km?

____

Name ______________________ Date ______________

12–2

Reteach

Problem-Solving Strategy: Determine Reasonable Answers

Erica takes a package of two paperback books to the post office. The package weighs 16 ounces. Erica estimates that the package weighs about 300 pounds. Is her estimate reasonable?

Step 1 Understand	**Be sure you understand the problem.** • What facts do you know? You know how many ounces the package weighs. • What do you need to find? You need to know whether Erica's estimate is reasonable.
Step 2 Plan	**Make a plan.** You want to compare the weight of the package to something that you know weighs about 300 pounds.
Step 3 Solve	**Carry out your plan.** A professional football player might weigh between 200 and 300 pounds. So, 300 pounds is much heavier than a package of two books. Therefore, the estimate is not reasonable. Erica multiplied to change a smaller unit to a larger one. She should have divided. $16 \div 16 = 1$ ← Remember: 1 pound = 16 ounces.
Step 4 Check	**Check for Reasonableness** • Does your answer make sense? • Did you answer the question? Yes. Erica's estimate was not reasonable. You found the mistake she made.

Is each estimate reasonable? Explain.

1. Jerry measures the hallway and finds that it is 240 feet long. He estimates that he will need a carpet that is 20 inches long in order to cover the hallway. Is Jerry's estimate reasonable?

____

____

12–2

Name ______________________ Date __________

Reteach

Problem-Solving Strategy: Determine Reasonable Answers (continued)

2. Leslie's computer weighs 165 ounces. She estimates that it weighs about 10 pounds. Is Leslie's estimate reasonable?

____

____

3. Rocky measures his bedroom and finds that it is 3 meters wide and 6 meters long. He thinks he can easily fit a desk that is 275 centimeters long in his room. Is this a reasonable guess?

____

____

____

4. Haruko wants to make a dress. The pattern she is using called for 2 yards of material. Haruko estimates that she will need to buy 2 feet of material. Is her estimate reasonable?

____

____

____

5. Eli weighs 900 ounces. He guesses that he can get on a ride at the amusement park that allows children from 30 to 80 pounds. Is his estimate reasonable?

____

____

____

Name ______________________ Date ______________

12–2

Skills Practice

Problem-Solving Strategy: Determine Reasonable Answers

Is each estimate reasonable? Explain.

1. Sandra needs to buy a phone cord that will reach a distance of at least 12 yards. At the store, all of the packages are marked in feet. Sandra estimates that the package with 40 feet of cord will be enough. Is her estimate reasonable?

____

____

2. Kyle and Julie are watching a television program on weightlifting. A man is going to lift 210 pounds. Julie comments that he is going to lift 4,000 ounces. Is her estimate reasonable?

____

____

3. Ryan and Tyler are going to the pet shop to buy 12 cans of dog food. They are trying to decide whether they should take their wagon to help carry the dog food home. The cans weigh 15 ounces each. They estimate that the dog food will weigh 10 pounds. Is the estimate reasonable?

____

____

4. Nicole is trying out a new recipe. The recipe calls for 4 pints of broth. Nicole has only a 1-cup measuring cup. She estimates that she will need 16 cups of broth. Is her estimate reasonable?

____

____

Name ______________________ Date ____________

12–3

Reteach

Units of Mass

Mass is the amount of matter in an object. The **kilogram (kg)** and the **gram (g)** are metric units of mass.

The mass of a large paper clip is about 1 g.

The mass of your math book is about 2 kg.

Metric Units of Mass
1 kilogram (kg) = 1,000 grams (g)
1 gram (g) = 1,000 milligrams (mg)

Complete. 4 kg = ■ g

You are changing from a larger unit to a smaller unit, so multiply.

4 kg = 4 × 1,000 g = 4,000 g

Complete. 4,000 mg = ■ g

You are changing from a smaller unit to a larger unit, so divide.

4,000 mg ÷ 1,000 mg = 4 g

Complete.

1. 7 g = ■ mg

1 g = ______ mg

7 g = 7 × ______ mg = ______ mg

2. 7,000 g = ■ kg

1 kg = ______ g

7,000 g ÷ ______ g = ______ kg

3. 4 g = ______ mg **4.** 5 kg = ______ g **5.** 2,000 mg = ______ g

6. 8,000 g = ______ kg **7.** 48 g = ______ mg **8.** 6,000 mg = ______ g

9. 2,000 mg = ______ g **10.** 3,000 mg = ______ g **11.** 1,000 mg = ______ g

12. 17 g = ______ mg **13.** 800 mg = ______ g **14.** 1,400 mg = ______ g

15. 10 kg = ______ g **16.** 51,000 g = ______ kg **17.** 0.9 g = ______ mg

Name ______________________ Date __________

12–3

Skills Practice

Units of Mass

Complete.

1. 7,000 g = ________ kg

2. 3,000 mg = ________ g

3. 4,000 mg = ________ g

4. 13 kg = ________ g

5. 1.5 kg = ________ g

6. 46 g = ________ mg

7. 65 kg = ________ g

8. 1,600 g = ________ kg

9. 5,000 mg = ________ g

10. 4,000 g = ________ kg

11. 7 kg = ________ g

Replace ◯ with <, >, or = to make a true statement.

12. 520.8 g ◯ 5,208 mg

13. 320 g ◯ 3.2 kg

14. 295 g ◯ 29.5 kg

15. 6.34 g ◯ 63.4 mg

16. 4,300 g ◯ 0.43 kg

17. 0.9 g ◯ 900 mg

18. 2.45 kg ◯ 245 g

19. 0.384 g ◯ 3,840 mg

Solve.

20. Marc was telling his friends about his new baby sister. Is her mass more likely to be 40 milligrams or 4 kilograms?

____

21. Gavin likes to hold his pet cat, Shadow. Is Shadow's mass more likely to be 6 kilograms or 6 grams?

____

Name ______________________ Date ____________

12–4

Reteach

Units of Capacity

The **liter (L)** and the **milliliter (mL)** are metric units of capacity.

A teaspoon holds about 5 mL of liquid.

A water bottle might hold about 1 L of liquid.

Metric Units of Capacity
1 liter (L) = 1,000 (mL)

Multiply to change larger units to smaller units.

3 L = ▇ mL

Liters are larger units than milliliters.

1 liter = 1,000 milliliters.

So multiply by 1,000.

3 × 1,000 = 3,000

3 L = 3,000 mL

Divide to change smaller units to larger units.

900 mL = ▇ L

900 mL = $\frac{900}{1,000}$ L or 0.9.

900 mL = 0.9 L

Complete.

1. 42 mL = ▇ L

_______ liter = 1,000 milliliters

So divide by _______.

42 mL = _______ L

42 mL = _______ L

2. 5.9 L = ▇ mL

1 liter = _______ milliliters

So multiply by _______.

5.9 × _______ = _______

5.9 L = _______ mL

3. 50 L = _______ mL **4.** 64 mL = _______ L **5.** 348 mL = _______ L

6. 9,000 mL = _______ L **7.** 12 L = _______ mL **8.** 40 mL = _______ L

9. 2 L = _______ mL **10.** 420 L = _______ mL **11.** 3 L = _______ mL

12. 52 mL = _______ L **13.** 738 mL = _______ L **14.** 2.5 L = _______ mL

15. 86 L = _______ mL **16.** 2,250 mL = _______ L

Name ______________________ Date ______________

12–4

Skills Practice

Units of Capacity

Complete.

1. 46 L = __________ mL

2. 602 L = __________ mL

3. 7 L = __________ mL

4. 350 mL = __________ L

5. 93 L = __________ mL

6. 13.5 L = __________ mL

7. 56 mL = __________ L

8. 19 mL = __________ L

9. 12 mL = __________ L

10. 3.07 L = __________ mL

11. 0.3 L = __________ mL

12. 4.2 mL = __________ L

13. 62 mL = __________ L

14. 6,400 L = __________ mL

15. 25 mL = __________ L

16. 1,500 mL = __________ L

17. 8.2 L = __________ mL

18. 900 L = __________ mL

Replace ◯ with <, >, or = to make a true statement.

19. 20.8 L ◯ 208 mL

20. 20 mL ◯ 0.2 L

21. 95 mL ◯ 9.5 L

22. 6.3 L ◯ 63 mL

23. 2,000 mL ◯ 20 L

24. 4.027 L ◯ 4,027 mL

25. 129 mL ◯ 12.9 L

26. 56.8 L ◯ 568 mL

27. 3,000 mL ◯ 0.03 L

Solve.

28. Jacob has 0.5 L of milk to use in two recipes. Each recipe uses 300 mL. Does he have enough? Explain.

____

____

Name ______________________________ Date ________________

12–5 Reteach

Integers and Graphing on Number Lines

You can represent positive and negative integers on a number line.

Use integers to represent these situations. Then graph the integers on a number line.

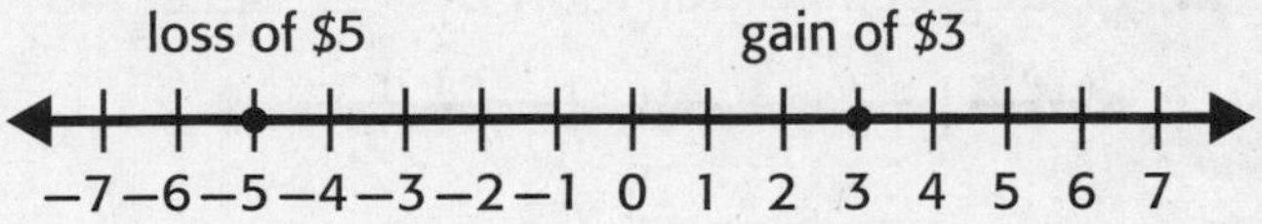

a loss of $5: −5
a gain of $3: +3 or 3

Write an integer to represent each situation. Then graph the integer on a number line.

1. 9 runs scored in baseball __________

2. 7 degrees below zero __________

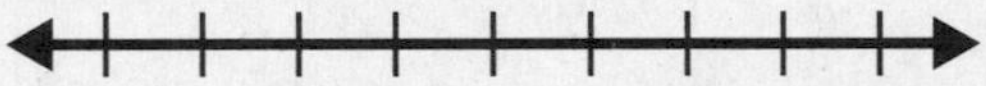

3. a loss of 3 years in football __________

4. a deposit of $23 __________

5. add 2 cups of flour __________

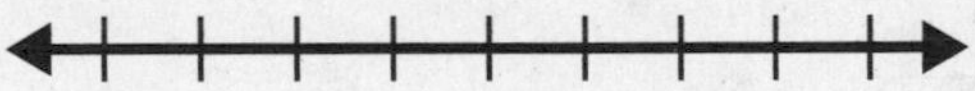

6. loss of 18 ounces __________

Write an integer to represent each situation. Then write its opposite.

7. 23 feet below sea level __________

8. loss of 18 pounds __________

9. profit of $74 __________

10. 5 degrees below zero __________

11. 14 feet above the ground __________

12. gain of 3 kilograms __________

13. 10 degrees above zero __________

14. loss of 5 ounces __________

Name ______________________ Date ____________

12–5 Skills Practice

Integers and Graphing on Number Lines

Write an integer to represent each situation. Then graph the integer on a number line.

1. spent $15 ________

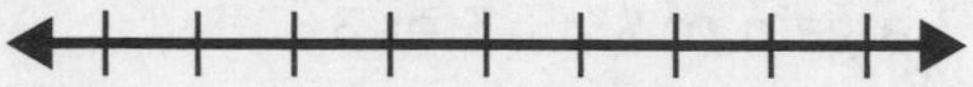

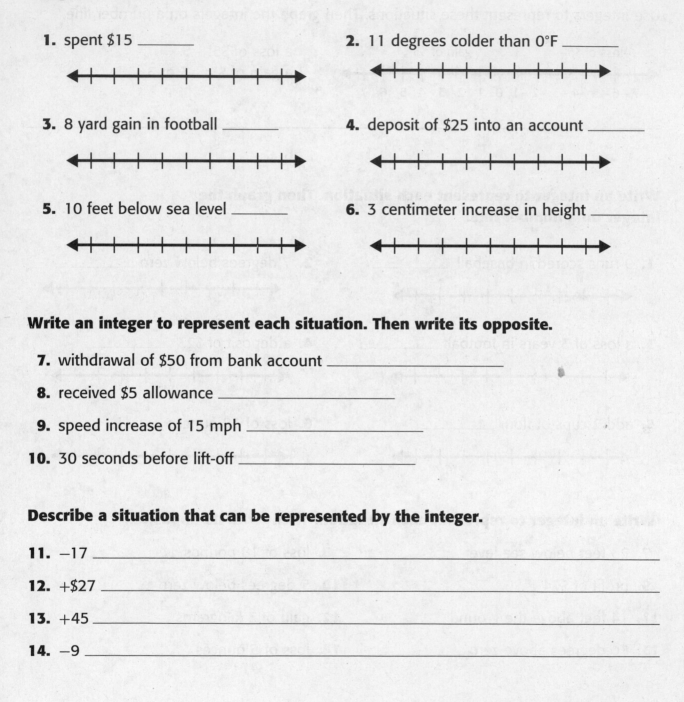

2. 11 degrees colder than 0°F ________

3. 8 yard gain in football ________

4. deposit of $25 into an account ________

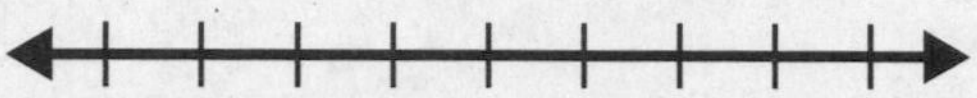

5. 10 feet below sea level ________

6. 3 centimeter increase in height ________

Write an integer to represent each situation. Then write its opposite.

7. withdrawal of $50 from bank account ________________

8. received $5 allowance ________________

9. speed increase of 15 mph ________________

10. 30 seconds before lift-off ________________

Describe a situation that can be represented by the integer.

11. –17 ________________________________

12. +$27 ________________________________

13. +45 ________________________________

14. –9 ________________________________

Name ________________________ Date ____________

12–6

Reteach

Units of Temperature

Two common temperature scales are the Celsius (°C) and Fahrenheit (°F) scales.

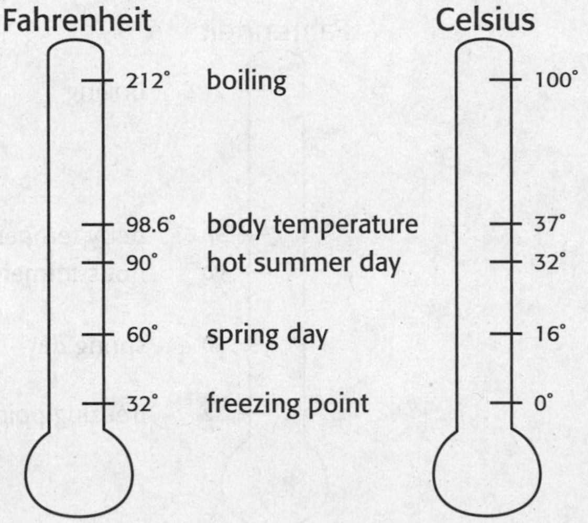

The boiling point of water is 100°C or 212°F.

The freezing point of water is 0°C or 32°F.

Which is a more reasonable temperature for a warm summer day: 75°F or 40°F?

Since 40°F is close to the freezing point of water, 75°F is the more reasonable temperature for a warm summer day.

In the morning the temperature was 15°C. By the afternoon, the temperature had risen to 28°C. Find the change in temperature. Use an integer to represent the change.

change in temperature = higher temperature − lower temperature

= 28° − 15°

= 13°

Ther temperature increased 13 degrees. The change can be represented by the integer +13 or 13.

Choose the more reasonable temperature for each situation. Use the thermometers above if needed.

1. glass of juice: 6°C or −20°C ________

2. a winter snowfall: 35°F or 35°C ________

3. hot water: 150°F or 50°F ________

4. cup of hot coffee: 82°C or 82°F ________

Find each change in temperature. Use an integer to represent the change.

5. 28°C to 42°C ________

6. 82°F to 64°F ________

7. 45°F to 57°F ________

8. 37°C to 12°C ________

Name ______________________ Date ______________

12–6 Skills Practice

Units of Temperature

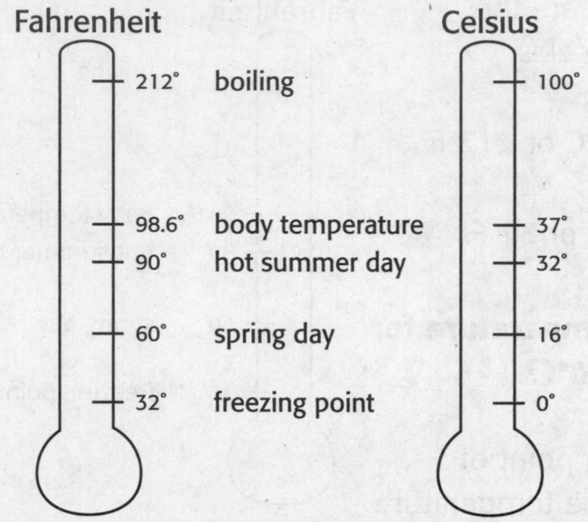

Choose the more reasonable temperature for each situation. Use the above thermometers if needed.

1. comfortable room temperature: 68°C or 68°F ______________

2. cup of hot chocolate: 75°C or 25°C ______________

3. warm day: 27°C or 27°F ______________

4. glass of cold milk: 55°C or 55°F ______________

5. icy day: 40°F or 65°F ______________

6. body temperature: 98°F or 198°F ______________

Find each change in temperature. Use an integer to represent the change.

7. 77°F to 90°F ________

8. 21°C to 0°C ________

9. 35°F to 79°F ________

10. 14°C to 26°C ________

11. 78°F to 24°F ________

12. 22°C to 17°C ________

12–7

Name ______________________ Date ______________

Reteach

Problem-Solving Investigation: Choose the Best Strategy

Dominique made invitations on her computer for a party. She distributed $\frac{1}{2}$ of the invitations, while her friend gave out 11. There are 5 more invitations that need to be delivered. How many invitations were there to begin with?

Step 1 Understand	**Be sure you understand the problem.** Read carefully. What facts do you know? • Dominique distributed ______ of the invitations. • Her friend gave out ______ invitations. • There are ______ invitations that still need to be delivered. What do you need to find? • The ________________ there were to begin with.
Step 2 Plan Choose a Strategy • Logical reasoning • Make an organized list • Determine reasonable answers • Use logical reasoning	**Make a plan.** Choose a strategy. You can work backward to solve the problem. Start with the number of invitations that still need to be delivered. Add the number of invitations that Dominique's friend gave out. Double the sum to find the number of invitations there were to begin with.

12–7

Name ______________________ Date __________

Reteach

Problem-Solving Investigation: Choose the Best Strategy (continued)

Step 3 Solve	**Carry out your plan.** Add the number of invitations that still need to be delivered and the number of invitations that Dominique's friend gave out. _____ + _____ = _____ So, there were _____ invitations left after Dominique distributed her invitations. Think: Dominique distributed _____ of the invitations. If there are _____ left over, they are the other half. Add the number of invitations that Dominique distributed to the number of invitations left after she distributed hers. _____ + _____ = _____ How many invitations were there to begin with? ______________________
Step 4 Check	**Is the solution reasonable?** Reread the problem. How can you check your answer by working forward? ______________________ ______________________ ______________________ ______________________

Practice

1. The coach gives uniforms to $\frac{1}{2}$ of the players on a soccer team. Brad helps out, giving uniforms to 3 players. James gives the remaining uniforms to 5 players. How many players are on the soccer team?

   ____

2. Leslie is $\frac{1}{2}$ as old as Carey. Carey is 2 years older than Jennifer. Jennifer is 18 years old. How old is Leslie?

   ____

12–7

Name ______________________ Date ____________

Skills Practice

Problem-Solving Investigation: Choose the Best Strategy

Use any strategy to solve each problem.

1. Matt bought a tennis racket that usually costs $73.95. He had a coupon for a discount of *d* dollars. The net price of the racket with the discount was *c* dollars. Write an equation to find the cost after the discount.

____

2. Michael needs to arrive at school at 8:15 A.M. It takes him 20 minutes to walk to school, 15 minutes to eat breakfast, and 50 minutes to get ready. What time does he need to set his alarm clock for to get to school on time?

____

3. Joel, Santiago, and Tiffani each have a different pet: a hamster, a dog, and some fish. Joel likes to play fetch with his pet and Santiago does not own the dog or the fish. Who owns which pet?

____

4. Emile is thinking of three consecutive numbers that add up to 75. What are the numbers?

____

5. Brooke is making a necklace in which the first, fifth, ninth, and thirteenth beads are blue and the rest of the first 15 beads are not blue. If the necklace continues this pattern and has 50 beads in all, how many of them will be blue?

____

6. At Joseph's birthday party, everyone shook hands with everyone else. If there were a total of 21 handshakes, how many people were at the party?

____

Name ______________________ Date __________

13–1

Reteach

Geometry Vocabulary

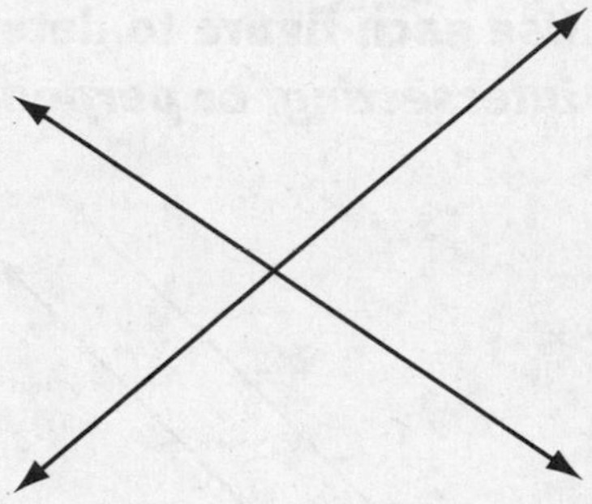

Look at the lines at the right.

Are these lines *parallel, intersecting,* or *perpendicular*?

Choose the most specific term.

You have three answer choices. Ask yourself questions to help choose the right answer.

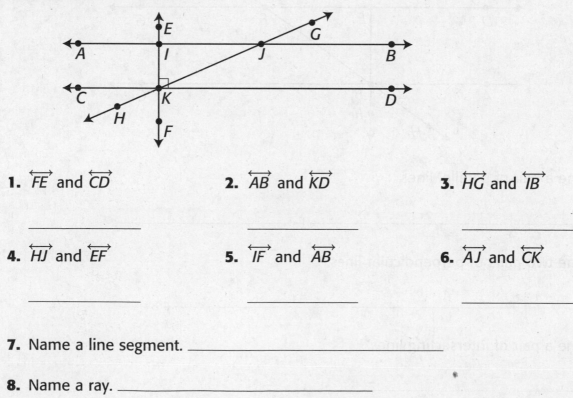

- Do the lines cross, or *intersect*, at a point? ______ If you answered yes, the lines are not parallel. If you answered no, they are.
- Do the lines form a right angle? ______ If you answered no, the lines are not perpendicular. If you answered yes, they are.
- If you answered *yes* to Question 1 and *no* to Question 2, then the lines must be *intersecting*.

Use the figure to determine if each pair of lines is *parallel, perpendicular,* or *neither*.

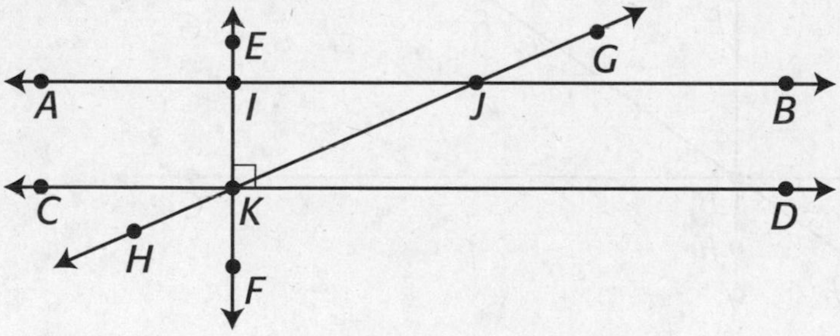

1. $\overleftrightarrow{FE}$ and $\overleftrightarrow{CD}$ ______

2. $\overleftrightarrow{AB}$ and $\overleftrightarrow{KD}$ ______

3. $\overleftrightarrow{HG}$ and $\overleftrightarrow{IB}$ ______

4. $\overleftrightarrow{HJ}$ and $\overleftrightarrow{EF}$ ______

5. $\overleftrightarrow{IF}$ and $\overleftrightarrow{AB}$ ______

6. $\overleftrightarrow{AJ}$ and $\overleftrightarrow{CK}$ ______

7. Name a line segment. ______________________

8. Name a ray. ______________________

Name ______________________ Date ______________

13–1

Skills Practice

Geometry Vocabulary

Use each figure to determine if the pair of lines is *parallel, intersecting,* or *perpendicular*. Choose the most specific term.

1.

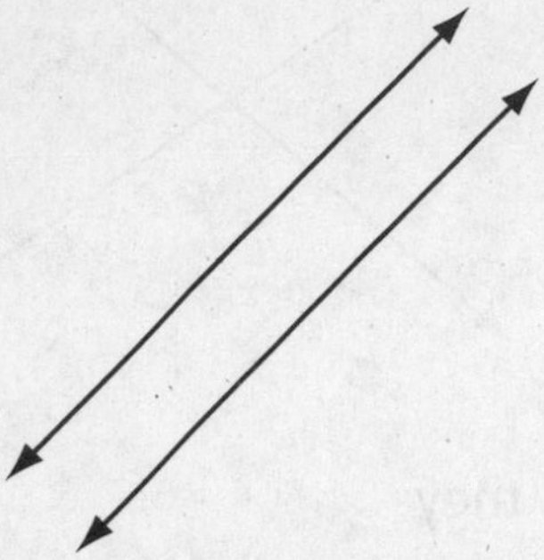

____

2.

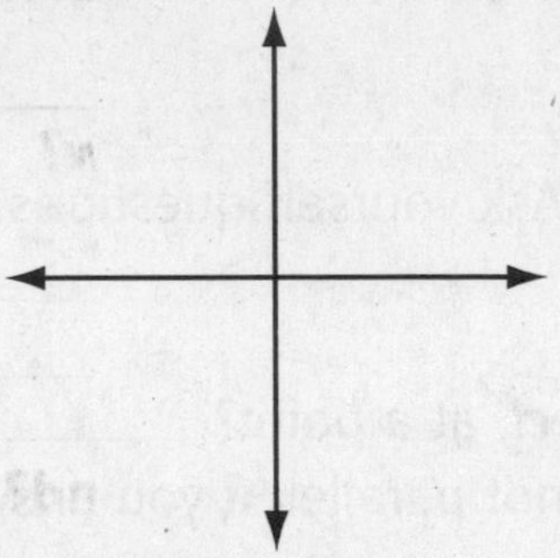

____

3.

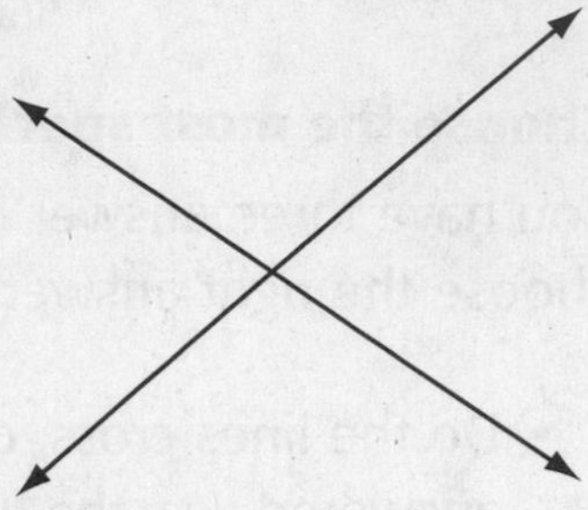

____

Use the figure for Exercises 4–6.

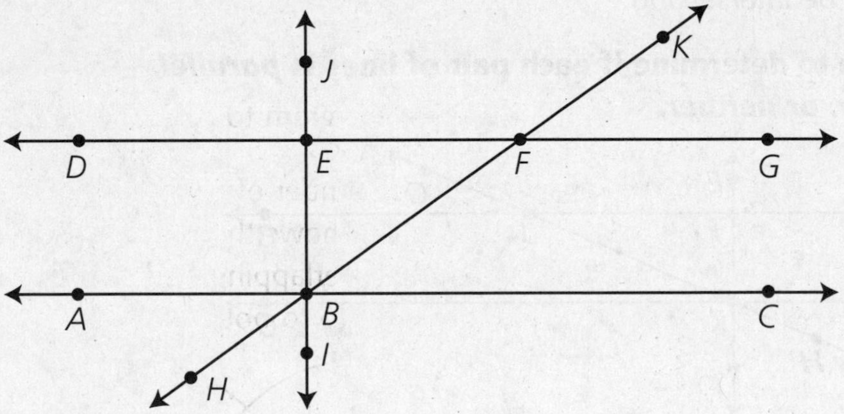

4. Name a pair of parallel lines.

____

5. Name two pairs of perpendicular lines.

____

6. Name a pair of intersecting lines.

____

Name ____________________ Date ____________

13–2 Reteach

Problem-Solving Strategy: Use Logical Reasoning

Of a group of people surveyed, 28 said they go to baseball games and 14 said they go to hockey games. Seven of the people said they go to both. How many people said they go to hockey games but not baseball games?

<table>
<tr>
<td>Step 1
Understand</td>
<td>What facts do you know?

• Of those surveyed, ______ go to baseball games, ______ go to hockey games, and ______ go to both types of games.

What do you need to find?

• The number of people ____________________
____________________</td>
</tr>
<tr>
<td>Step 2
Plan

• Logical reasoning
• Draw a picture or diagram
• Make a graph
• Act it out
• Make a table
• Look for a pattern
• Guess and check
• Work backward
• Solve a simpler problem</td>
<td>Make a plan.

Choose a strategy.

You can draw a Venn diagram to solve the problem.

One circle shows the number of people who go to baseball games. The other circle shows the number of people who go to hockey games. The overlapping part of the circles shows the number of people who go to both.

</td>
</tr>
</table>

Name ______________________ Date ____________

13–2

Reteach

Problem-Solving Strategy: Use Logical Reasoning (continued)

<table>
<tr><td>Step 3
Solve</td><td>Carry out your plan. How many people go to both types of games? Write the number in the overlapping section of the Venn diagram.
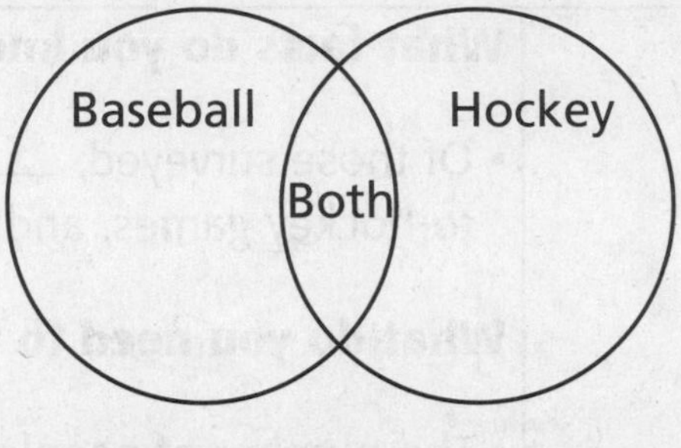

The two sections of the circle for hockey must add up to 14. You can write and solve an equation to find the number of people who only go to hockey games.

Let x = ______________________

Use the Venn diagram. So, ______ + ______ = ______

Solve the equation and complete the Venn diagram. ______

How many people go to hockey games, but not baseball games? ______________________</td></tr>
<tr><td>Step 4
Check</td><td>Is the solution reasonable? Look back. Have you answered the question? ______

How can you check your answer?

______________________</td></tr>
</table>

Solve.

1. Of 25 pet owners surveyed, 16 have a dog and 12 have a cat. Three people have both a cat and a dog. How many of the pet owners have only dogs?

____

13–2

Name ____________________ Date ____________

Skills Practice

Problem-Solving Strategy: Use Logical Reasoning

1. Of 26 people surveyed, 19 said they go to basketball games and 12 said they go to football games. Five of the people said they go to both. How many people said they go to basketball games, but not to football games?

   ____

2. Of 40 teachers surveyed, 34 said they listen to classical music and 17 said they listen to opera. Eleven of the teachers said they listen to both classical music and opera. How many teachers listen to classical music, but not to opera?

   ____

3. Of 24 students surveyed, 17 students said they like board games and 12 said they like card games. Five students said they like both. How many students said they like board games, but not card games?

   ____

4. Of the 50 people surveyed at a recreation center, 32 said they used the basketball courts and 24 said they used the racquetball courts. Six of the people said they used both courts. How many people said they use the racquetball courts, but not the basketball courts?

   ____

5. Nathan wants to buy trading cards. Superstar packages cost $3.23 each and mixed packages cost $1.78 each. Nathan buys 7 packages and spends a total of $15.36. How many of each type of package did he buy?

   ____

6. An after-school club is building a clubhouse that is 8 feet by 6 feet. They are also including a trampoline with a radius of 4 feet. What is the total area of the clubhouse and the trampoline, to the nearest square foot?

   ____

7. A band is performing on a rectangular stage that is 36 feet by 24 feet. The manager wants to set up lights every 4 feet around the stage, including the corners. How many lights will he need?

   ____

8. Write a problem that you could use logical reasoning to solve. Share it with a classmate.

   ____

13–3

Name ______________________ Date ______________

Reteach

Triangles

You can classify triangles by the lengths of their sides.

equilateral

all sides congruent

isosceles

at least two sides congruent

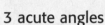

scalene

no sides congruent

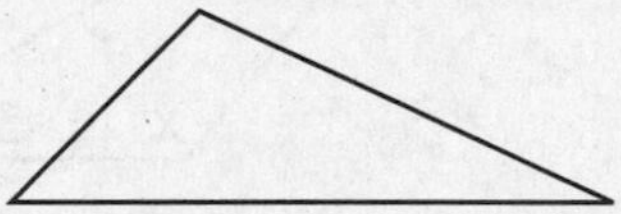

You can also classify triangles by the measures of their angles.

right

1 right angle

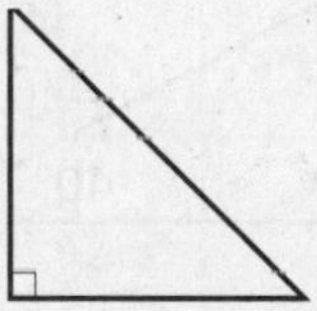

acute

3 acute angles

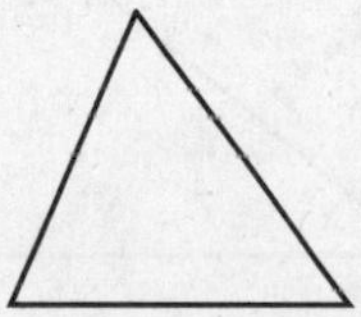

obtuse

1 obtuse angle

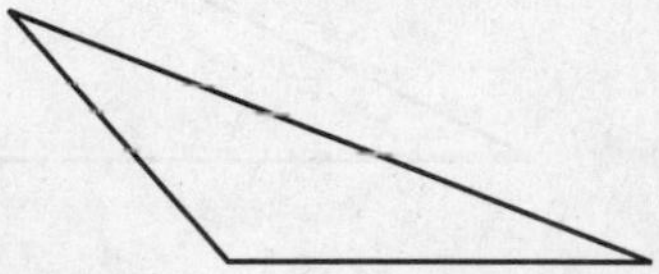

Circle the characteristics of each triangle. Then classify the triangle as *equilateral, isosceles,* or *scalene* and *right, acute,* or *obtuse.*

1. 3 congruent sides

2 congruent sides

no congruent sides

1 right angle

3 acute angles

1 obtuse angle

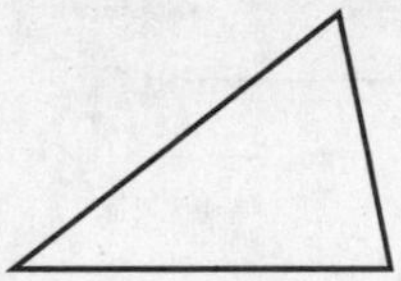

____

____

2. 3 congruent sides

2 congruent sides

no congruent sides

1 right angle

3 acute angles

1 obtuse angle

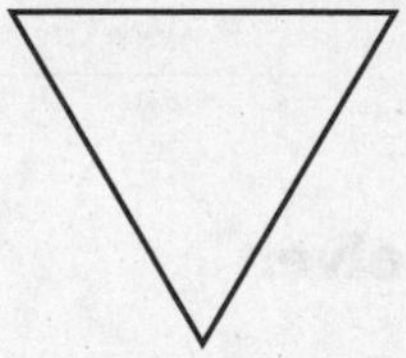

____

____

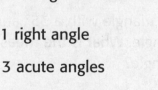

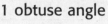

Name ______________________ Date ____________

13–3 Skills Practice

Triangles

Classify each triangle as *acute, right,* or *obtuse*. Then classify each triangle as *scalene, isosceles,* or *equilateral*.

1.

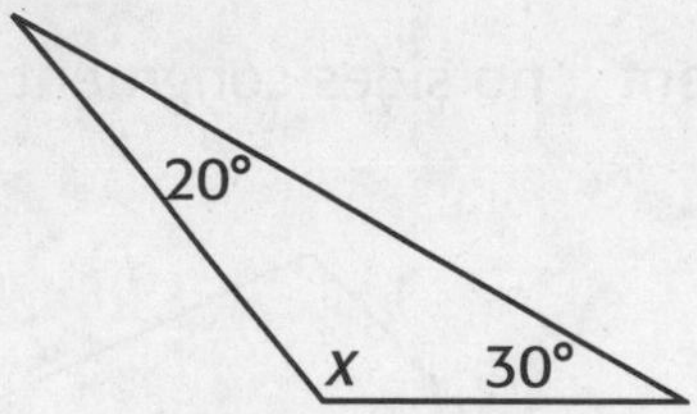

____

2.

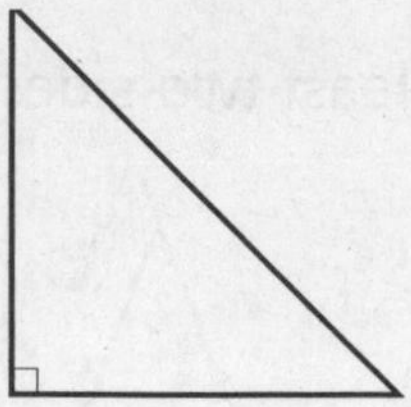

____

3.

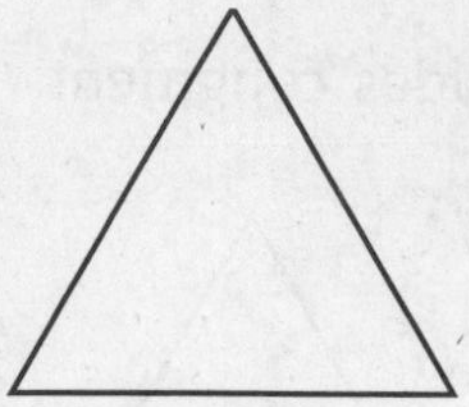

____

The sum of the measures of the angles of a triangle is 180°. Find the value of *x* in each triangle drawn or having the given angle measures.

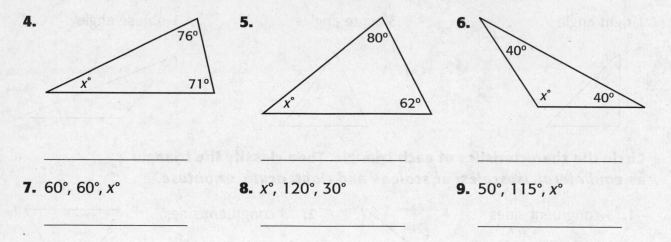

4.

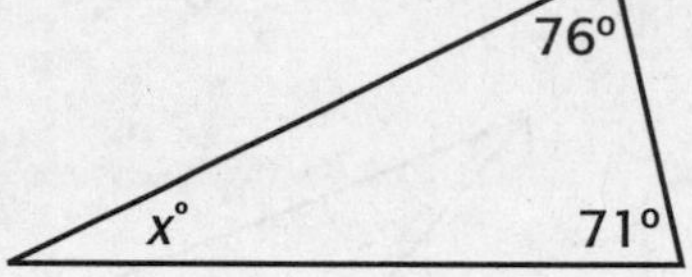

____

5.

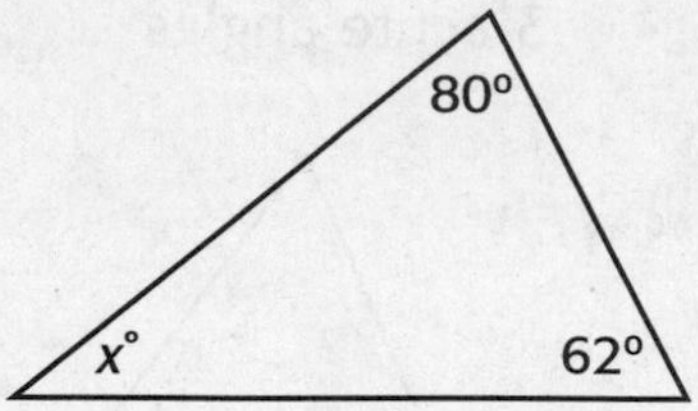

____

6.

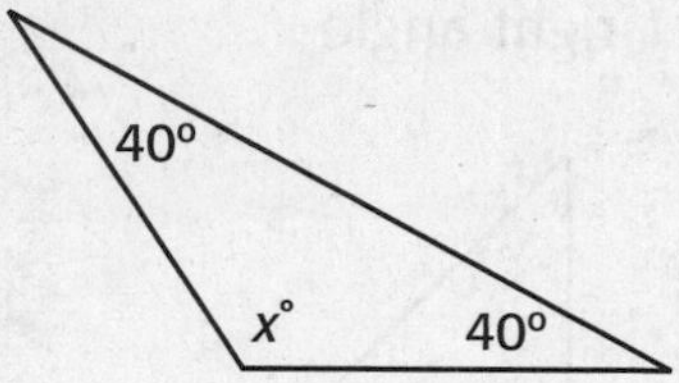

____

7. 60°, 60°, x°

____

8. x°, 120°, 30°

____

9. 50°, 115°, x°

____

Solve.

10. Tyler draws a triangle with a 35° angle and an 85° angle. What is the measure of the third angle?

____

11. Amber draws an obtuse triangle with a 110° angle. The other two angles are congruent. What are the measures of the other two angles?

____

13–4

Name ______________________ Date ______________

Reteach

Quadrilaterals

You can classify quadrilaterals by their sides and angles.

Parallelogram

opposite sides congruent

opposite sides parallel

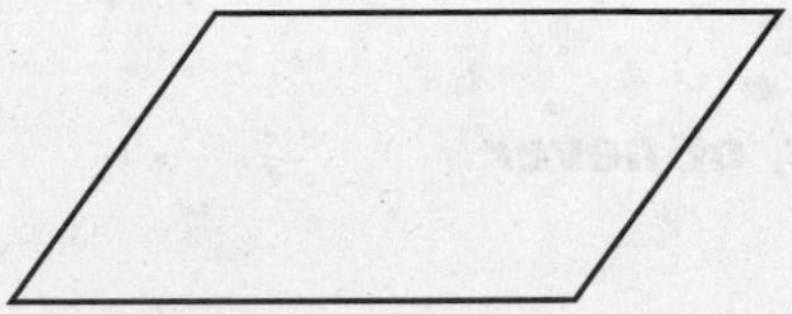

Rectangle

opposite sides congruent

opposite sides parallel

4 right angles

Square

all sides congruent

opposite sides parallel

4 right angles

Rhombus

all sides congruent, opposite sides parallel

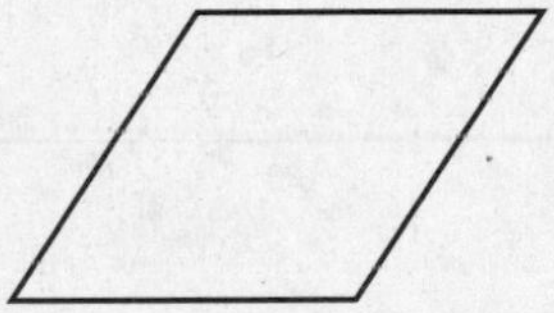

Trapezoid

exactly one pair of parallel sides

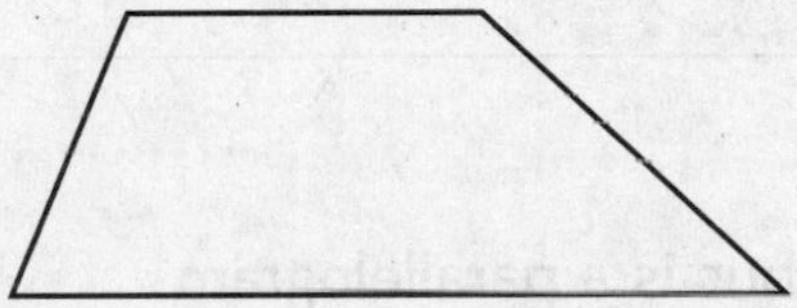

Circle the characteristics of each quadrilateral. Then classify the quadrilateral in as many ways as possible.

1.

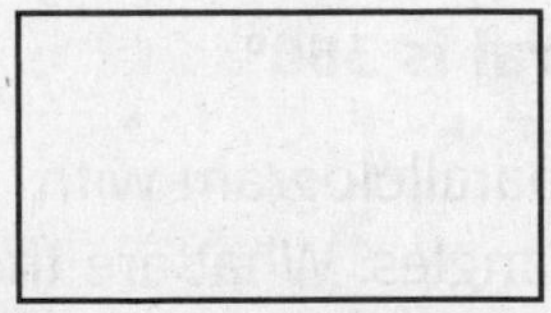

opposite sides congruent

all sides congruent

opposite sides parallel

exactly one pair of parallel sides

4 right angles

____

2.

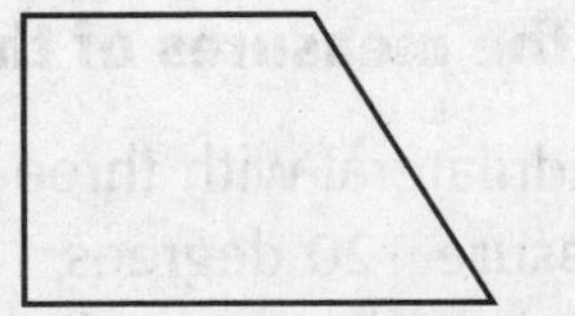

opposite sides congruent

all sides congruent

opposite sides parallel

exactly one pair of parallel sides

4 right angles

____

Name ________________________ Date ______________

13–4

Skills Practice

Quadrilaterals

What term best describes each quadrilateral?

1.

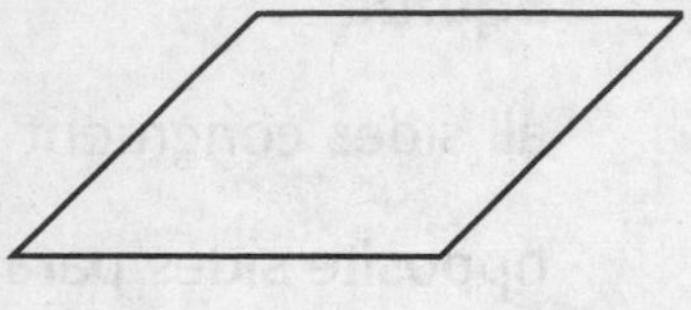

____

2.

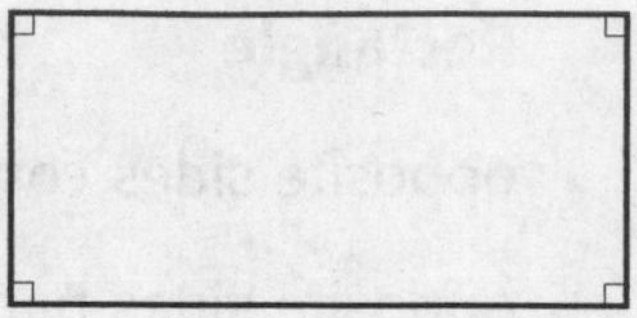

____

3.

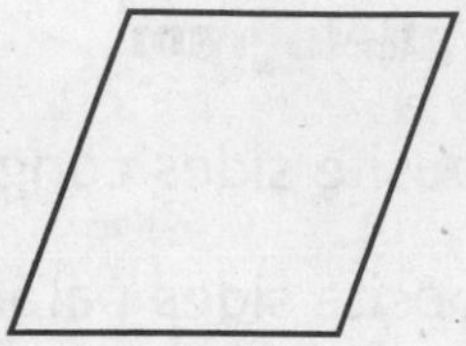

____

Determine whether each statement is *sometimes, always,* or *never* true. Explain your reasoning.

4. A square is a rhombus.

____

____

5. A trapezoid has exactly one pair of congruent sides.

____

____

6. A rhombus is a parallelogram.

____

____

Solve. The sum of the measures of the angles of a quadrilateral is 360°.

7. Lee drew a quadrilateral with three angles that measure 120 degrees, 110 degrees, and 70 degrees. What is the measure of the fourth angle?

____

8. Robert drew a parallelogram with two 55-degree angles. What are the measures of the other two angles?

____

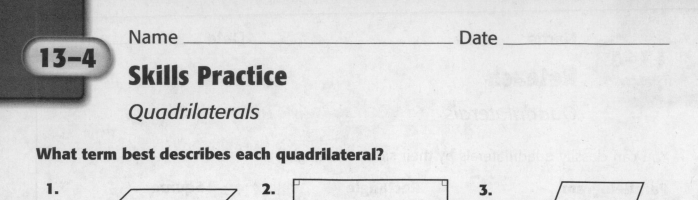

Name ______________________________ Date ______________

13–5

Reteach

Problem-Solving Investigation: Choose the Best Strategy

Which part of the pizza is larger, $\frac{3}{8}$ of the first pizza or $\frac{2}{6}$ of the second pizza?

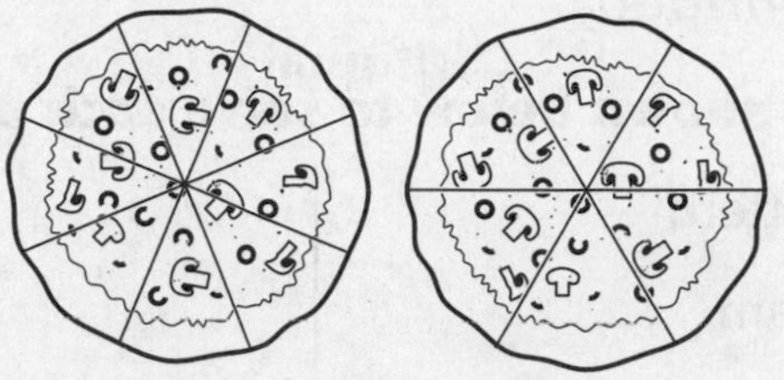

Step 1 Understand	Be sure you understand the problem. You need to compare the two parts of the pizzas, and find which one is larger.
Step 2 Plan • Look for a pattern • Draw a diagram • Guess and check	Make a plan. Choose a strategy. You already have a diagram of the two pizzas. You can also use the four-step plan. Decide what facts you know. Plan what you will do and in what order. Use your plan to solve the problem. Then check your solution to make sure it makes sense.
Step 3 Solve	Carry out your plan. The pizza parts are close in size, so change each fraction to an equivalent fraction with a like denominator. The least common denominator of 8 and 6 is 24. $\frac{3}{8} = \frac{3 \times 3}{8 \times 3} = \frac{9}{24}$ $\frac{2}{6} = \frac{2 \times 4}{6 \times 4} = \frac{8}{24}$ Since $\frac{9}{24} > \frac{8}{24}$, $\frac{3}{8} > \frac{2}{6}$.
Step 4 Check	Is the solution reasonable? Reread the problem. How can you check your answer? ____________________ ______________________________

Name ______________________ Date ____________

13–5

Reteach

Problem-Solving Investigation: Choose the Best Strategy (continued)

Use any strategy shown below to solve each problem.

- Look for a pattern
- Draw a diagram
- Guess and check

1. Which is more, $\frac{7}{8}$ of an apple pie or $\frac{8}{9}$ of the same pie?

____

2. On Monday, Veronica had 20 minutes of homework. On Tuesday, she had 30 minutes, and on Wednesday, she had 40 minutes. If the pattern continues, how much homework will she have on Friday?

____

3. Charo is three times as old as Lorena. In 5 years, Lorena will be half Charo's age. How old are Lorena and Charo now?

____

4. Justin has 6 shirts and 5 pairs of pants. If he wears a different combination each day, how many days will pass before he has to repeat a combination?

____

5. An artist drew a circle, two lines, and a triangle. Then the artist drew another two lines. What shape will the artist draw next?

____

6. At a party, everyone said hello to everyone else exactly once. There were a total of 28 pairs of "hellos" in the room. How many people were at the party?

____

Name ______________________ Date ______________

13–5

Skills Practice

Problem-Solving Investigation: Choose the Best Strategy

Use any strategy shown below to solve each problem.

- Look for a pattern
- Draw a diagram
- Guess and check

Use the picture to answer Exercises 1 and 2.

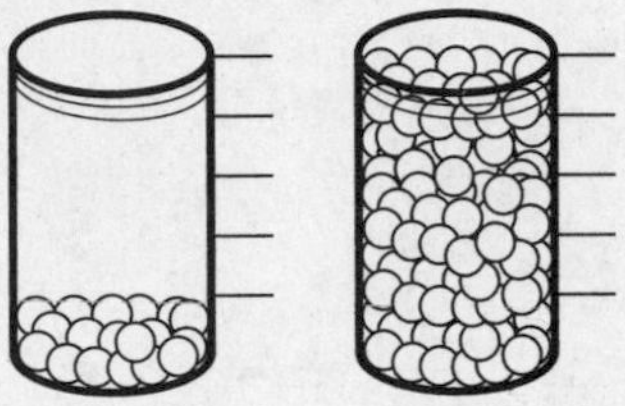

1. Suppose there are 125 marbles in the jar on the right and 25 marbles in the jar on the left. Write a fraction to show the empty part of the first container. Assume the jar on the right is full.

____

2. What fraction represents the difference between the amounts in each container?

____

3. In 2006 you sold 25 rolls of wrapping paper for a fundraiser. In 2007 you sold 30 rolls. If the trend continues, how many rolls will you sell in 2008?

____

4. Look at the pattern below. What are the next three bugs?
ladybug, ladybug, bee, ant, ladybug, ladybug, bee, ant, ladybug

____

13–6

Name ______________________ Date ______________

Reteach

Translations and Graphs

A **translation** is a type of transformation, or movement of a figure. Sliding a figure in a straight line – horizontally, vertically, or diagonally – is called a translation. To translate a figure, move all the vertices in the same direction for the same distance.

Triangle *ABC* has vertices at *A*(5, 2), *B*(7, 6), and *C*(9, 4). Graph △*ABC* and its translation 3 units left and 2 units up. Write the ordered pairs for the new vertices.

Step 1: Graph the original triangle.

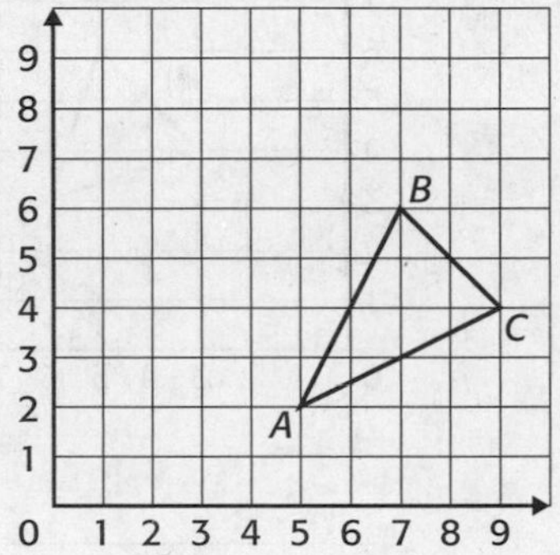

Step 2: Graph the translated image.

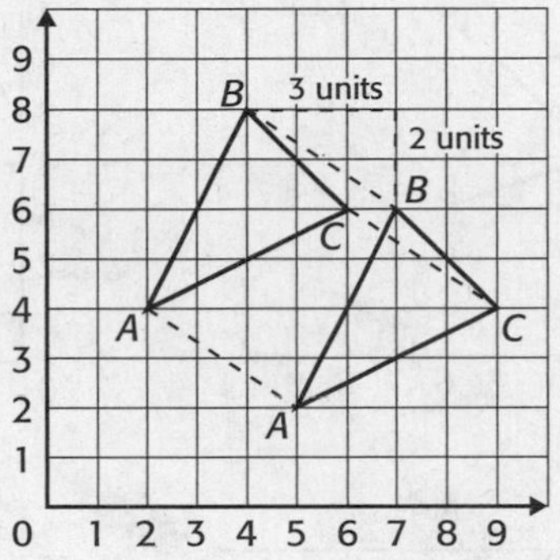

Step 3: Locate the new vertices.

The new vertices are at *A*(2, 4), *B*(4, 8), and *C*(6, 6).

A triangle has vertices (2, 3), (3, 5), and (6, 3). Graph the image after each translation. Then write the ordered pairs for the new vertices.

1. 2 units left

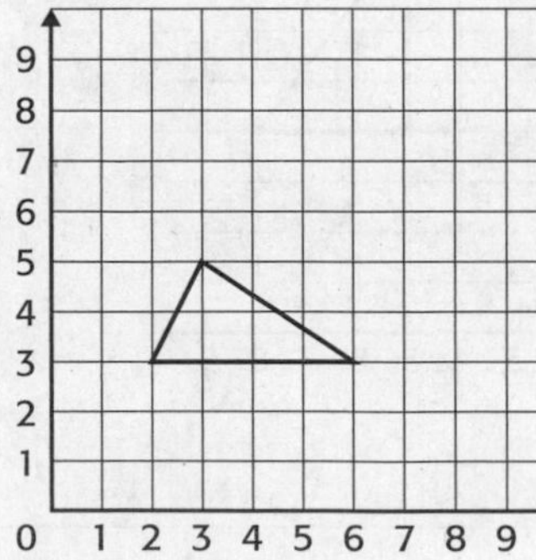

____

2. 3 units down

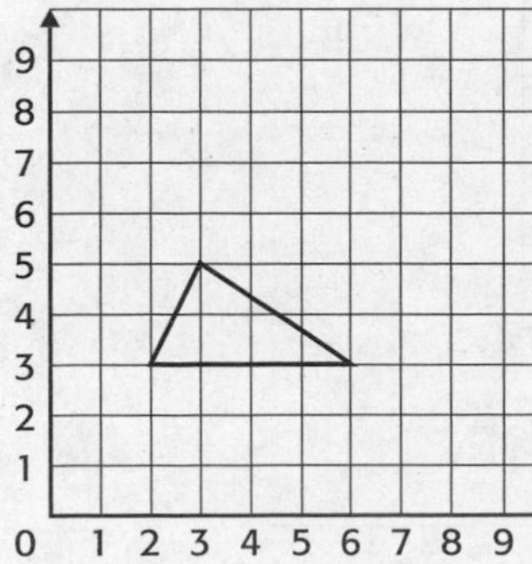

____

3. 3 units right, 5 units up

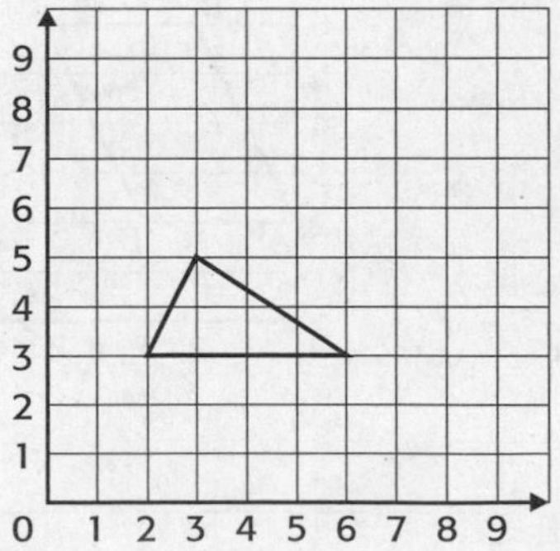

____

Name ______________________________ Date ____________

13–6

Skills Practice

Translations and Graphs

A triangle has vertices (3, 4), (5, 6), and (6, 3). Graph the triangle. Then graph the image after each translation. Then write the ordered pairs for the new vertices.

1. 3 units right

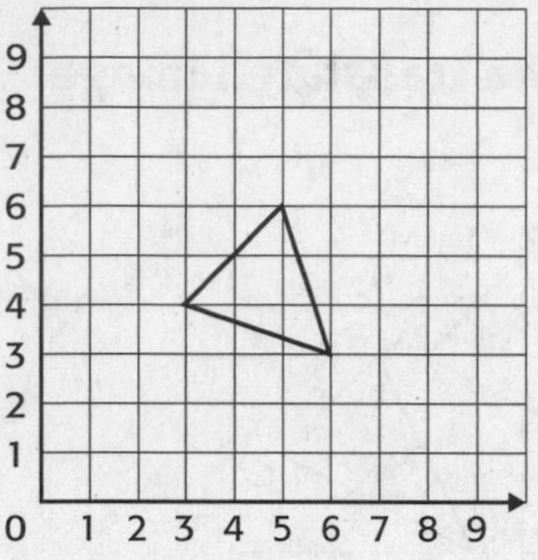

____

2. 4 units up

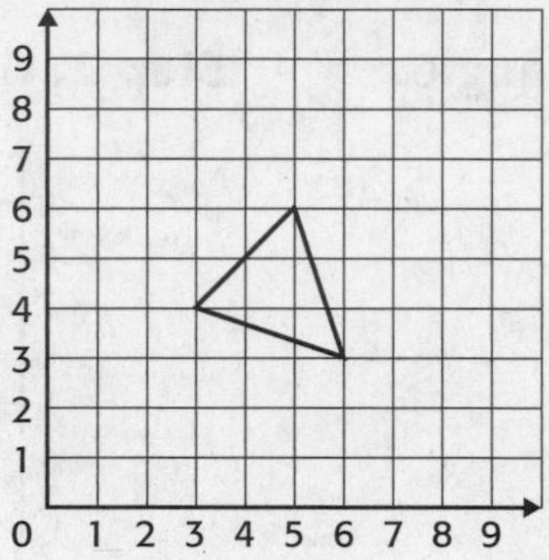

____

3. 1 unit left, 3 units down

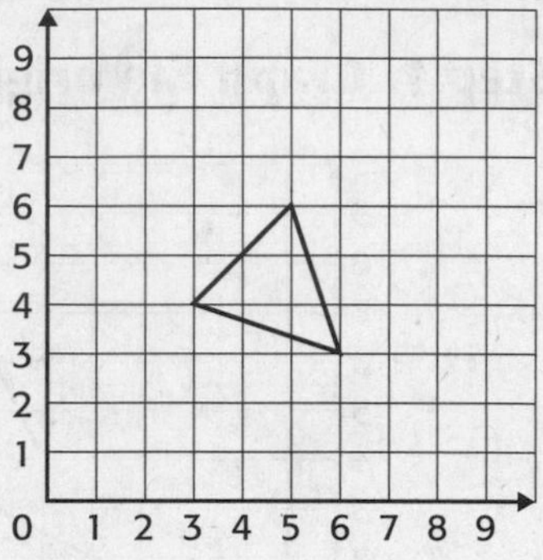

____

Graph each figure and the translation described. Write the ordered pairs for the new vertices.

4. quadrilateral *ABCD* with vertices A(0, 2), *B*(2, 6), *C*(5, 6), *D*(3, 2); translated 4 units right

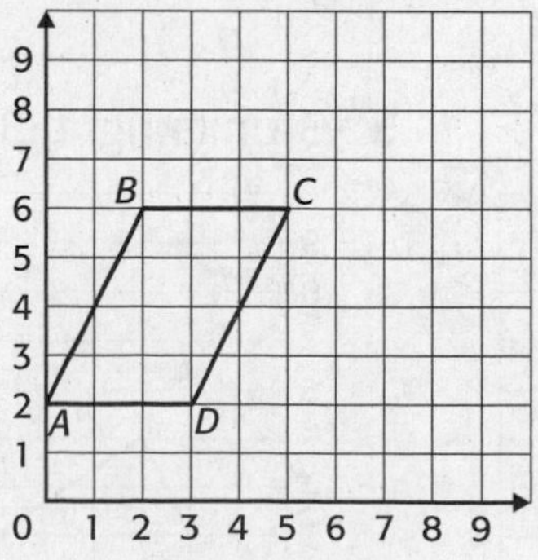

____

5. triangle *FGH* with vertices *F*(5, 5), *G*(5, 9), *H*(8, 5); translated 3 units left, 1 unit down

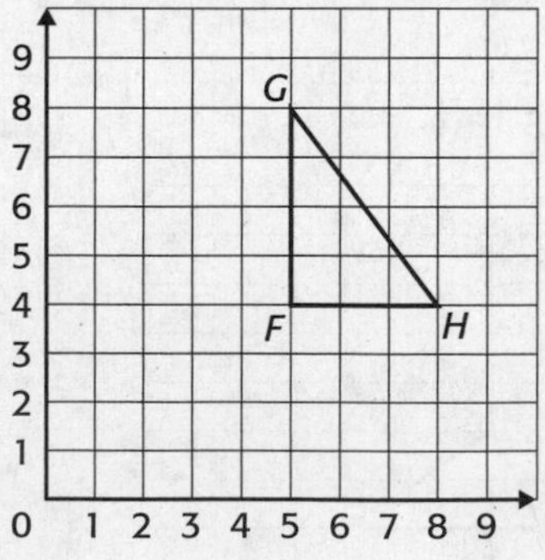

____

Name ______________________ Date ____________

13–7 Reteach

Reflections and Graphs

A **reflection** is another transformation that does not change the size or shape of a figure. In a reflection, a figure is flipped over a line to create a mirror image of the figure. The line is called a **line of reflection**. The corresponding vertices of a figure and its reflection are the same distance from the line of reflection.

To sketch a reflection across a horizontal line:

Step 1: Graph the original figure.

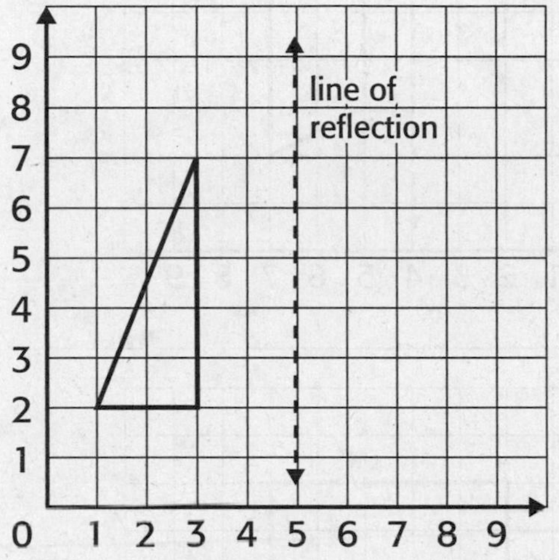

Step 2: Graph the reflected image.

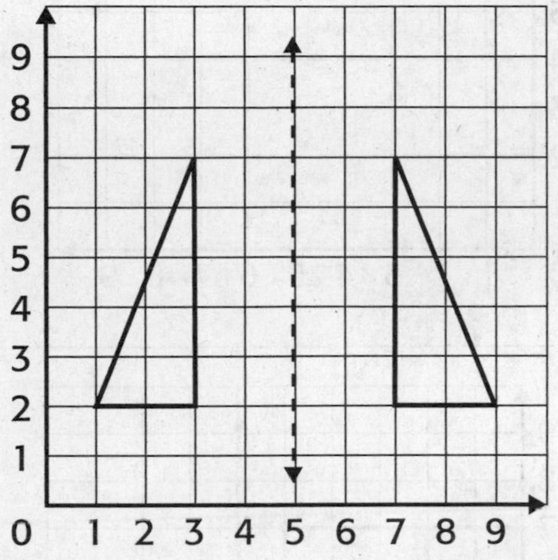

Step 3: Locate the new vertices.

The new vertices are at (7, 2), (7, 7), and (9, 2).

Graph each image after a reflection across the line. Then write the ordered pairs for the new vertices.

1.

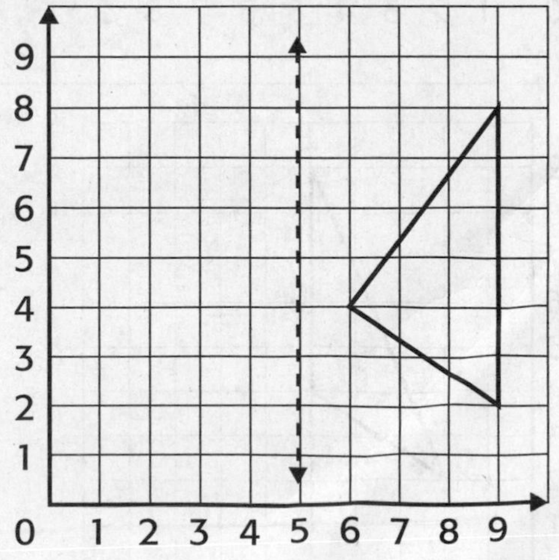

____

2.

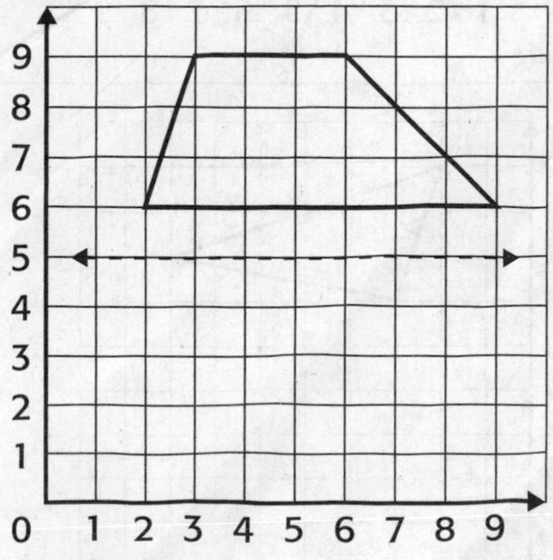

____

Name ______________________ Date ______________

13–7 Skills Practice

Reflections and Graphs

Graph each figure after a reflection across the line. Then write the ordered pairs for the new vertices.

1.

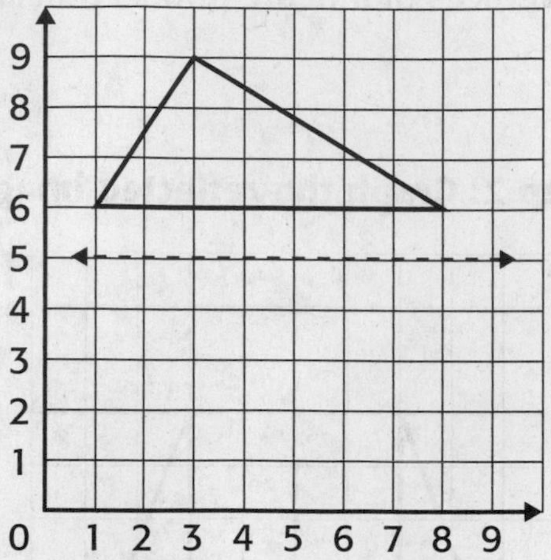

2.

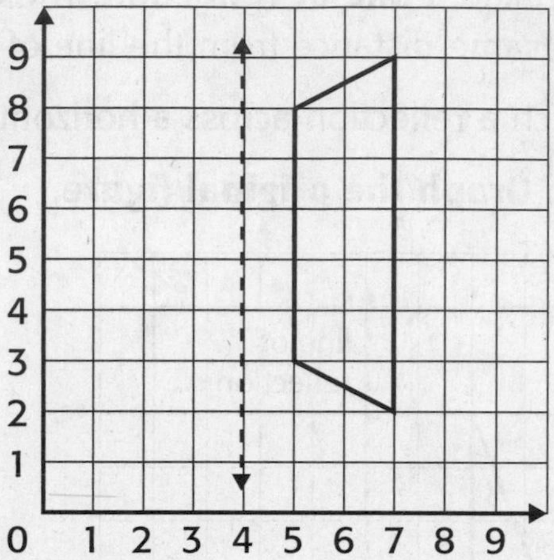

3.

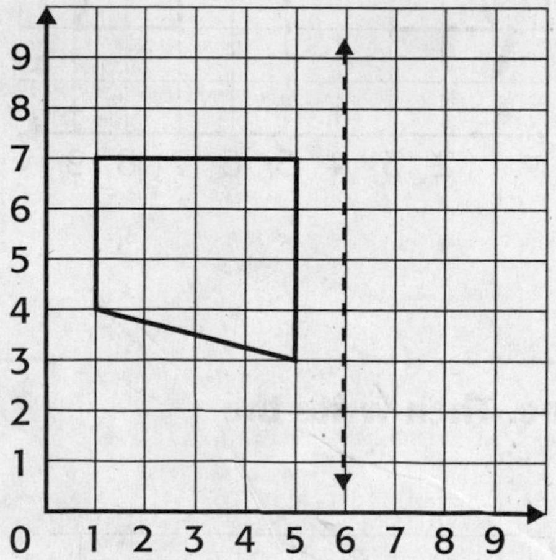

4.

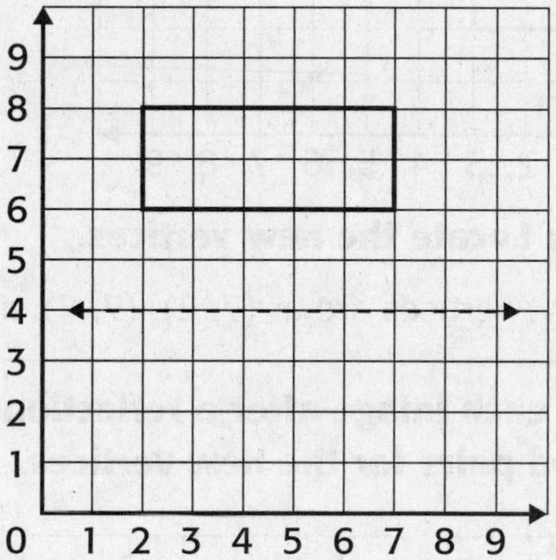

5.

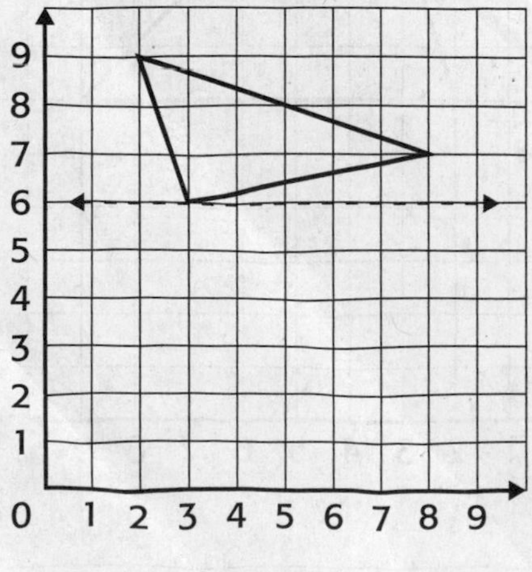

6.

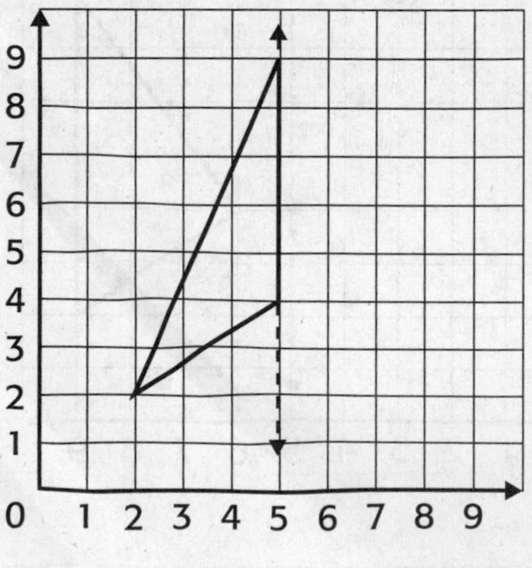

Name ____________________ Date ____________

13–8

Reteach

Rotations and Graphs

A **rotation** is another kind of transformation that does not change the size or shape of a figure. In a rotation, a figure is rotated around a point.

To sketch a rotation:

Step 1: Graph the original figure.

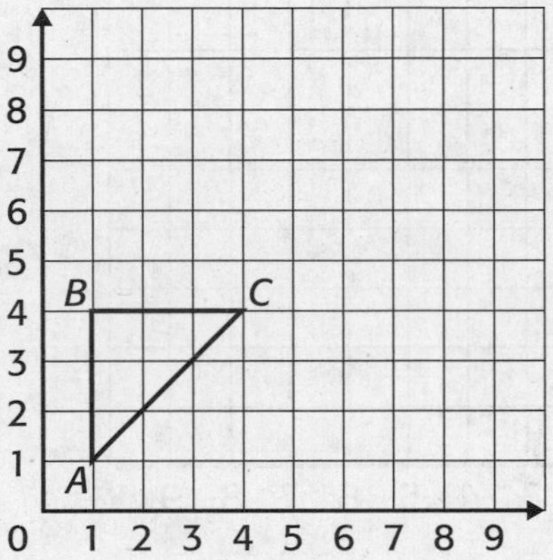

Step 2: Graph the rotated image.

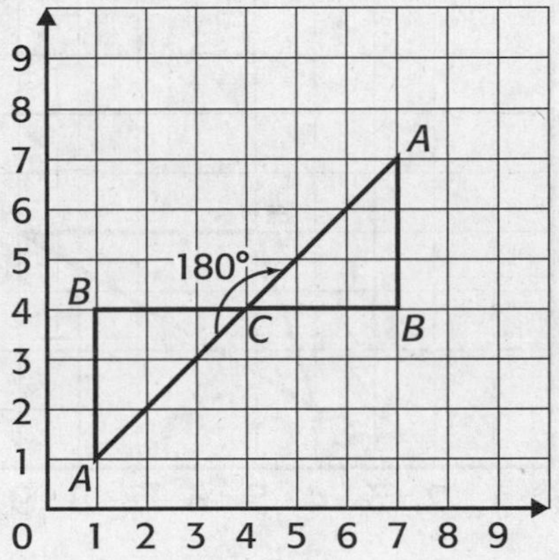

Step 3: Locate the new vertices.

The new figure has vertices at *A*(7, 7), *B*(7, 4), and *C*(4, 4).

Graph the triangle after each rotation. Then write the ordered pairs for the new vertices.

1. 90° clockwise about point *A*

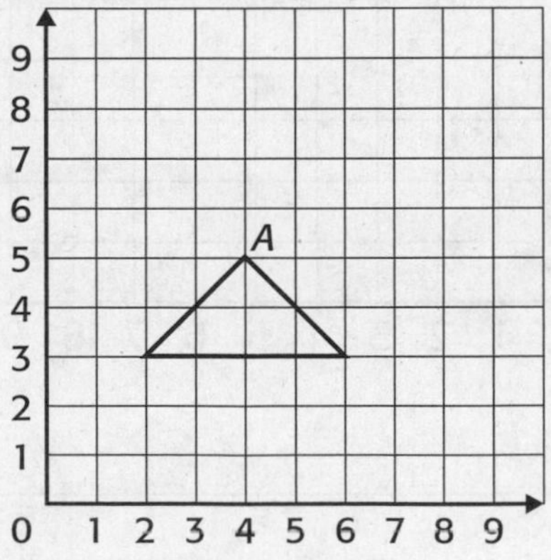

____

2. 180° counterclockwise about point *C*

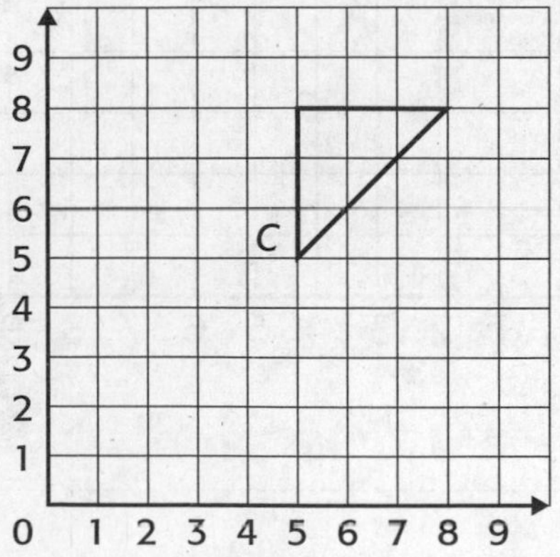

____

Name ______________________ Date ______________

13–8

Skills Practice

Rotations and Graphs

For Exercises 1–3, graph triangle *ABC*. Then graph the rotation image. Write the ordered pairs for the new vertices.

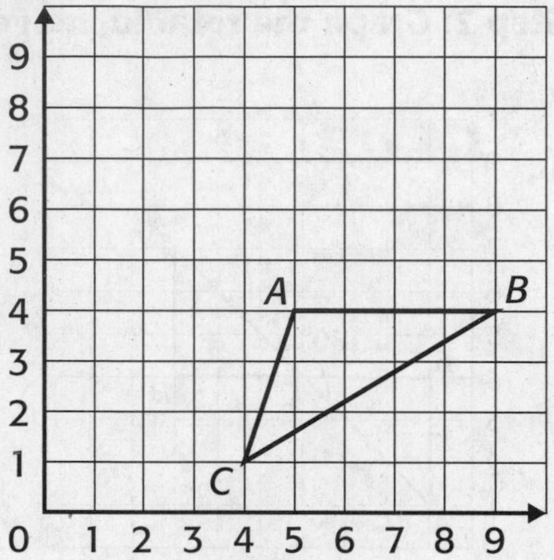

1. 90° counterclockwise about point *A*

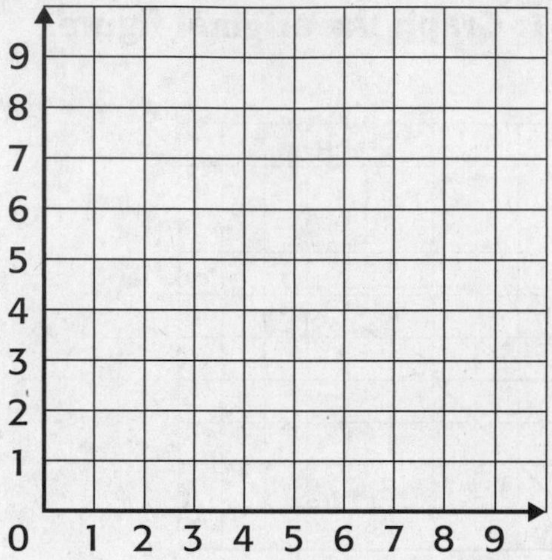

____

2. 180° clockwise about point *A*

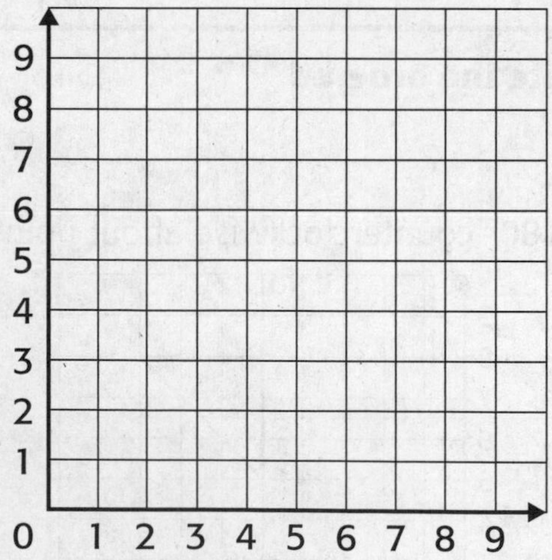

____

3. 90° counterclockwise about point *C*

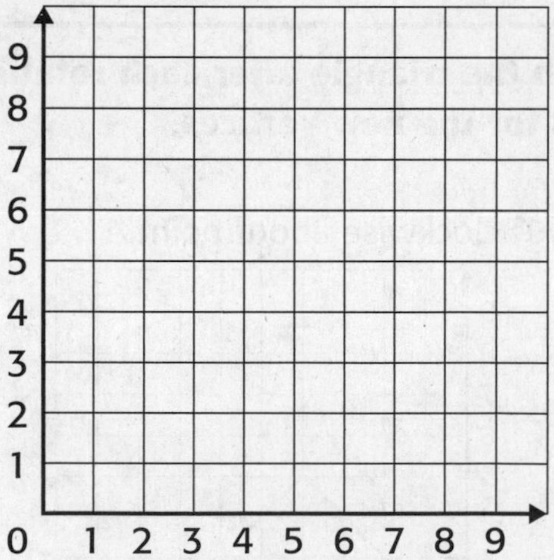

____

Name ______________________________ Date ______________

13–9

Reteach

Identify Transformations

You can transform figures by using translations, reflections, or rotations.

In a **translation,** a figure **slides** along a line.

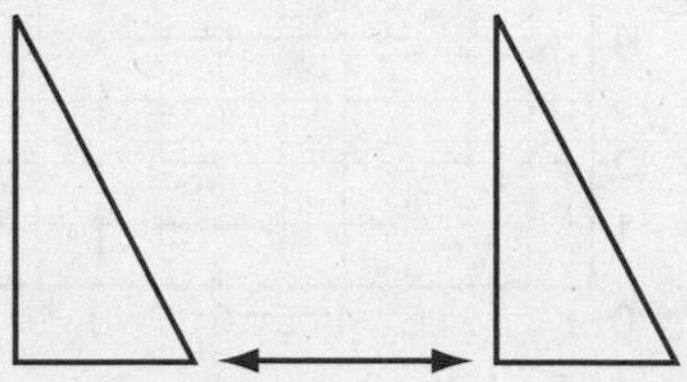

In a **reflection**, a figure **flips** over a line.

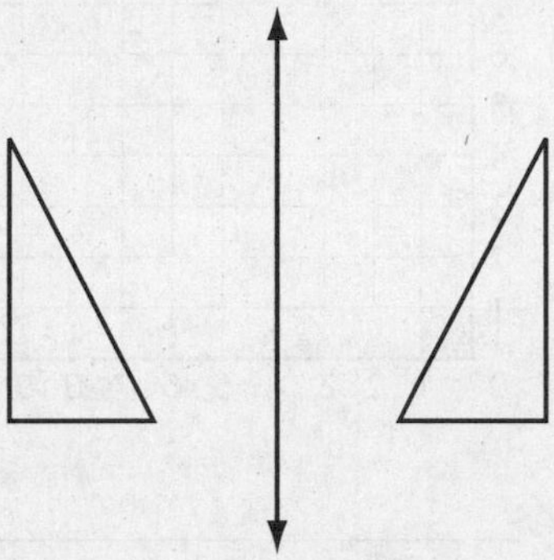

In a **rotation**, a figure **turns** around a point.

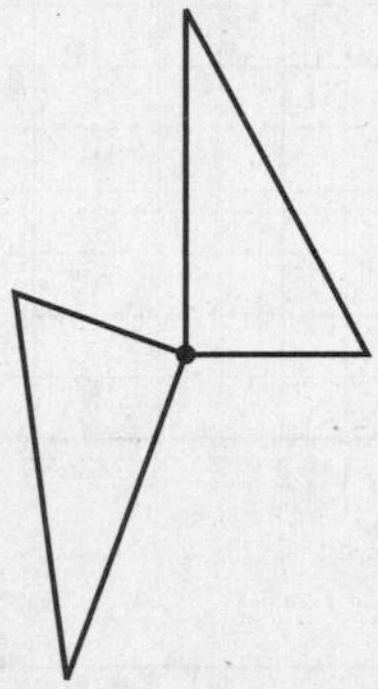

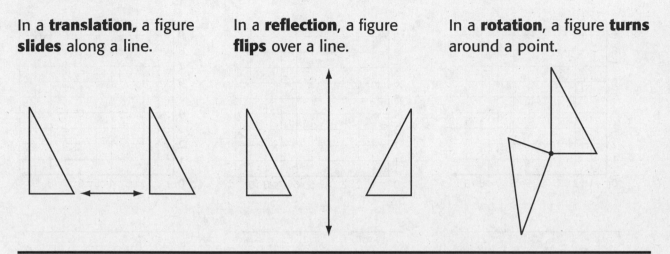

Complete the statement about each transformation that was made.

1.

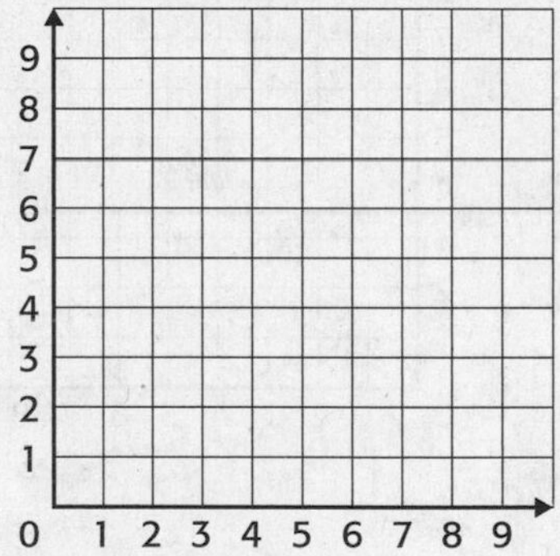

The figure was ____________ over an imaginary line, creating a ____________.

2.

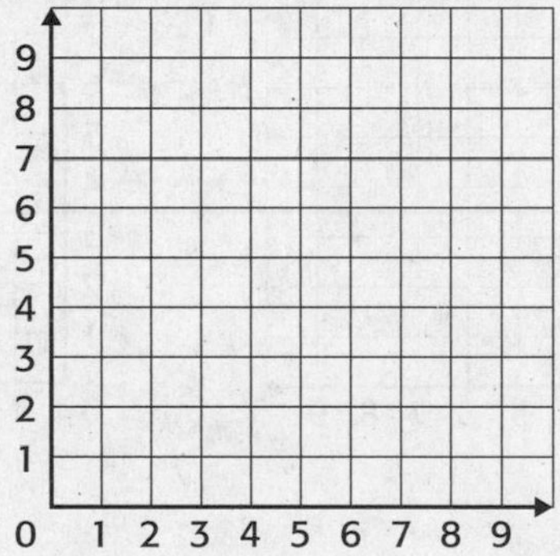

The figure was ___________ around a __________, to form a ______________.

Determine whether each transformation is a *translation, reflection,* or *rotation*.

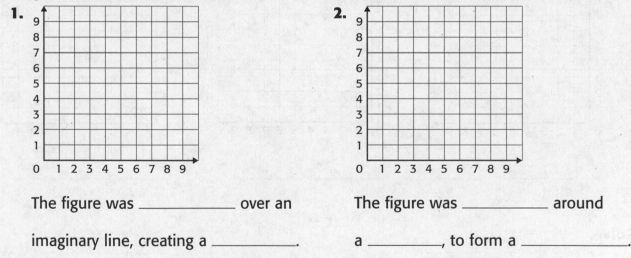

3.

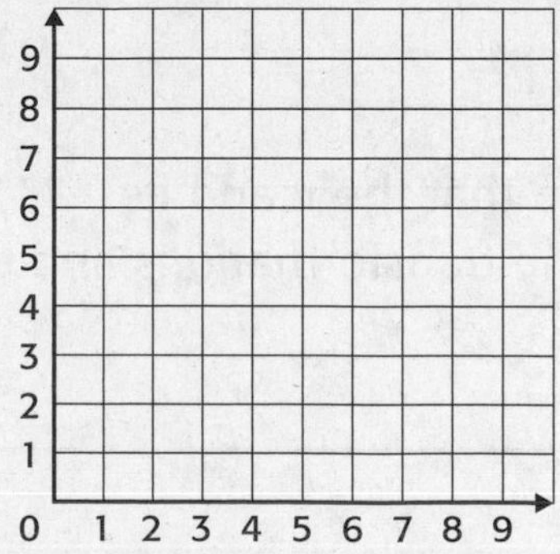

____

4.

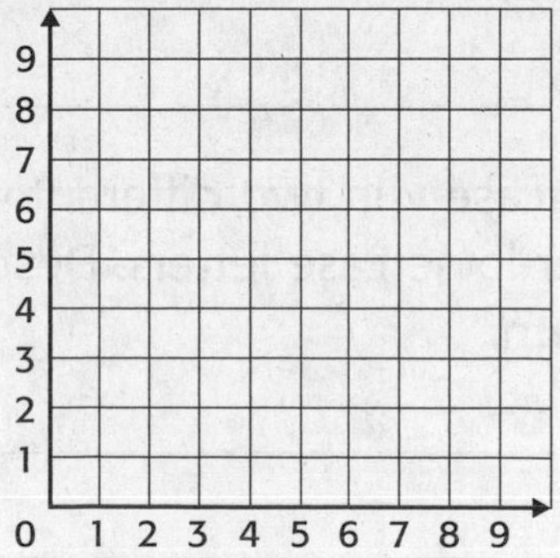

____

5.

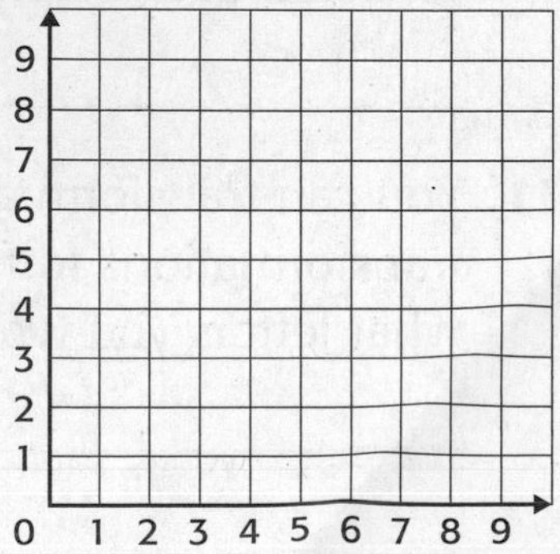

____

Name ______________________ Date ____________

13–9

Skills Practice

Identify Transformations

Determine whether each transformation is a *translation, reflection,* or *rotation.*

1.

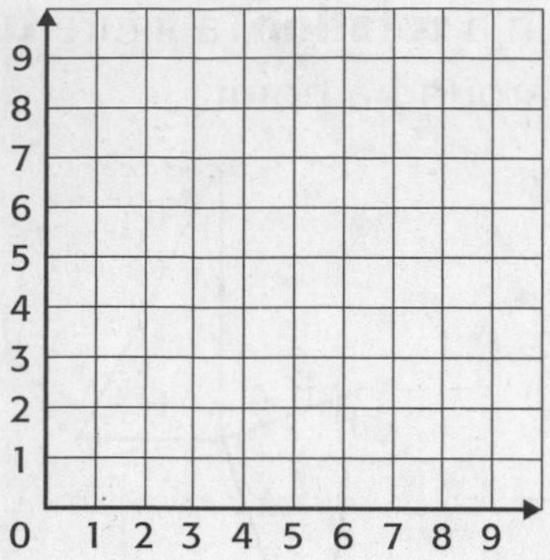

____

2.

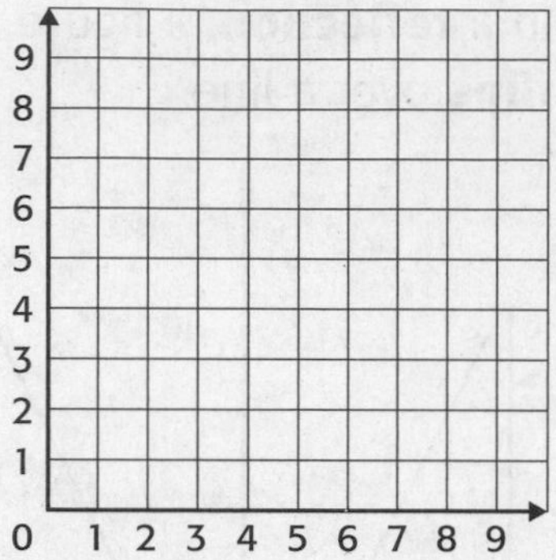

____

6.

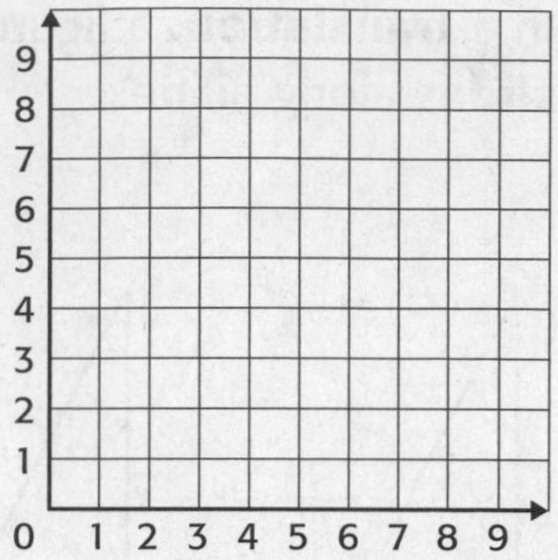

____

7.

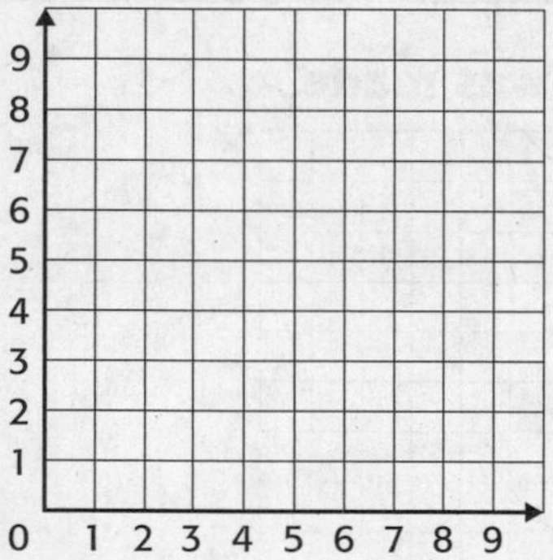

____

8.

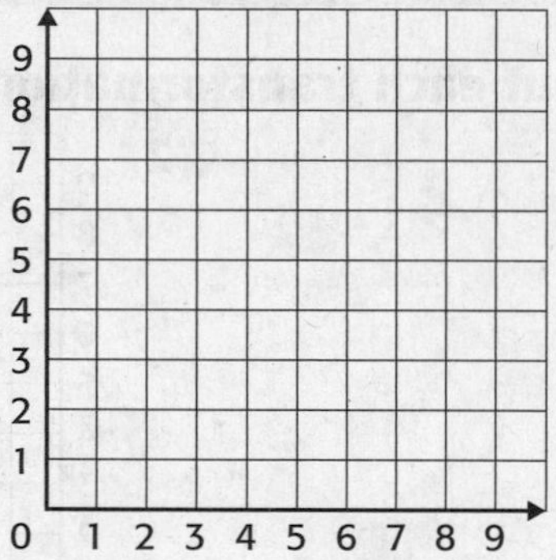

____

9.

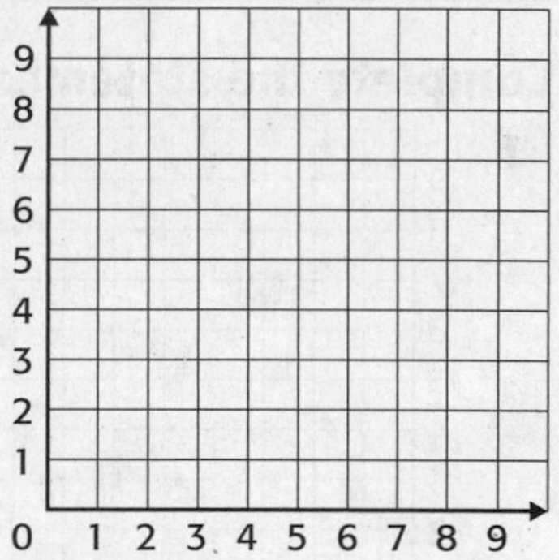

____

Solve.

10. Which uppercase letters look like different uppercase letters when they are reflected over a horizontal line?

____

11. You can transform a lowercase *v* in two different ways so that the *v* and its transformations form other lowercase letters. Describe the transformations and tell what letters you would form.

____

____

Name ______________________ Date ______________

14–1

Reteach

Perimeters of Polygons

Perimeter is the distance around a closed figure.

To find the perimeter of a figure, add the lengths of all the sides.

$P = 6\text{ cm} + 7\text{ cm} + 4\text{ cm} + 2\text{ cm} + 5\text{ cm} + 8\text{ cm}$

$P = 32\text{ cm}$

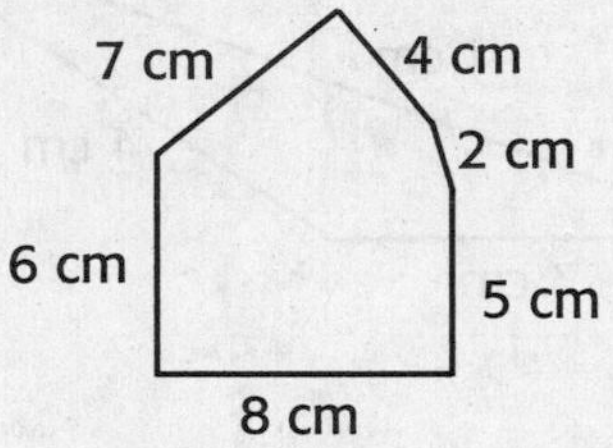

Find the perimeter of each figure.

1.

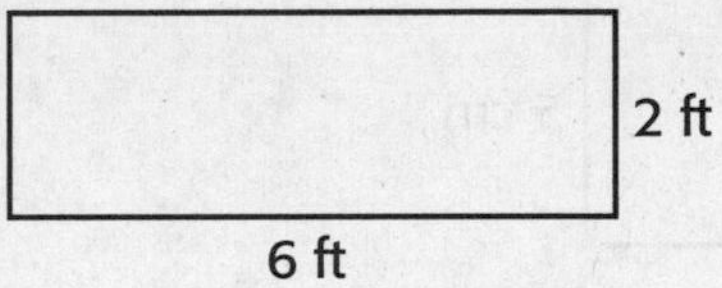

____

2.

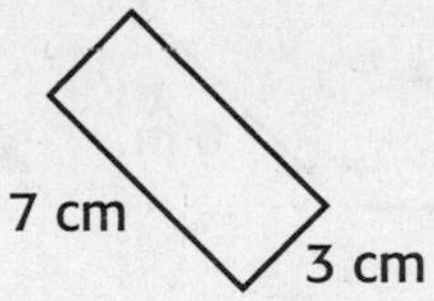

____

3.

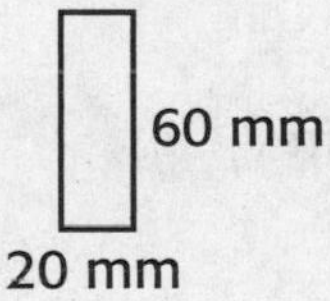

____

4.

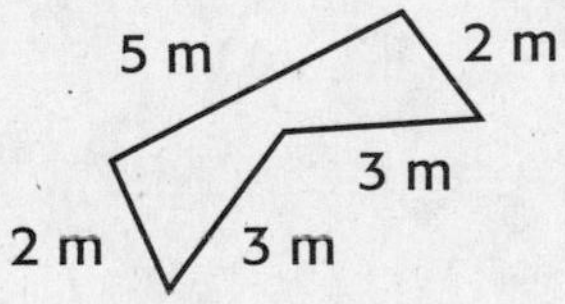

____

5.

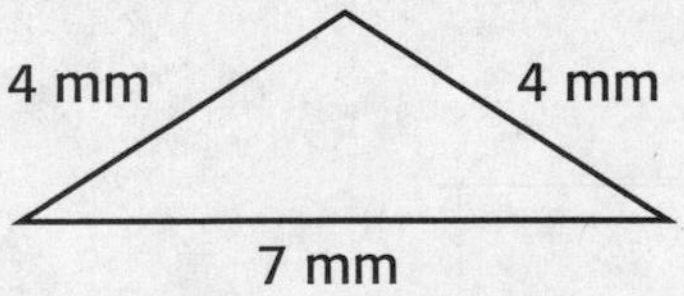

____

6.

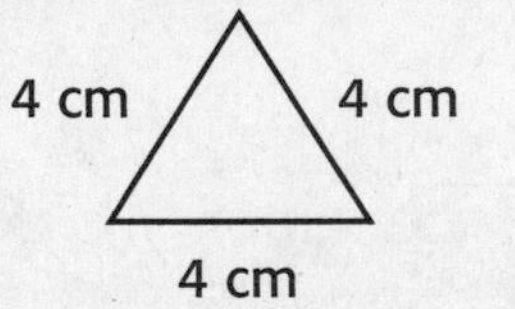

____

7.

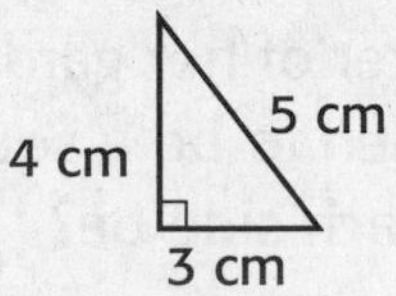

____

8.

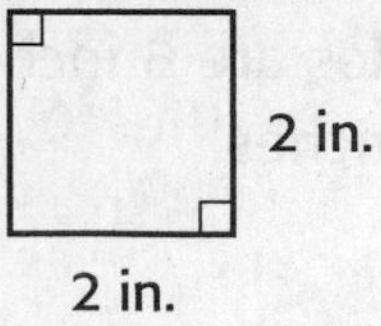

____

14–1

Name ______________________ Date ____________

Skills Practice

Perimeters of Polygons

Find the perimeter of each figure.

1.

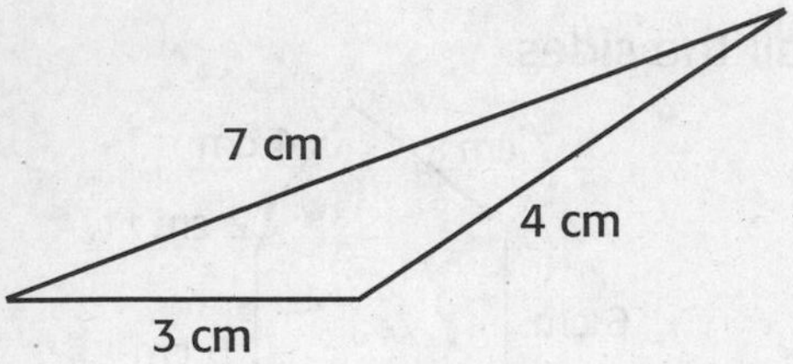

____

2.

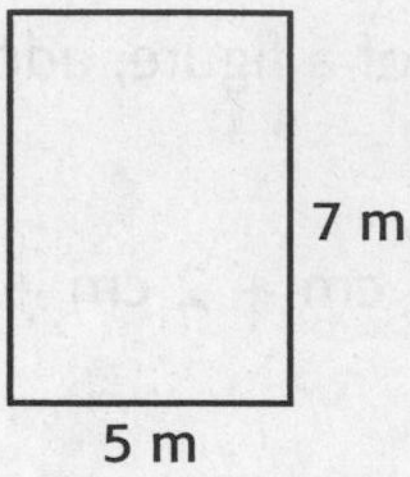

____

3.

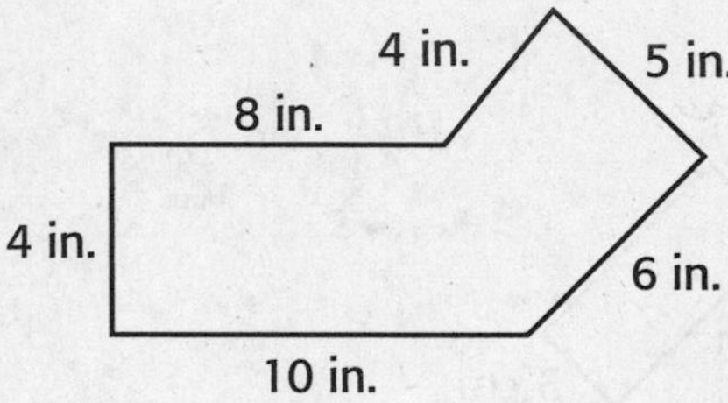

____

4.

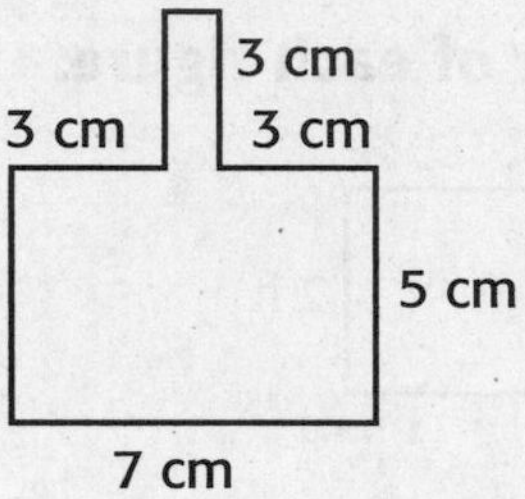

____

5.

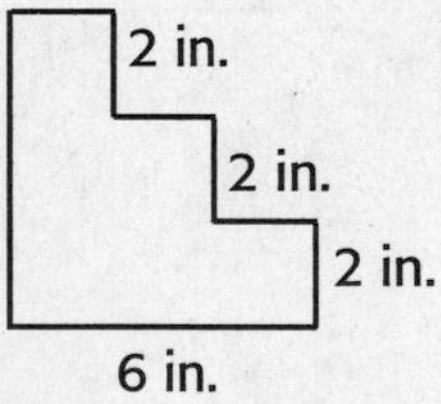

____

6.

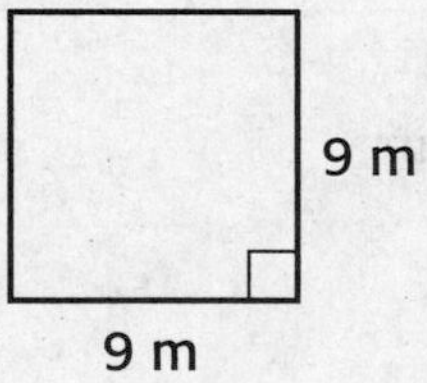

____

Solve.

7. Find the perimeter of an isosceles triangle whose sides are 8 inches and whose base is 4 inches.

____

8. Molly has 60 feet of fencing to go around the perimeter of her garden. She wants the garden to be a square. How long should each side be?

____

Name ______________________ Date ______________

14–2

Reteach

Area

Area is the number of square units that cover the surface of a closed figure. One way to find the area of a figure is to use grid paper and count the number of square units.

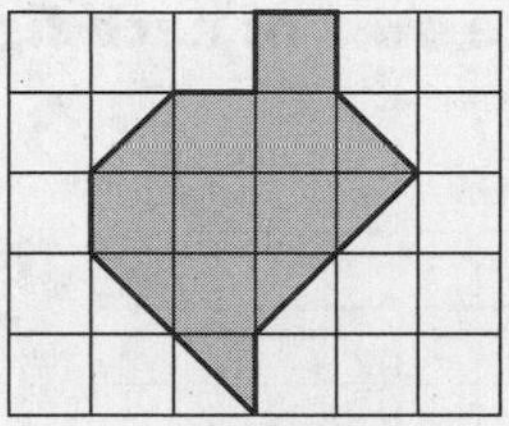

There are 7 whole squares and 6 half squares.

 = 1 square unit

The 6 half squares equal 3 whole squares.

The area of the figure is 10 square units.

When you cannot count square units or half square units exactly, you can estimate the area.

Step 1 Count the whole squares. There are 20 whole squares.

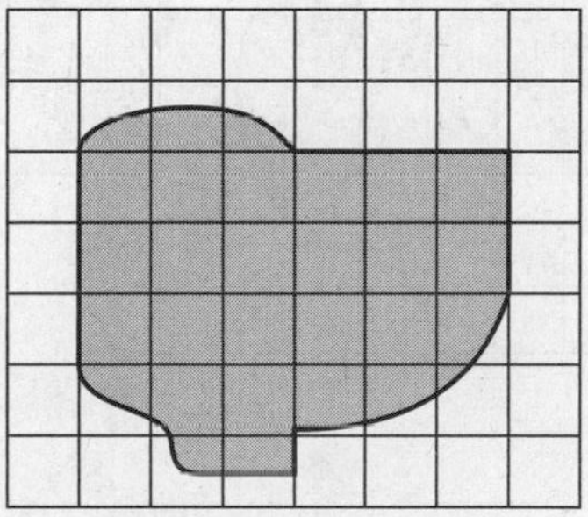

Step 2 Count the squares that are partly covered and divide that number by 2.

$8 \div 2 = 4$

Step 3 Add the numbers from Step 1 and Step 2.

$20 + 4 = 24$

The area of the figure is 24 square units.

Estimate the area of each figure. Each square represents 1 square centimeter.

1.

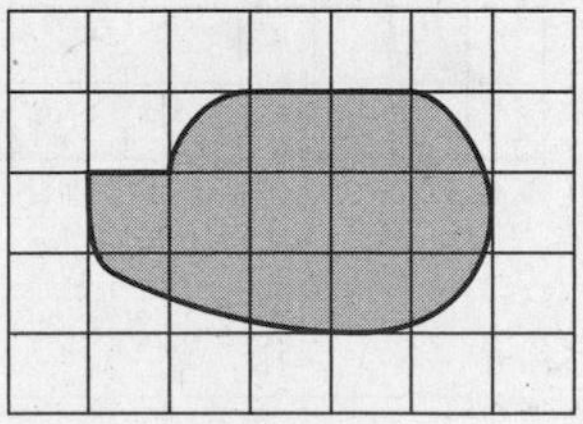

A = ______ square centimeters

2.

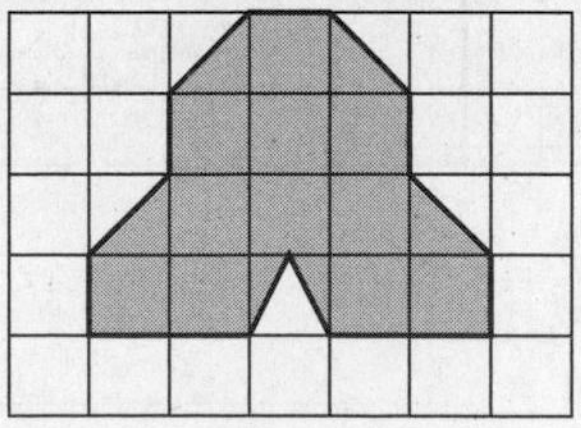

A = ______ square centimeters

3.

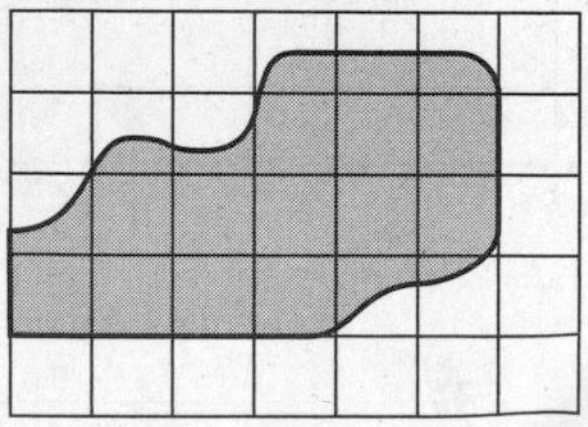

A = ______ square centimeters

Name ______________________ Date ______________

14–2

Skills Practice

Area

Estimate the area of each figure. Each square represents 1 square centimeter.

1. 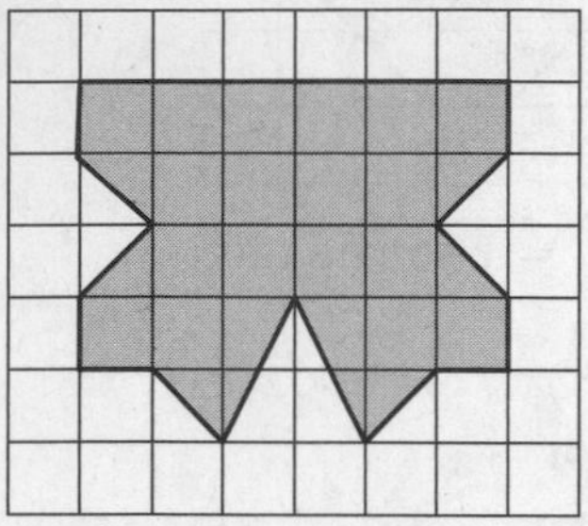

$A =$ ______________

2. 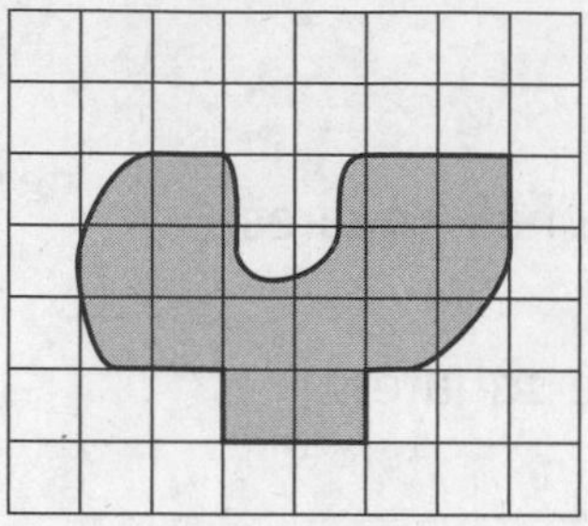

$A =$ ______________

3. 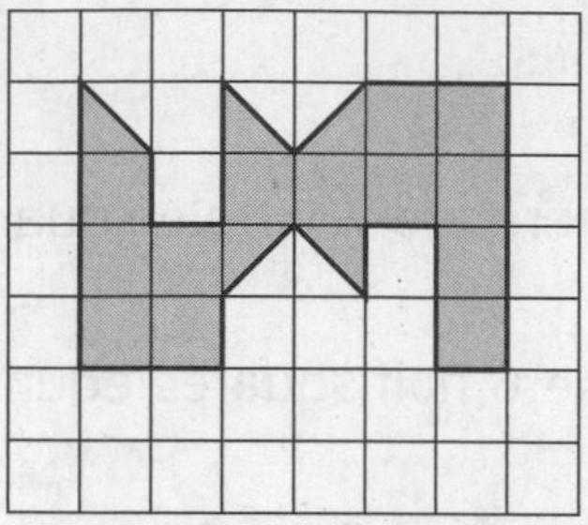

$A =$ ______________

4. 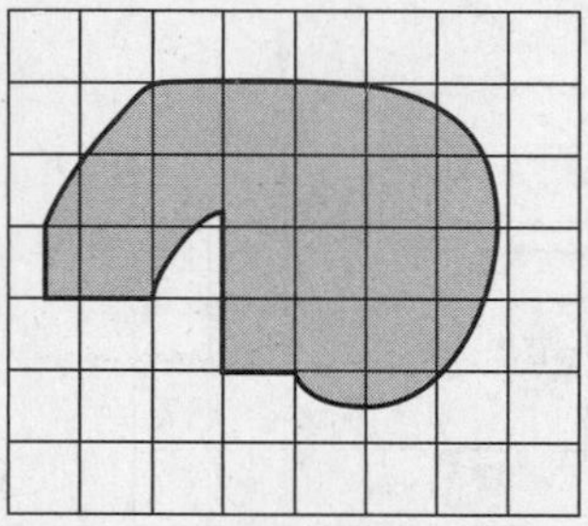

$A =$ ______________

5. 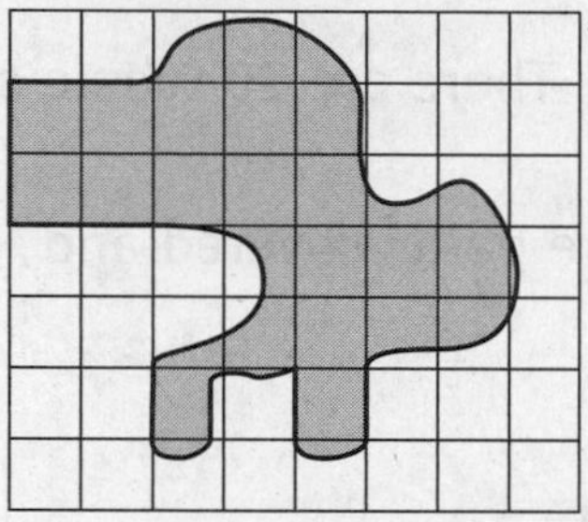

$A =$ ______________

6. 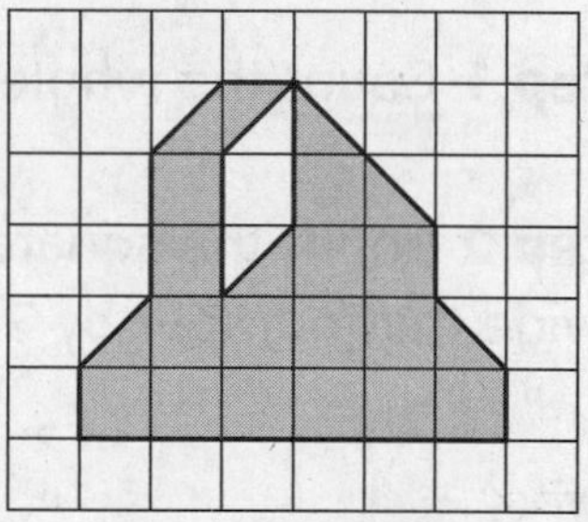

$A =$ ______________

7. 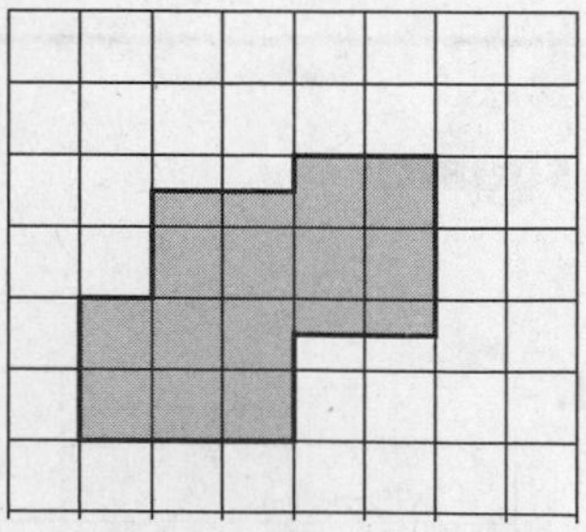

$A =$ ______________

8. 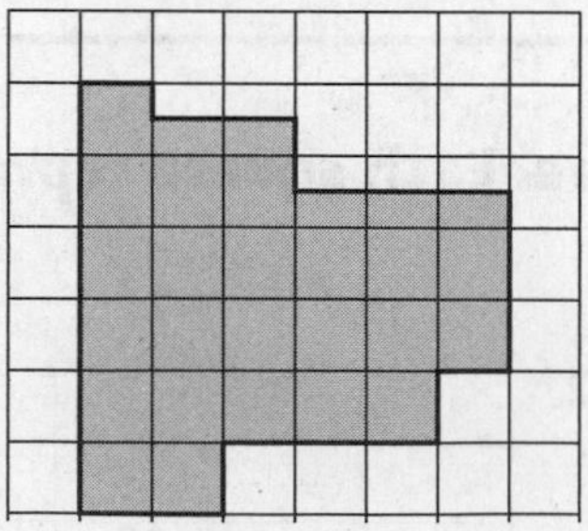

$A =$ ______________

9. 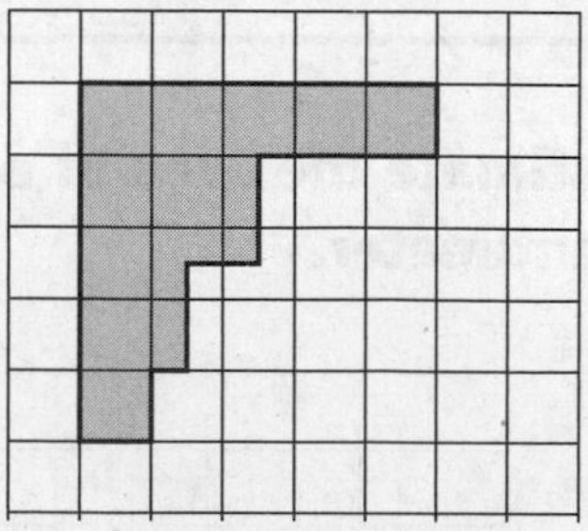

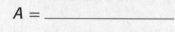

$A =$ ______________

Name ______________________________ Date ____________

14–3

Reteach

Areas of Rectangles and Squares

Area is the number of square units needed to cover a figure. To find the area of a rectangle or square, you can multiply its length times its width. This can be shown by a formula.

Find the area of the rectangle. Use the formula $A = \ell w$, where A = area, ℓ = length, and w = width.

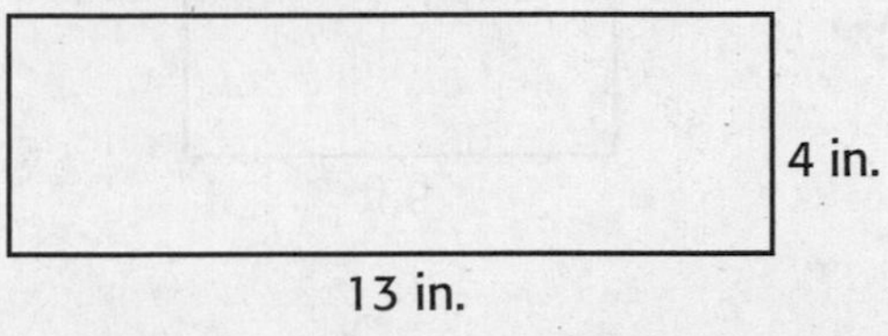

$A = \ell w$

$A = 13 \times 4$

$A = 52$ square inches

Find the area of the square. Use the formula $A = s \times s$ *or* s^2, where A = area and s = length of a side.

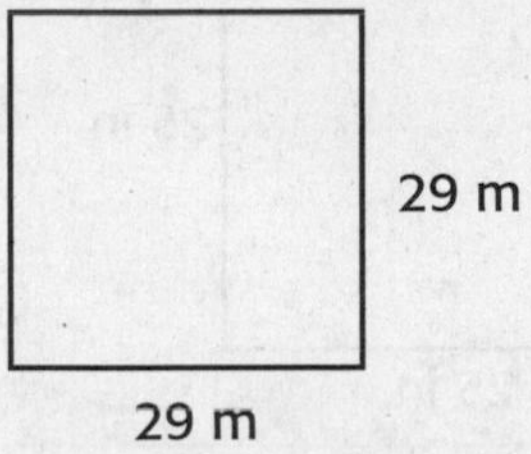

$A = s^2$

$A = 29 \times 29$

$A = 841$ square meters

Find the area of each rectangle or square.

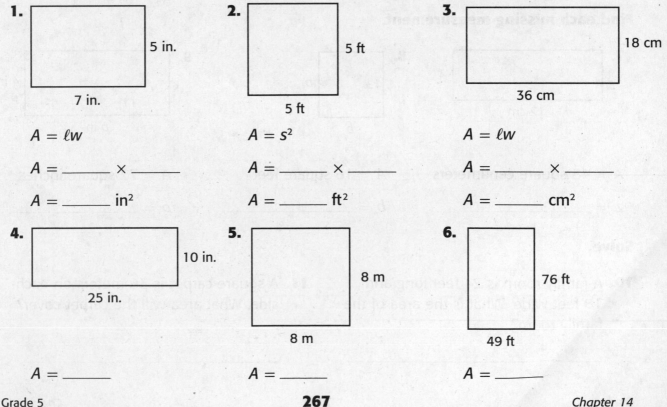

1.

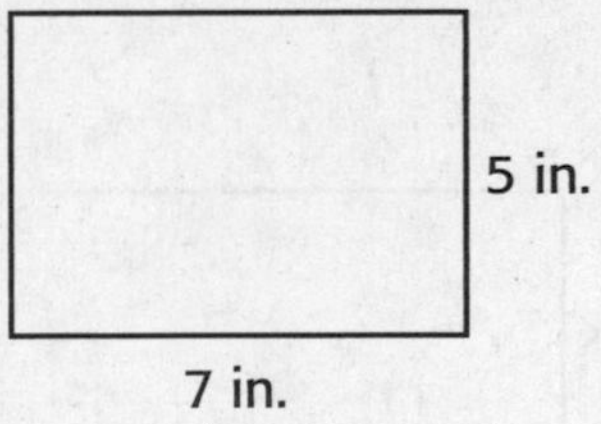

$A = \ell w$

$A =$ ______ $\times$ ______

$A =$ ______ in^2

2.

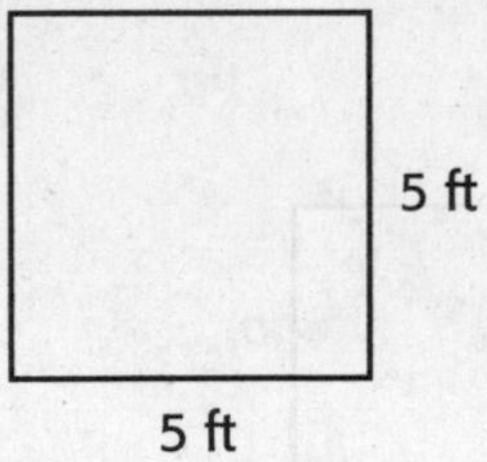

$A = s^2$

$A =$ ______ $\times$ ______

$A =$ ______ ft^2

3.

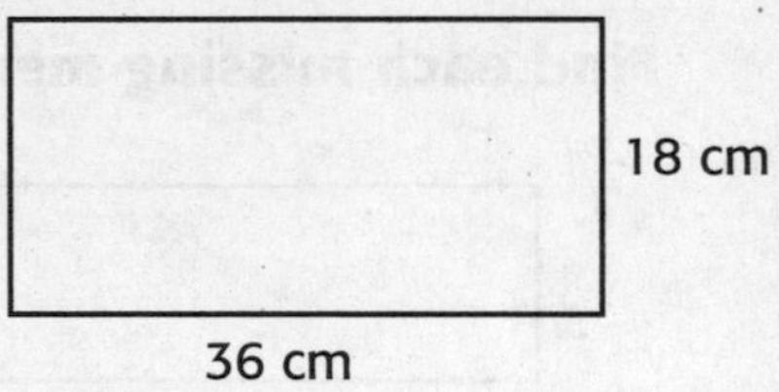

$A = \ell w$

$A =$ ______ $\times$ ______

$A =$ ______ cm^2

4.

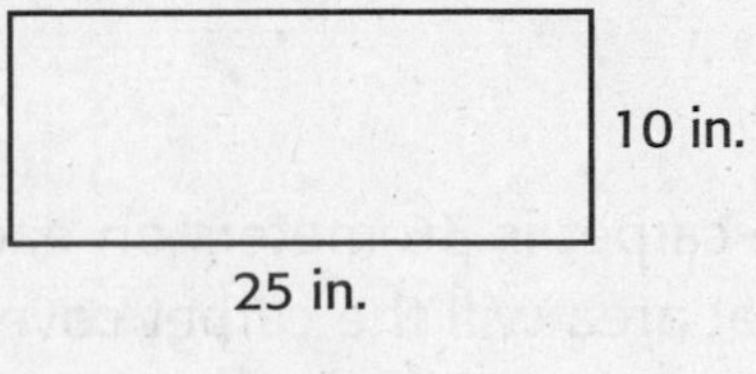

$A =$ ______

5.

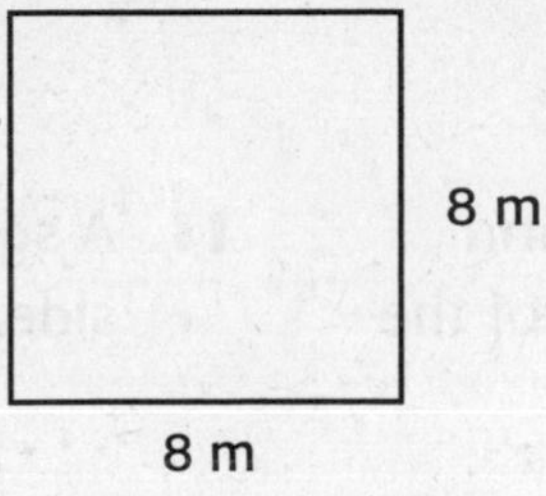

$A =$ ______

6.

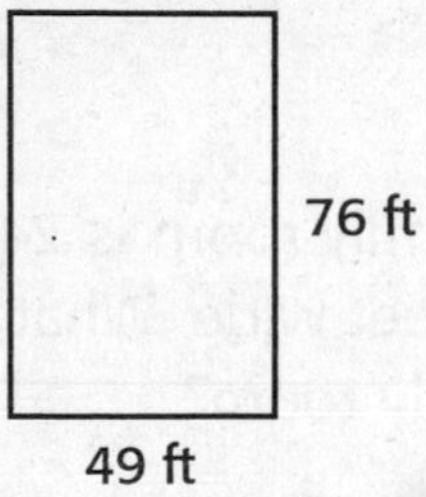

$A =$ ______

14–3

Name ______________________ Date ______________

Skills Practice

Areas of Rectangles

Find the area of each rectangle or square.

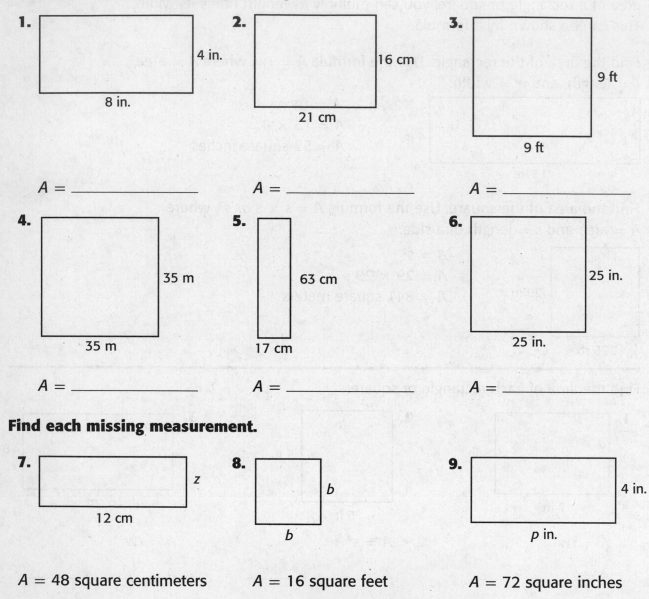

1.
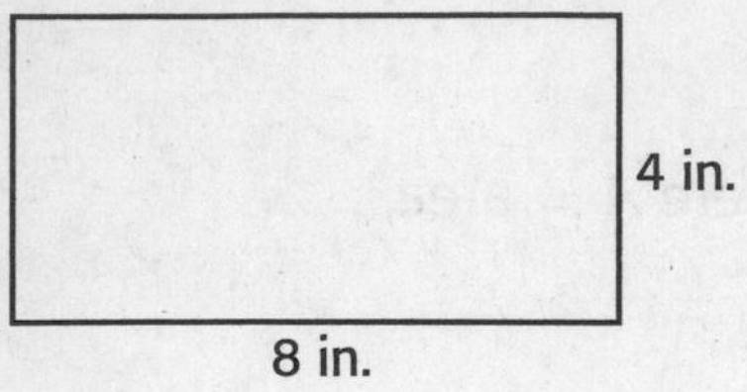

$A =$ ______________

2.
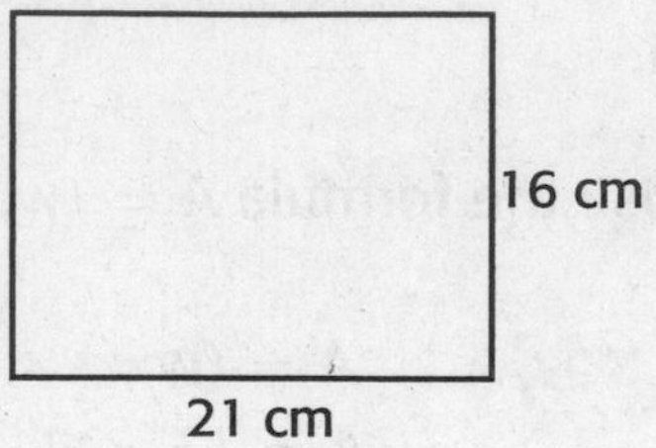

$A =$ ______________

3.
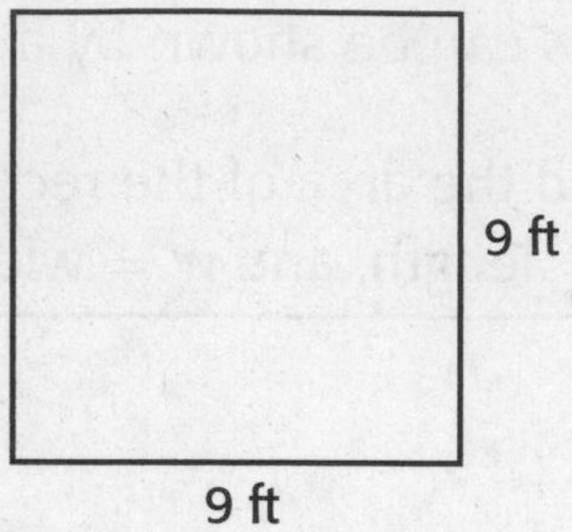

$A =$ ______________

4.
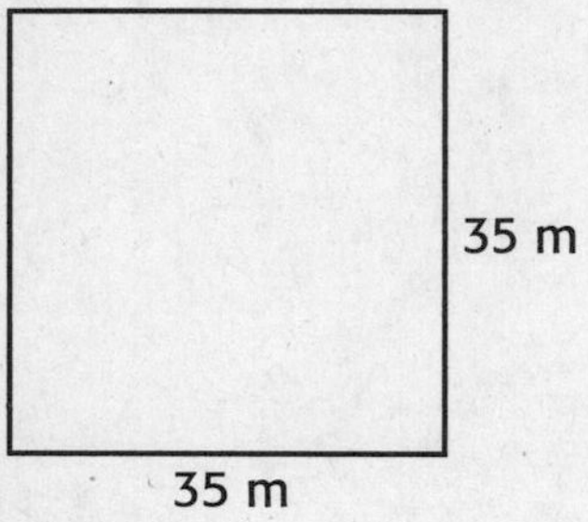

$A =$ ______________

5.
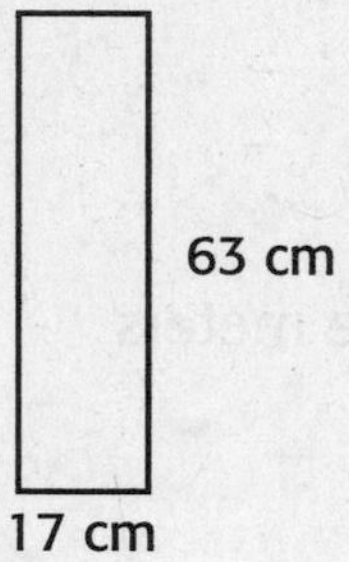

$A =$ ______________

6.
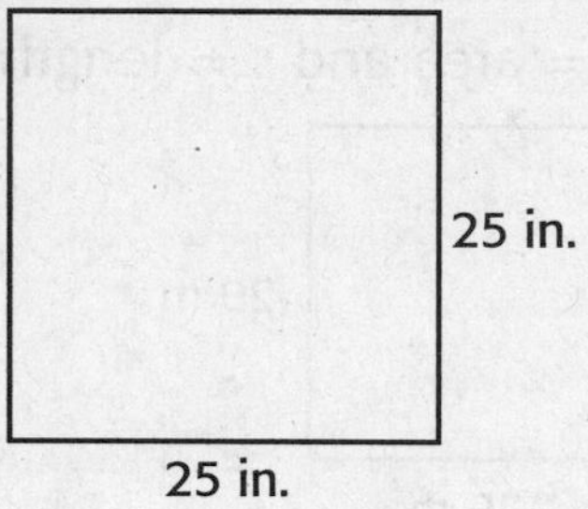

$A =$ ______________

Find each missing measurement.

7.
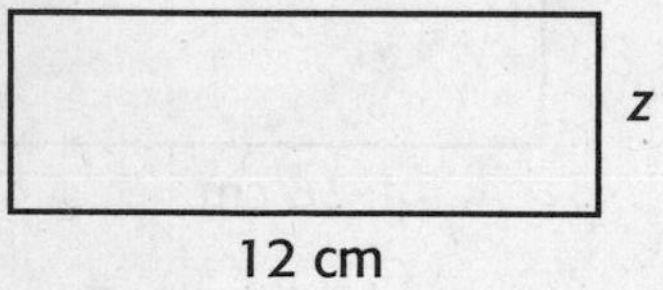

$A = 48$ square centimeters

$z =$ ______________

8.
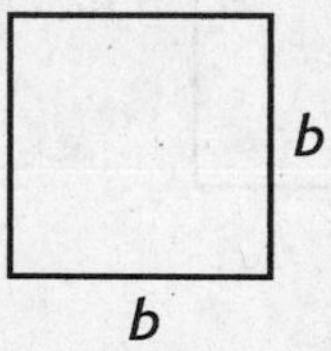

$A = 16$ square feet

$b =$ ______________

9.
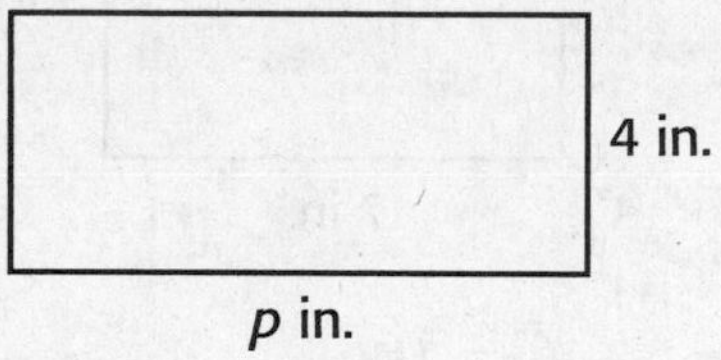

$A = 72$ square inches

$p =$ ______________

Solve.

10. A family room is 24 feet long and 18 feet wide. What is the area of the family room?

____

11. A square carpet is 36 meters on each side. What area will the carpet cover?

____

Name ______________________ Date ______________

14–4 Reteach

Geometry: Three-Dimensional Figures

Prisms are three-dimensional figures. Their parts have special names.

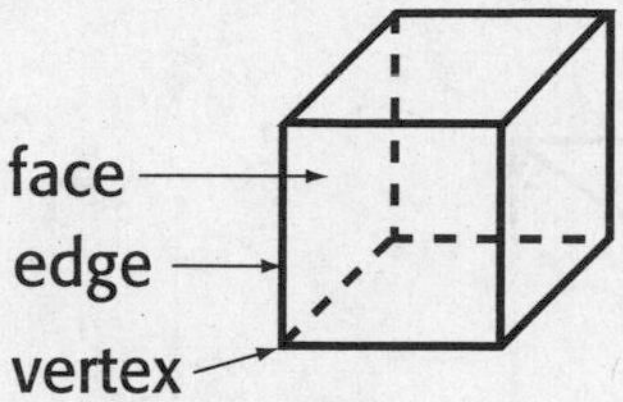

Face: flat surface on a prism or pyramid
Edge: segment where 2 faces meet
Vertex: point where edges meet
Prisms can be named by the shape of their bases.

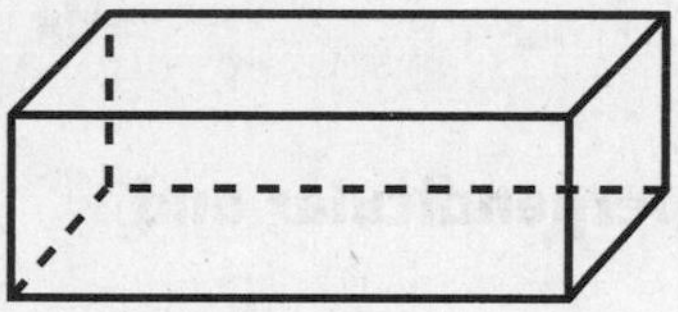

6 faces
12 edges
8 vertices

The bases are rectangular.
This prism is a rectangular prism.

Describe parts of each figure that are parallel and congruent. Then identify the figure.

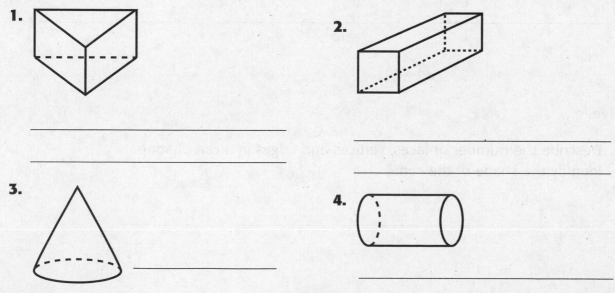

1.

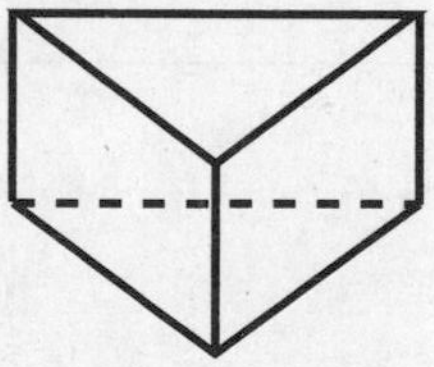

____

____

2.

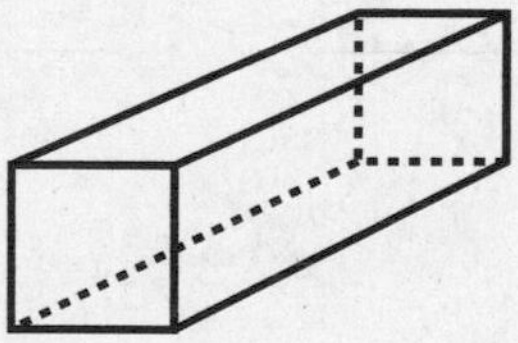

____

____

3.

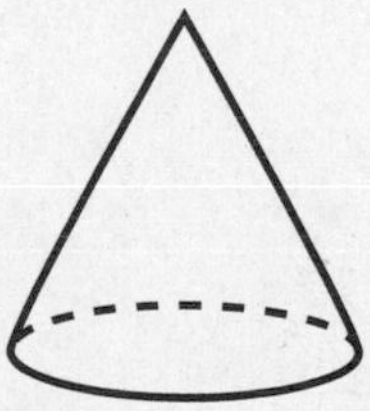

____

4.

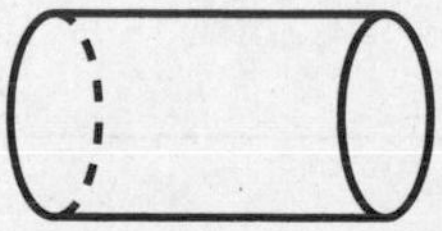

____

Name ______________________ Date ____________

14–4

Skills Practice

Geometry: Three-Dimensional Figures

Describe parts of each figure that are parallel and congruent. Then identify the figure.

1. 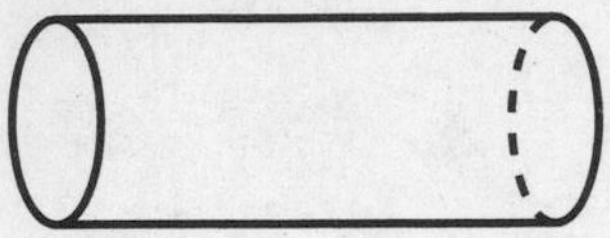

2. 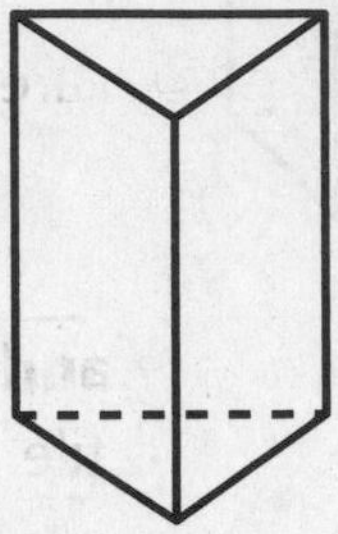

3. 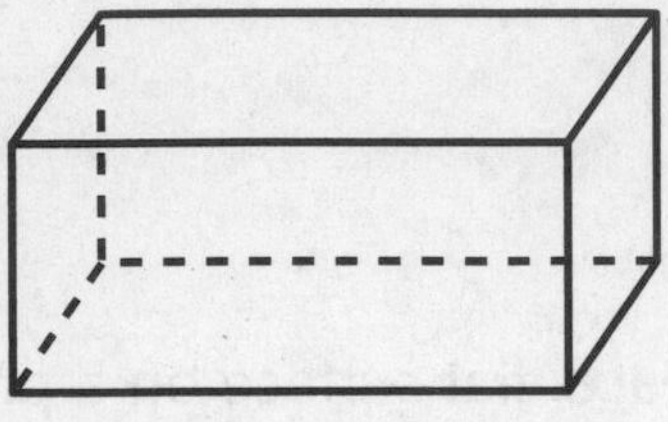

______________________ ______________________ ______________________

______________________ ______________________ ______________________

Describe parts of each figure that are perpendicular and congruent. Then identify the figure.

4. 

5. 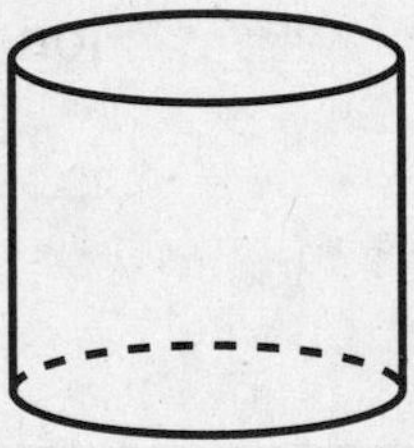

6. 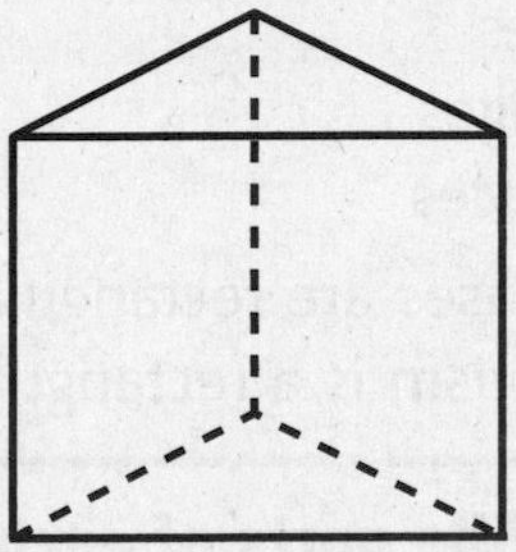

______________________ ______________________ ______________________

______________________ ______________________ ______________________

Solve.

7. Describe the number of faces, vertices and edges in a can of soup. Identify the shape of the can.

____

14–5

Name ______________________ Date ____________

Reteach

Problem-Solving Strategy: Make a Model

Solve. Use the *make a model* strategy.

Pedro is laying out tiles for a design in his bathroom. The area is 20 inches by 16 inches, and the tiles are 2 inch squares. How many square tiles are needed to fill the area?

Step 1 Understand	**Be sure you understand the problem.** Pedro is laying 2-inch tile in a 20-inch by 16-inch area.
Step 2 Plan Make a model using paper to find the number of tiles needed.	**Make a plan.** You can use a piece of construction paper and small square pieces of paper to represent the tiles.
Step 3 Solve	**Carry out your plan.** Make a model of the area by measuring out a 20″ × 16″ rectangle on construction paper. 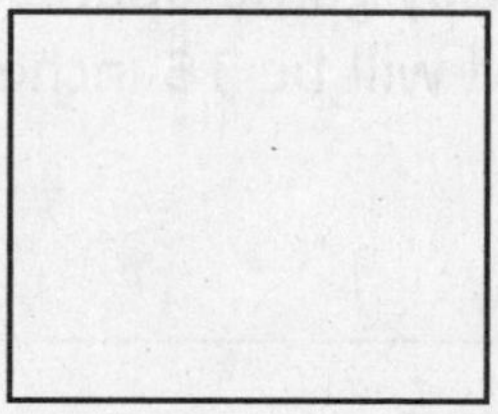 Cut out 2-inch squares from another piece of paper. Cover the 20″ × 16″ area completely with the squares. It will take 80 squares or tiles.
Step 4 Check	**Is the solution reasonable?** Reread the problem. Calculate to check your answer. Find the area of 20″ × 16″. It is 320 square inches. Each 2 inch tile has an area of 2″ × 2″ = 4 square inches. 320 square inches ÷ 4 square inches = 80 tiles

Name ______________________ Date ____________

14–5

Reteach

Problem-Solving Strategy: Make a Model (continued)

Solve. Use the *make a model* strategy.

1. Hugo is making a block tower. Each block is a 4-inch square and is 1 inch thick. If he has 35 blocks, what is the tallest height he can make with the blocks?

____

2. Susan wants to organize her bookshelf in her bedroom. It measures 36 inches long, and there are three shelves. If she has 25 two-inch wide books, 15 three-inch wide books, and 32 one-inch wide books, will she be able to fit them on the three shelves? If not, how many of each book will not fit?

____

____

3. Patricia is making a clay game board. Each square needs to be 2 inches. If the board will be 16 inches square, how many total squares will it have?

____

4. Pablo has a sheet of stickers that is 11 inches long. Each sticker is a 1 inch circle and there are 10 in each row. How many stickers are there on one page?

____

5. Charo is making a picture frame with shells she found. Each shell is 2 inches long. If she makes a rectangular frame out of 20 shells, how large can she make the frame?

____

14–5

Name ______________________ Date ______________

Skills Practice

Problem-Solving Strategy: Make a Model

Solve. Use the *make a model* strategy.

1. Ping and Kuri are designing a small end table using 1-inch tiles. If Kuri picks three times as many tiles out than Ping, and Ping picks out 24 tiles, how many total tiles are there? The area of the table is 19 inches by 5 inches. Will they have enough tiles to cover the tabletop?

____

2. The Miller family is redoing their garden. If they have a garden that is 500 square feet, and one side is 10 feet long, what is the length of the other side of the garden? If they plant 5 trees that need to be 5 feet apart and 5 feet away from the fence around the garden, will they have the space?

____

3. Bob is organizing his pantry. If he has cracker boxes that measure 12 inches high, 2 inches wide, and 10 inches long, how many boxes can he fit on a 24-inch-long shelf that is 14 inches deep?

____

4. You are packing picnic baskets for a day camp. Each basket needs to carry 8 square sandwiches, 8 apples, and 8 juice boxes. Would the best basket be an 18″ × 15″ × 9″ basket, a 72″ × 40″ × 18″ basket, or a 12″ × 6″ × 8″ basket?

____

5. Roberto wants to build a long train track. If each piece of track is 6 inches long, and he has 42 pieces, can he make a track that is 20 feet long? Can he make a track that is 22 feet long?

____

14–6

Name ______________________ Date ______________

Reteach

Volume of Prisms

Volume is the amount of space a three-dimensional figure encloses. To find the volume of a rectangular prism, you can use a formula.

Find the volume of the rectangular prism. Use the formula $V = \ell wh$, where V = volume, ℓ = length, w = width, and h = height.

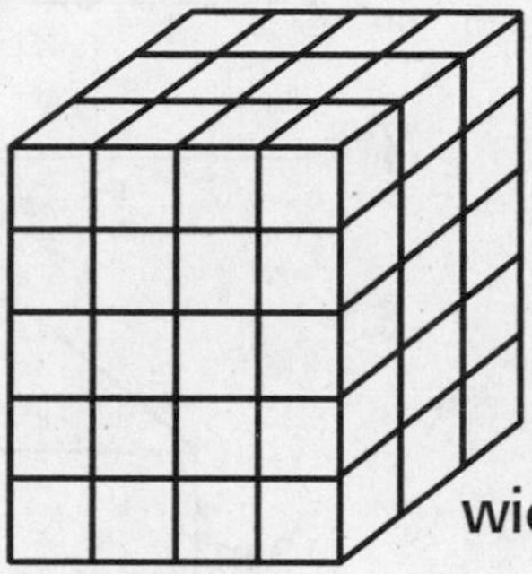

$V = \ell wh$

$V = 4 \times 3 \times 5$

$V = 60$ cubic units

Find the volume of each prism.

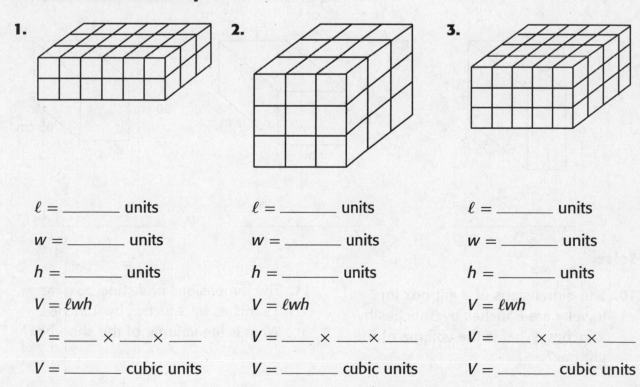

1.

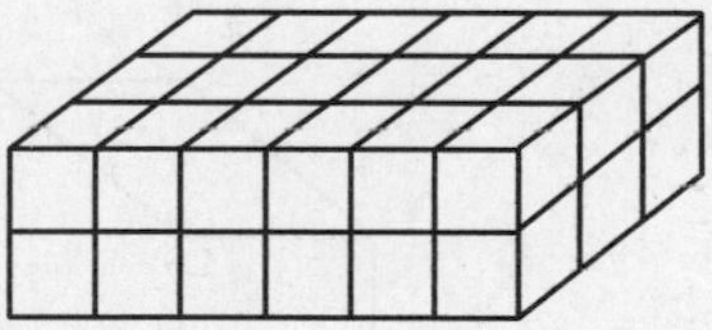

ℓ = ______ units

w = ______ units

h = ______ units

$V = \ell wh$

V = ____ × ____ × ____

V = ______ cubic units

2.

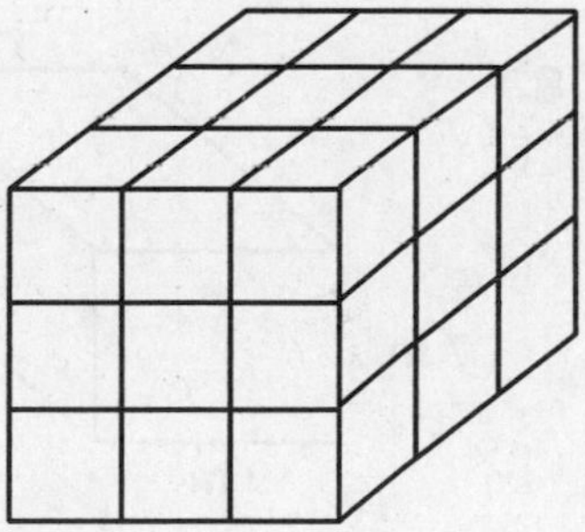

ℓ = ______ units

w = ______ units

h = ______ units

$V = \ell wh$

V = ____ × ____ × ____

V = ______ cubic units

3.

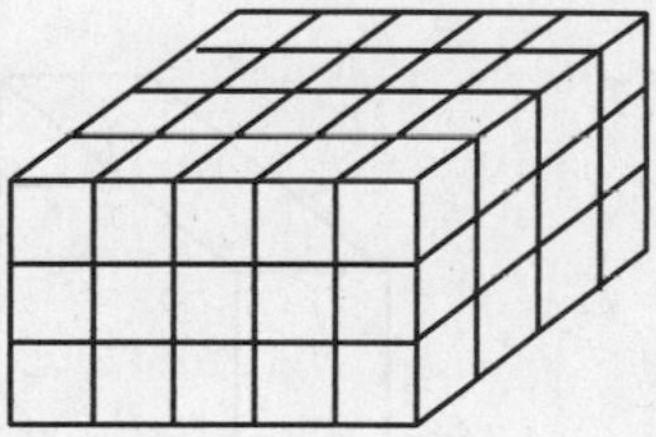

ℓ = ______ units

w = ______ units

h = ______ units

$V = \ell wh$

V = ____ × ____ × ____

V = ______ cubic units

Name ______________________ Date ____________

14–6

Skills Practice

Volume of Prisms

Find the volume of each prism.

1.

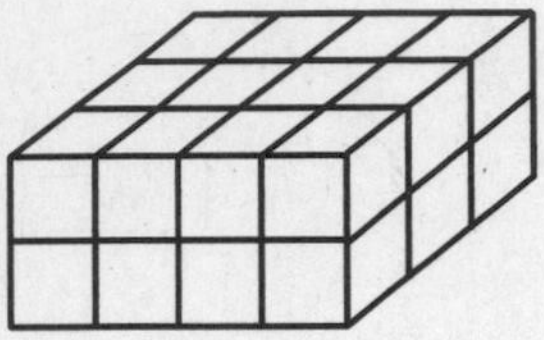

$V =$ ____________

2.

$V =$ ____________

3.

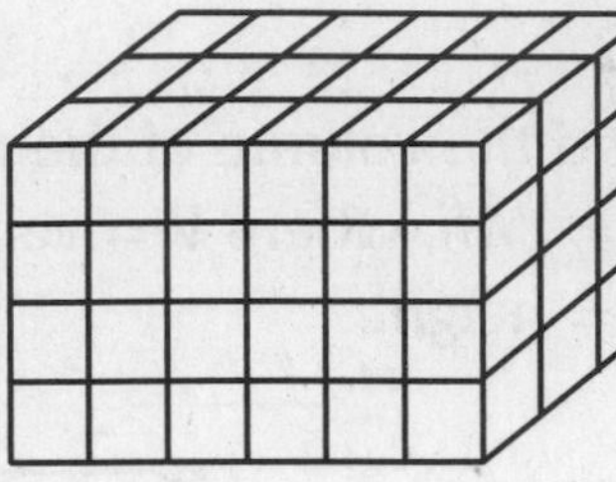

$V =$ ____________

4.

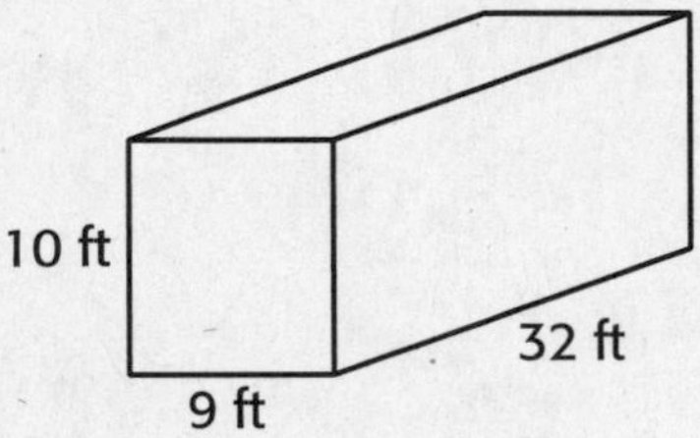

$V =$ ____________

5.

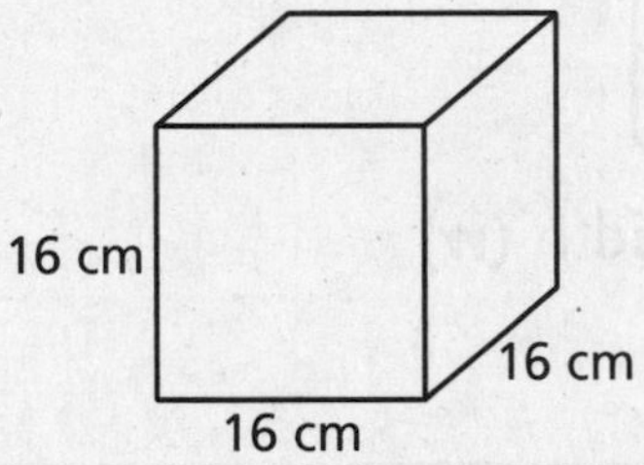

$V =$ ____________

6.

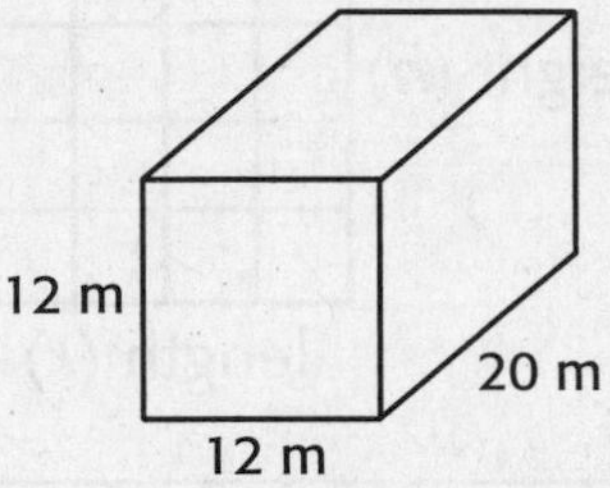

$V =$ ____________

7.

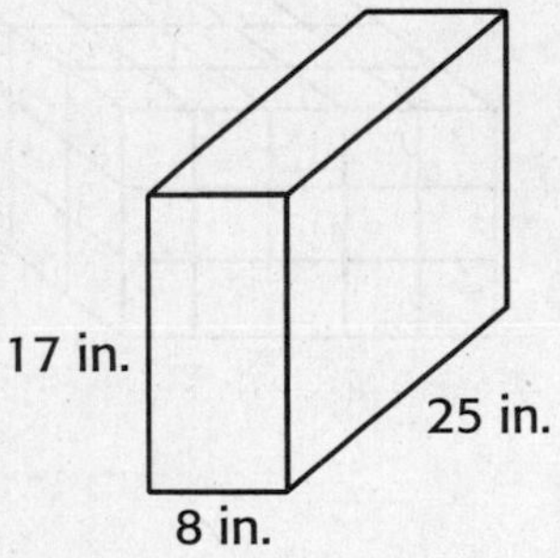

$V =$ ____________

8.

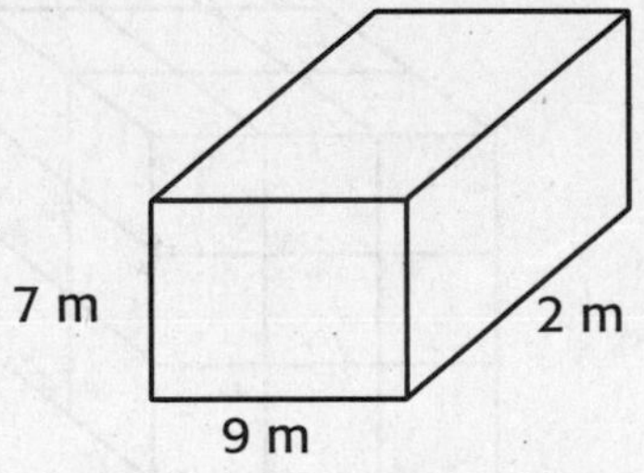

$V =$ ____________

9.

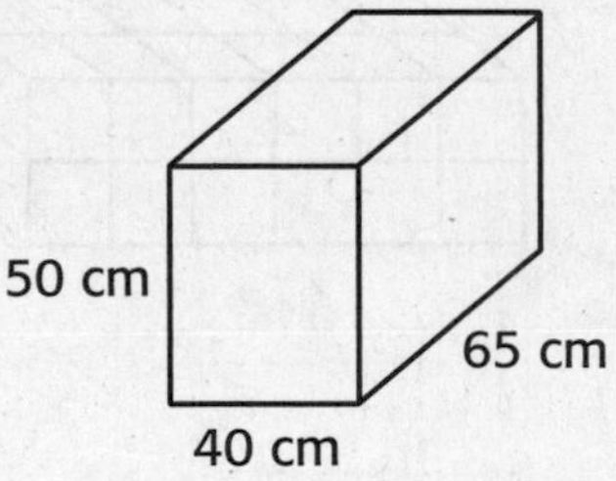

$V =$ ____________

Solve.

10. The dimensions of a gift box for jewelry are 6 inches by 3 inches by 2 inches. What is the volume of the gift box?

____

11. The dimensions of a shoe box are 13 inches by 9 inches by 4 inches. What is the volume of the shoe box?

____

14–7

Name ____________________________ Date ______________

Reteach

Surface Areas of Prisms

You can find the **surface area** of a rectangular prism by finding the total area of all its faces. Each face is a rectangle, so use the formula $A = lw$ to find the area of each face.

Find the surface area of this rectangular prism.

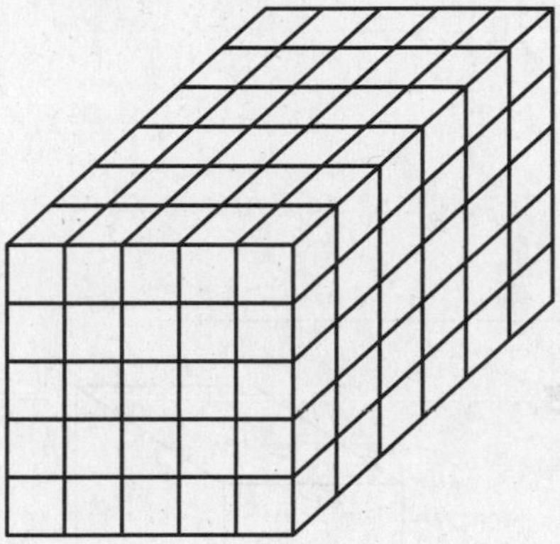

Front face:	$5 \times 5 = 25$ square units
Back face:	$5 \times 5 = 25$ square units
Top face:	$5 \times 6 = 30$ square units
Bottom face:	$5 \times 6 = 30$ square units
Right face:	$5 \times 6 = 30$ square units
Left face:	$5 \times 6 = 30$ square units
Total surface area:	170 square units

Find the surface area of each rectangular prism.

1.

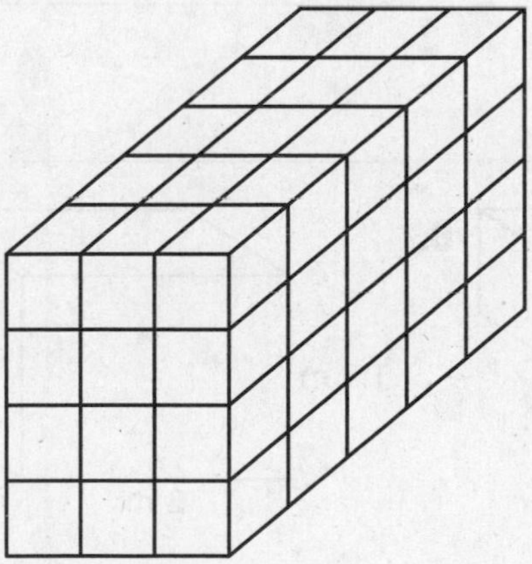

Front face: _____ × _____ = _____ square units

Back face: _____ × _____ = _____ square units

Top face: _____ × _____ = _____ square units

Bottom face: _____ × _____ = _____ square units

Right face: _____ × _____ = _____ square units

Left face: _____ × _____ = _____ square units

Total surface area: _____ square units

2.

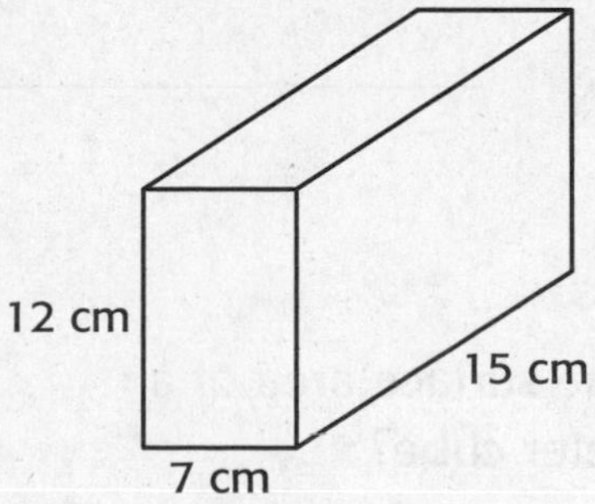

Front face: _____ × _____ = _____ cm^2

Back face: _____ × _____ = _____ cm^2

Top face: _____ × _____ = _____ cm^2

Bottom face: _____ × _____ = _____ cm^2

Right face: _____ × _____ = _____ cm^2

Left face: _____ × _____ = _____ cm^2

Total surface area: _____ cm^2

Name ______________________ Date ____________

14–7

Skills Practice

Surface Areas of Prisms

Find the surface area of each rectangular prism.

1.

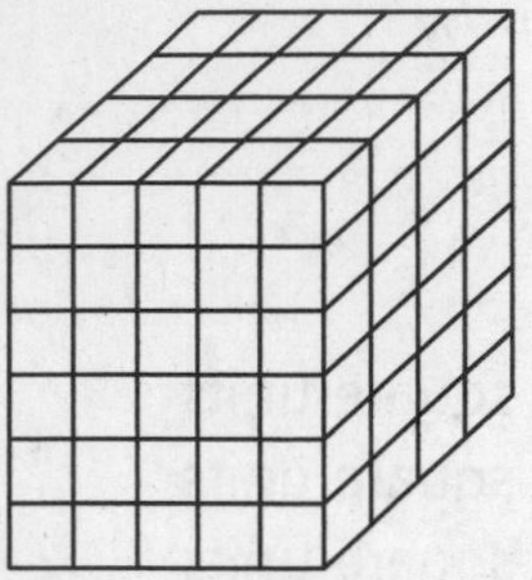

2.

3.

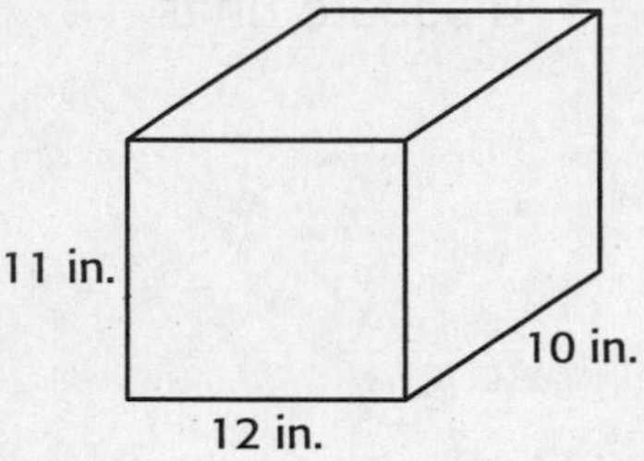

4.

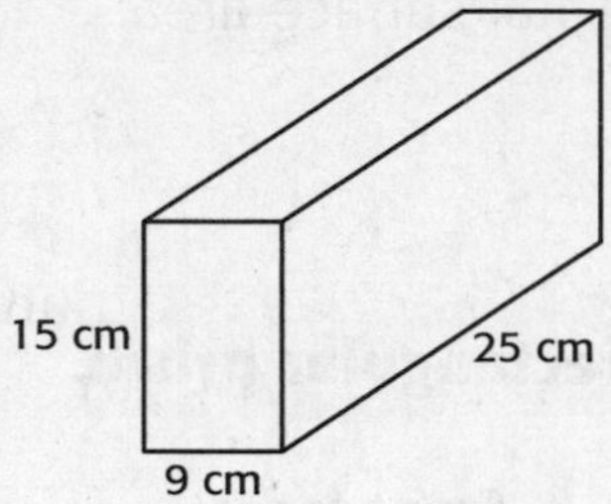

5.

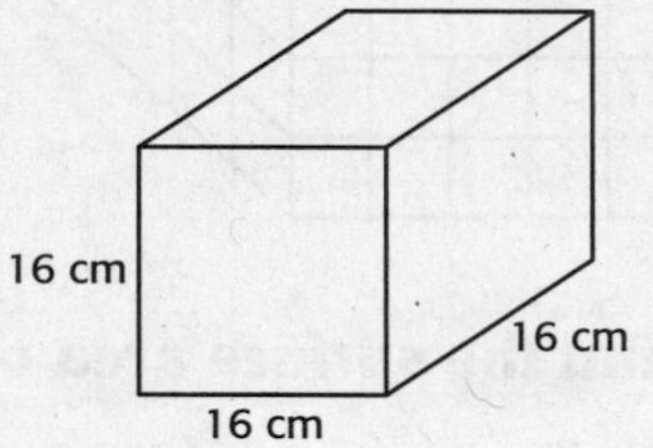

6.

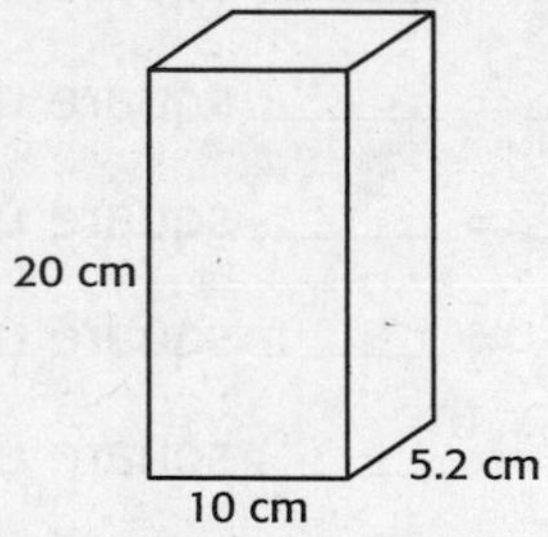

7.

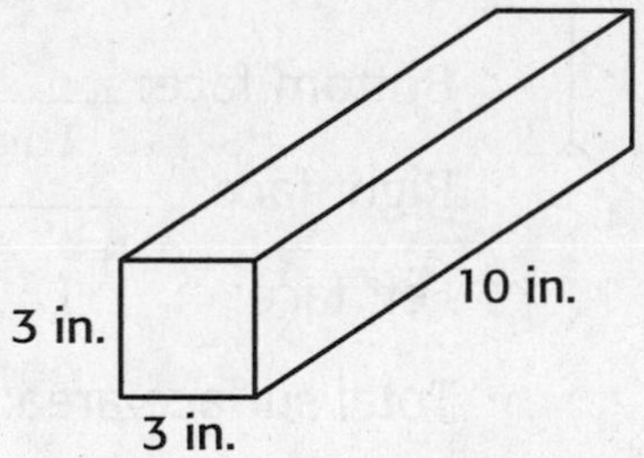

8.

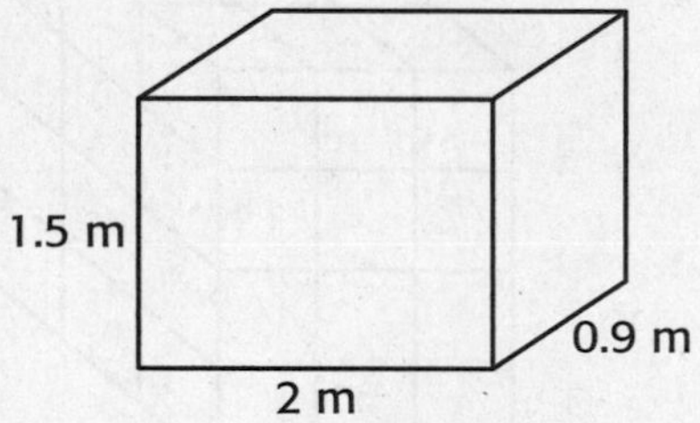

Problem Solving

Solve.

9. What is the surface area of a cardboard shipping box that is 26 inches long, 26 inches wide, and 18 inches high?

10. What is the surface area of a 9-centimeter cube?

Name ______________________ Date ____________

Reteach

Select Appropriate Measurement Formulas

Mr. Gonzalez wants to enclose a field for his horse. The field is 20 feet wide and 40 feet long. How much fencing will Mr. Gonzalez need? Should he find the perimeter or area of the field? Solve the problem.

The field is 20 feet by 40 feet.
You need to find how much fencing is needed.

Draw a diagram of the field. Label the length of each side.

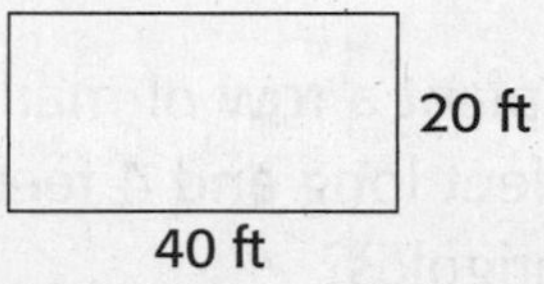

Think: **Perimeter** is the distance around a closed figure. $P = 2\ell + 2w$
Area is the number of square units inside a closed figure. $A = \ell w$
Volume is the space enclosed by a figure. $V = \ell wh$

You need to find the **perimeter**, or the distance around the field.
Perimeter = 2 × (length + width) = 2 × (40 + 20)

Mr. Gonzalez needs 120 feet of fencing.

Determine whether you need to find the perimeter, area, or volume. Then solve.

1. A rectangular banner is 4 feet wide and 8 feet long. How much ribbon is needed to trim the borders of the banner?

2. The floor of a room needs new carpet. The room is 10 feet wide and 12 feet long. How much carpet is needed to cover the floor?

____

Name ______________________ Date ______________

14–8

Skills Practice

Select Appropriate Measurement Formulas

Determine whether you need to find the perimeter, area, or volume. Then solve.

1. Hayden wants to make a rectangular herb garden that is 4 feet long and 3 feet wide. She wants to plant lavender in half of the garden. How much of the garden will be covered with lavender?

____

2. Daniel wants to plant a row of marigolds along the border of his vegetable garden. The garden is 6 feet long and 4 feet wide. How much of the garden will need to be covered with marigolds?

____

3. Ms. Carmichael is building a deck with two levels. The lower level is a square. The length of each side is 5 feet. The upper level is rectangular in shape, 12 feet long and 8 feet wide. How much wood will she need to construct each level?

____

____

____

4. Ms. Carmichael wants to use the space underneath the lower level as storage space. If the lower level of the deck is 4 feet high off the ground, how much storage space will she have?

____

5. Jamison has 70 square feet of plywood to make a floor for a two-room clubhouse he is building. The floor of one room is 8 feet long and 6 feet wide. The floor of the other room is 5 feet long and 4 feet wide. How can he decide if he has enough plywood?

____

____

6. Amy wants to make a frame for a painting that is 24 inches long and 18 inches wide. She found a wood molding she would like to use. How can she decide how much molding she needs to make the frame?

____

Name ______________________ Date ______________

14–9

Reteach

Problem-Solving Investigation: Choose the Best Strategy

Alberto often goes along with his sister, Sonia, to videotape her soccer games. He records each $1\frac{1}{2}$ hour game. If she played 11 games, would Alberto be able to fit all her games on one DVD if each DVD holds 15 hours of video?

Step 1 Understand	**Be sure you understand the problem.** Alberto will videotape Sonia's soccer games. Each game is $1\frac{1}{2}$ hours. Sonia played 11 games. The DVD will hold 15 hours of video.
Step 2 Plan • Make a model • Draw a diagram • Look for a pattern	**Make a plan.** Choose a strategy. You can draw a diagram. Draw a line segment that is 15 inches long. Then mark intervals that are $1\frac{1}{2}$ inches long. Count the intervals to see whether you have 11 intervals.
Step 3 Solve	**Carry out your plan.** Two games take 3 hours. So, in 15 hours Alberto can fit 2×5 or 10 games on his DVD. So 11 games will *not* fit on one DVD.
Step 4 Check	**Is the solution reasonable?** Reread the problem. How can you check your answers?

Name ______________________ Date ____________

14–9

Reteach

Problem-Solving Investigation: Choose the Best Strategy (continued)

Use any strategy shown below to solve each problem.

- Make a model
- Draw a diagram
- Look for a pattern
- Use logical reasoning

1. Mitchell spent some money on his haircut. He paid the cashier three $5-bills. He received $4.25 back from the cashier. How much did he pay for the haircut?

____

2. Callie is throwing a party and spends a total of $135. She spends $20 on cake, $40 on food, and $25 for decorations. If the rest of the money was spent on music, how much did the music cost?

____

3. Meredith spent $125 on new clothes. She also purchased school supplies that totaled $45. She received 10% back on her total purchase. How much did she receive back?

____

4. Jordan works at a pool during the week. Monday he worked for 30 minutes, Tuesday he worked for 40 minutes, Wednesday he worked for 50 minutes. If the pattern continues, how long will he work on Friday?

____

5. Roberto is looking for the better deal on a bag of pens. One bag has 6 pens for $3.65. Another bag is $4.98 for 8 pens. Which one should Roberto buy?

____

14–9

Name ______________________________ Date ____________________

Skills Practice

Problem-Solving Investigation: Choose the Best Strategy

Use any strategy shown below to solve each problem.

• Make a model • Draw a diagram • Look for a pattern • Use logical reasoning

1. A pet store is building new cages for their birds. They have 8 cockatiels, 32 parakeets, and 28 finches. How many cages will they need if each cage will hold either 2 cockatiels, 10 parakeets, or 14 finches. The different types of birds are all kept separate.

____

2. You decide to do an even exchange on an outfit that you received for your birthday. The top and pants total \$32. If you pick another top for \$14, how much is the highest price of the pants, that you can pick out?

____

3. Danielle picks fruit from her family's lemon tree. She picked 28 lemons. If each lemon makes $\frac{1}{2}$ cup of lemonade after adding water, how many cups of lemonade can she make?

____

4. Meredith is making a dress. She has 5 feet of ribbon. She needs 12 inches of ribbon for the neck and two 6-inch pieces for the cuffs. How many cuts will she need to make to get 6 equal lengths from the rest of the ribbon for bows?

____

5. Taye ran for 3 miles each week. On each fourth week, he ran an extra mile. How many miles did he run after 4 weeks? How many miles did he run after 7 weeks?

____

Name ______________________ Date __________

15–1

Reteach

Probability

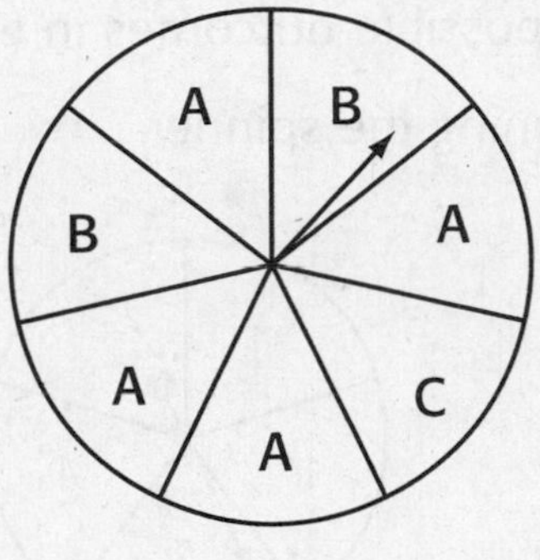

Probability is the chance an event will happen.

If you were to spin this spinner, it could land on A, B, or C. A, B, and C are the possible **outcomes.**

Words such as *certain, impossible, unlikely, equally likely,* and *likely* are used to describe the chance an outcome will happen.

The likelihood of landing on a particular outcome depends on how many of that outcome are on the spinner.

4–A sections	Landing on A is likely.
1–C section	Landing on C is unlikely.

Use the spinner at the right for Exercises 1–3.

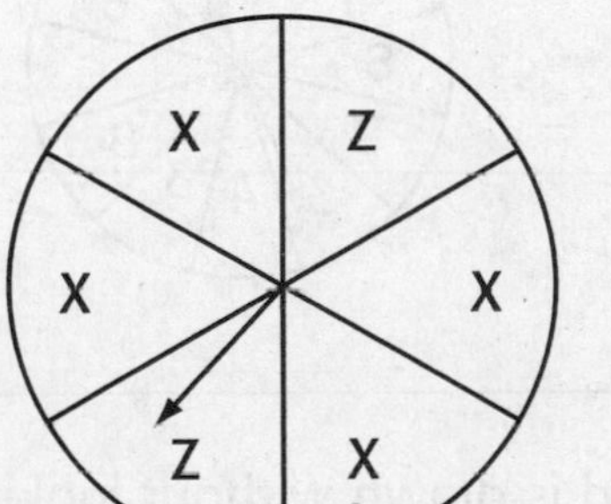

1. There are ______ outcomes, ______ and Z.

2. Landing on ______ is likely, because ______ sections are ______.

3. Landing on ______ is unlikely, because ______ sections are ______.

Use the spinner at the right for Exercises 4–7.

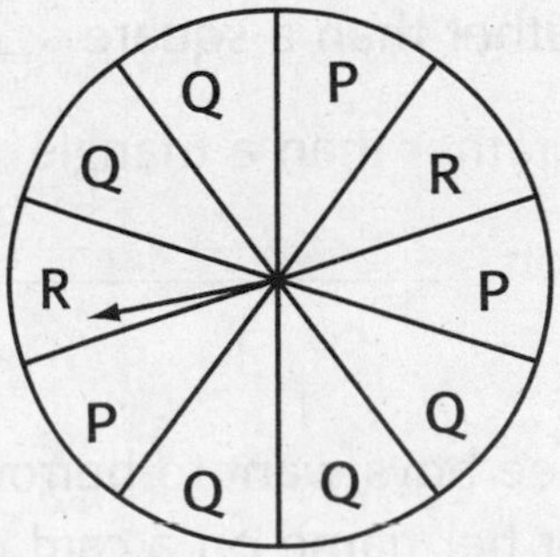

4. What are the possible outcomes?

____

5. Which outcome is least likely?

____

6. Which outcome is likely?

____

7. If you spin the spinner 50 times, which letter do you think you will get most often?

____

15–1

Name ______________________ Date ____________

Skills Practice

Probability

List the possible outcomes in each probability experiment.

1. spinning the spinner

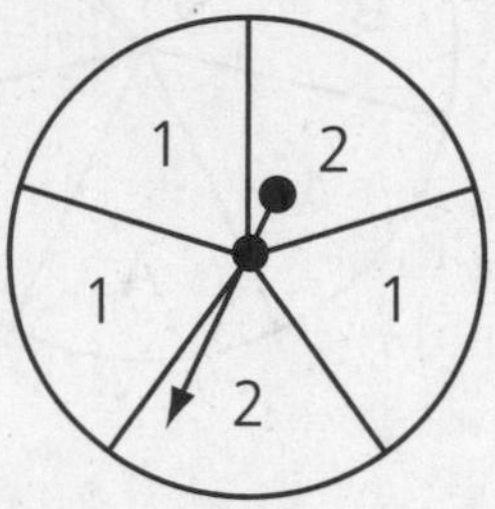

____

2. Selecting a marble from the bag without looking.

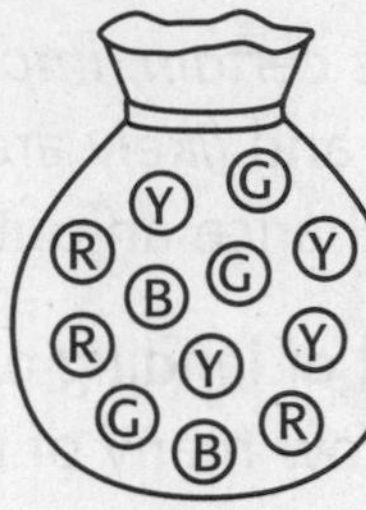

____

3. spinning the spinner without looking

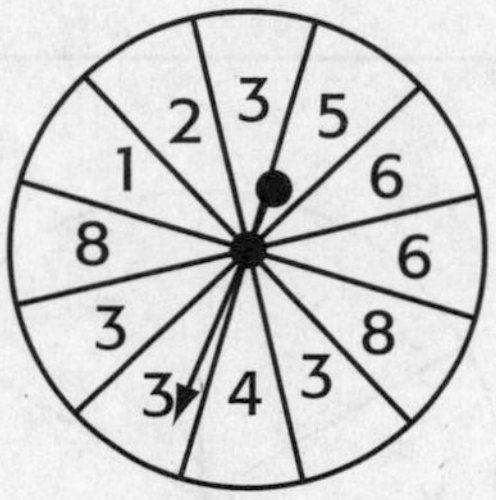

____

4. randomly choosing a card

A	P	E	Q	A

____

One card is drawn without looking. Describe the probability of drawing each card. Write *certain, impossible, unlikely, equally likely* or *likely.*

△	△	□	○	△	□	△	○	□	□	△	○	○	□

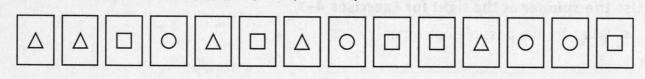

5. Picking a circle rather than a square ______________

6. Picking a square rather than a triangle ______________

7. Picking a pentagon ______________

Solve.

8. Two girls and three boys want to borrow the same book from the school library. Each writes his or her name on a card. If the librarian picks a card at random, describe the probability that a girl will be chosen to borrow the book.

____

Name ______________________ Date ______________

15–2

Reteach

Probability as a Fraction

The probability of an event can be written as a number from 0 to 1. It can be found by comparing the number of favorable outcomes to the number of possible outcomes

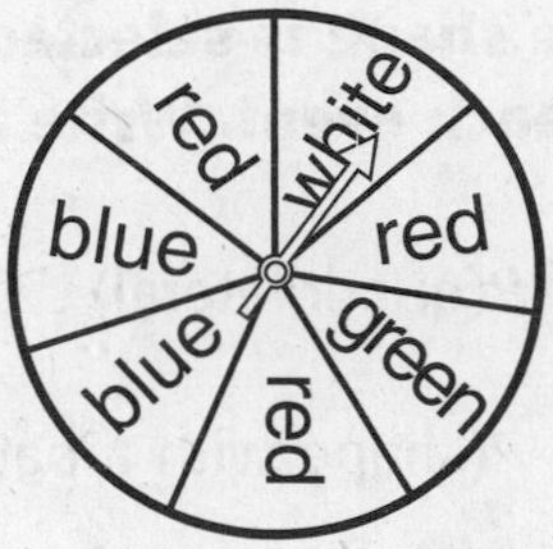

$$P(\text{event}) = \frac{\text{number of favorable outcomes}}{\text{number of possible outcomes}}$$

To find the probability of spinning "blue" on the spinner to the right, compare the number of times blue is a possible outcome (2) to the number of possible outcomes (7).

$P(\text{blue}) = \frac{2}{7}$

The spinner is spun once. Find the probability of each event. Write as a fraction in simplest form.

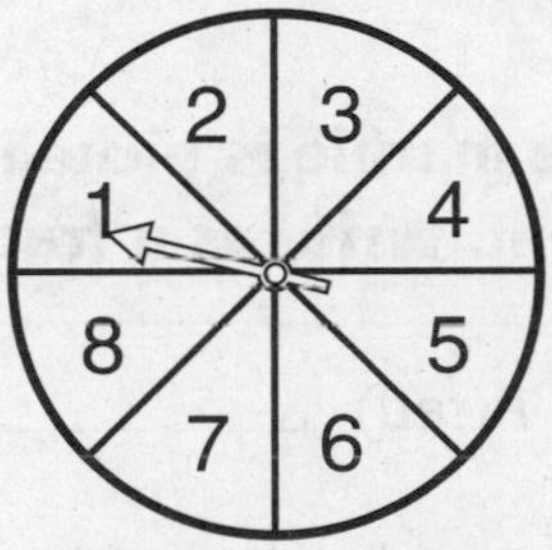

1. $P(7)$ ______________

2. $P(\text{even number})$ ______________

3. $P(\text{multiple of } 3)$ ______________

4. $P(\text{number greater than } 6)$ ______________

5. $P(\text{factor of } 12)$ ______________

Each letter in the word DIVISIBLE is written on a separate tile and placed in a bag. One letter is drawn at a time. Find the probability of each event. Write as a fraction in simplest form.

6. $P(\text{I})$ ______________

7. $P(\text{consonant})$ ______________

8. $P(\text{vowel})$ ______________

9. $P(\text{F})$ ______________

Name ______________________ Date ______________

15–2

Skills Practice

Probability as a Fraction

One shape is selected from the shapes shown. Find the probability of each event. Write as a fraction in simplest form.

1. *P*(quadrilateral) ______________

2. *P*(shape with a pattern) ______________

3. *P*(shape with polka dots) ______________

4. *P*(shape with no edges) ______________

5. *P*(shape with a vertex) ______________

One marble is picked from the bag. Find the probability of each event. Write as a fraction in simplest form.

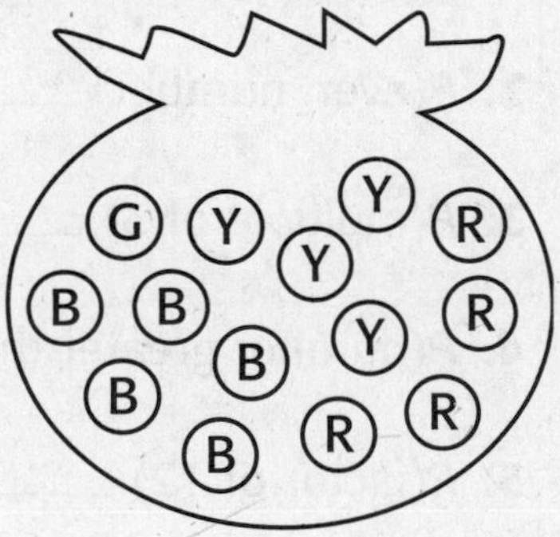

6. *P*(red) ______________

7. *P*(red, yellow, blue, or green) ______________

8. *P*(green) ______________

9. *P*(red or yellow) ______________

10. *P*(blue or green) ______________

Name ______________________ Date ______________

15–3

Reteach

Problem-Solving Strategy: Make an Organized List

Otto plays a game. He spins two spinners and finds the sum of the numbers he lands on. What sums can Otto make?

Spinner A

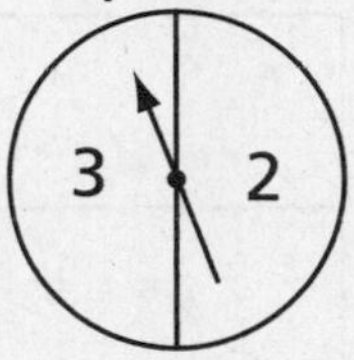

Spinner B

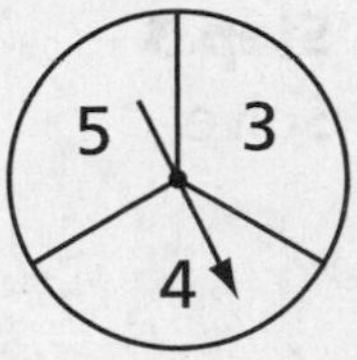

Step 1 Understand	**What do you know?** Spinner A is marked ________ and Spinner B is marked ________. **What do you need to find?** What ________ Otto can make.
Step 2 Plan	**Make a plan.** You can make an organized list to solve the problem. *Remember:* A sum is the answer to an addition problem.
Step 3 Solve	**Carry out your plan** Make a list of possible sums.

Spinner A		Spinner B		Sum
	+		=	
	+		=	
	+		=	
	+		=	

15–3

Name ______________________ Date ____________

Reteach

Problem-Solving Strategy: Make an Organized List (continued)

Step 3 Solve	___ + ___ = ___ ___ + ___ = ___ What sums can Otto make? ____________
Step 4 Check	**Is the solution reasonable?** Reread the problem. Have you answered the question? How can you check your answer? ____________________ ____________________ ____________________

Solve using the *make an organized list* strategy.

1. A spinner has 3 equal sections that are white, yellow, and green. Another spinner has 3 equal sections that are blue, purple, and red. How many different possibilities of colors are there if you spin each spinner once?

   ____

2. Liz has 4 different rings and 3 different bracelets. If she wears one ring and one bracelet, how many different possibilities of rings and bracelets can she wear?

   ____

15–3

Name ______________________ Date ______________

Skills Practice

Problem-Solving Strategy: Make an Organized List

Solve by *making an organized list*.

1. Tom has a blue shirt, a red shirt, and a yellow shirt. He also has a pair of blue jeans, a pair of khaki pants, and a pair of corduroys. How many different outfits are possible if he chooses one shirt and one pair of pants?

   ____

2. Jackson is making a sandwich. He can choose from ham, turkey, or roast beef, wheat, white, or rye bread, and mayonnaise or mustard. How many different sandwiches can he make? Hint: Choose only one meat, one bread, and one condiment.

   ____

3. Allie has square beads that are red, blue, and green. She has round beads that are yellow and white. If she chooses one color from each shape of beads, how many different possibilities of colors can she have?

   ____

4. Ms. Dawson eats a fruit and a vegetable for lunch each day. She selects an apple, a banana, an orange, or a pear for her fruit. She chooses carrot sticks, celery sticks, or green pepper slices for her vegetable. How many different ways can she choose 1 fruit and 1 vegetable?

   ____

5. There are three girls, Jackie, Janey, and Janelle. How many different ways can the girls be lined up?

   ____

6. Greta orders stickers that come with 12 sheets per package. Each sheet has 10 rows of stickers and each row has 8 stickers. How many stickers are in each package?

   ____

Name ______________________ Date ____________

15-4

Reteach

Counting Outcomes

You can use a tree diagram to show all the possible outcomes of an event.

Use a Tree Diagram to Show All Possible Outcomes

Use a tree diagram to find how many pizzas are possible from a choice of thin or thick pizza crust and a choice of pepperoni, mushrooms, or green peppers.

List each crust type. Then pair each crust choice with each topping choice.

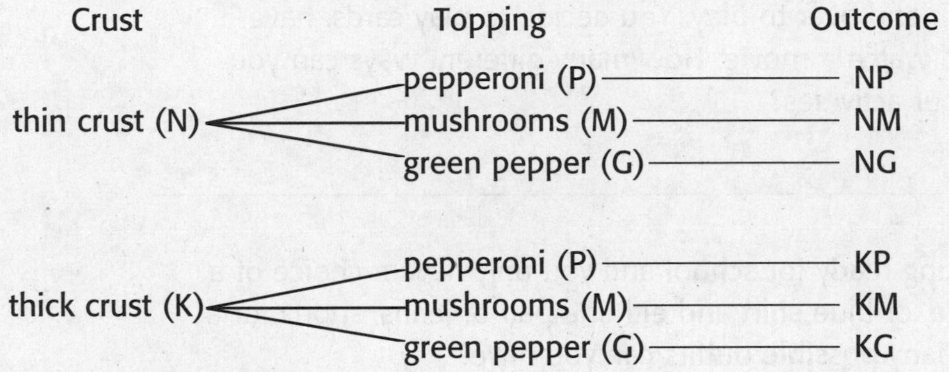

There are six possible pizzas.

Use a Tree Diagram to Find Probability

Use the tree diagram above to find the probability of choosing a thin crust pizza with pepperoni.

$P(\text{event}) = \dfrac{\text{number of favorable outcomes}}{\text{number of possible outcomes}}$

Since there are 6 possible pizzas that can be made from the choices given:

$P(\text{thin and pepperoni}) = \dfrac{1}{6}$

For lunch, Dominic can choose a ham or turkey sandwich and an apple, orange or banana.

1. Use a tree diagram to find all the possible outcomes. List all of the outcomes.

____

2. What is the probability of choosing a ham sandwich and a banana?

____

Name ______________________ Date ______________

15–4

Skills Practice

Counting Outcomes

Use a tree diagram to find the possible outcomes.

1. How many choices do you have for your lunch if you pick either an orange or apple and pretzels or carrots to go with your sandwich?

____

2. You have a friend over to play. You decide to play cards, have a snack, and watch a movie. How many different ways can you complete your activities?

____

3. You are getting ready for school and you only have a choice of a white, purple, or blue shirt and either a pair of jeans, shorts, or a skirt. How many possible outfits can you have?

____

For the following exercises, toss a number cube and spin the spinner shown.

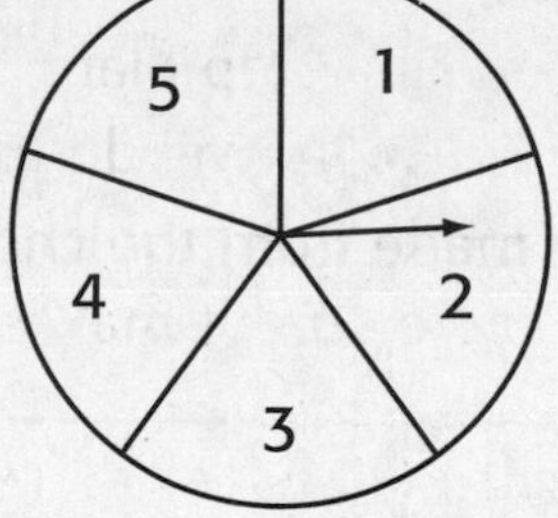

4. Find the number of possible outcomes.

____

5. Find the probability of tossing a four and spinning a number less than 3.

____

6. Find the probability of tossing a 1 and spinning a 3.

____

7. Find the probability of tossing an even number and spinning a number less than 5.

____

15–5

Name ______________________ Date ______________

Reteach

Problem-Solving Investigation: Choose the Best Strategy

Philip and his family caught a lot of fish over a one-week period when they were on vacation.

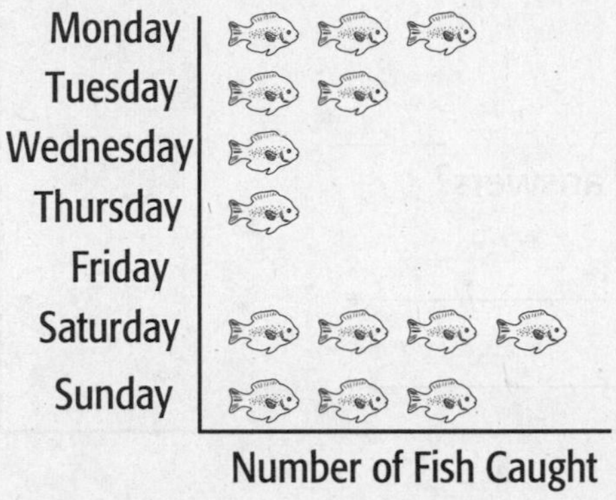

Philip fished on Monday, Wednesday, Friday, and Saturday. His sister, Nancy, fished on Tuesday, Thursday, Friday, and Sunday. Who caught more fish? How many total fish did they catch?

Step 1 Understand	**Be sure you understand the problem.** Philip fished on Monday, Wednesday, Friday, and Saturday. Nancy fished on Tuesday, Thursday, Friday, and Saturday.
Step 2 Plan • Work backwards. • Look for a pattern. • Solve a simpler problem.	**Make a plan.** Choose a strategy. You can use a four-step plan. Decide what facts you know. Plan what you will do and in what order. Use your plan to solve the problem. Then check your solution to make sure it makes sense.
Step 3 Solve	**Carry out your plan.** Count the number of fish each child caught. Philip caught $3 + 1 + 0 + 4 = 8$ Nancy caught $2 + 1 + 0 + 3 = 6$ For the total amount of fish caught, add up all the fish. You can either add $8 + 6 = 14$ or look at the chart and add them up using the amount from each day: $3 + 2 + 1 + 1 + 0 + 4 + 3 = 14$.

15–5

Name ______________________ Date ____________

Reteach

Problem-Solving Investigation: Choose the Best Strategy (continued)

Step 4 Check	**Is the solution reasonable?** Reread the problem. How can you check your answers? ______________________ ______________________

Use any strategy shown below to solve.

- Look for a pattern
- Work backward
- Solve a simpler problem

1. Aisha read 24 books over the summer. Jamil read half that many. Taye read twice as many as Aisha. Zina read three times as many as Jamil. Shawon read a third of the number of books that Zina read. Which two students read the same number of books?

____

2. Hugo spent some money on school supplies. He received $5 back from the cashier. If he spent $95, how much money did he give the cashier?

____

15–5

Name ______________________ Date ______________

Skills Practice

Problem-Solving Investigation: Choose the Best Strategy

Use any strategy shown below to solve each problem.

- Look for a pattern
- Work backward
- Solve a simpler problem

1. Digna packed up 10 dinners to deliver to the food shelter. Isabel packed twice as many dinners as Digna. Rosa packed $\frac{1}{4}$ the amount of meals as Isabel. Juanita packed three times as many dinners as Rosa. How many dinners in all did the girls prepare? Who prepared the most dinners? Who prepared the least number of dinners?

____

____

2. Refer to question number 1. If it takes the girls 1 hour to deliver 5 meals, in how many hours will they deliver all of the meals? If they break up into two groups, with 2 girls in each group and work at the same rate, how long will it take them to deliver the meals?

____

3. For every dollar Luisa puts into her savings account, her parents put in $0.50. If Luisa put $40 a week into her savings account, how much will she have saved up at the end of the month?

____

4. Keshia bought a new outfit. She chooses a top that cost $48.95 and leather boots that were twice as much as the top. The pants were one third of the price of the boots. If she received $20.52 back in change, how much money did she give to the cashier?

____